Making History for Stalin

Making History for Stalin

The Story of
the Belomor Canal

Cynthia A. Ruder

University Press of Florida
Gainesville Tallahassee Tampa Boca Raton
Pensacola Orlando Miami Jacksonville

Copyright 1998 by the Board of Regents of the State of Florida
Printed in the United States of America on acid-free paper ñ
All rights reserved

03 02 01 00 99 98   6 5 4 3 2 1

Library of Congress Cataloging-in-Publication Data
Ruder, Cynthia Ann, 1956–
Making history for Stalin: the story of the Belomor Canal / Cynthia A. Ruder.
p. cm.
Includes bibliographical references (p.   ) and index.
ISBN 0-8130-1567-7 (alk. paper)
1. Soviet Union—Social life and customs—1917–1970. 2. Soviet Union—History—1925–1953—Historiography. 3. White Sea–Baltic Canal (Russia)—History. 4. White Sea–Baltic Canal (Russia) in literature. 5. Russian literature—20th century—History and criticism. 6. Socialist realism in literature. I. Title.
DK268.3R83 1998 97-24059
947.084—dc21

The University Press of Florida is the scholarly publishing agency for the State University System of Florida, comprised of Florida A&M University, Florida Atlantic University, Florida International University, Florida State University, University of Central Florida, University of Florida, University of North Florida, University of South Florida, and University of West Florida.

University Press of Florida
15 Northwest 15th Street
Gainesville, FL 32611
http://nersp.nerdc.ufl.edu/~upf

For my mother
For Igor

Contents

List of Illustrations   ix

Preface   xi

Abbreviations   xv

Constructing the Problem Historically and Theoretically   1

1. Reconstructing the (F)Actual History of the Belomor Canal   12

2. Mythmaking and Mythbreaking: The (Hi)Story behind *The History of the Construction of the Stalin White Sea–Baltic Canal*   39

3. Literary Text as Historical Narrative: *The History of the Construction of the Stalin White Sea–Baltic Canal*   86

4. Converging Narratives and the Emerging Truth   154

5. The Legacy of Belomor   204

Appendixes   213

Notes   227

Bibliography   235

Index   245

Illustrations

1. Map of the route of the Belomor Canal   15
2. Canalarmyists hauling away soil from the construction site of a dike, 1932   23
3. Canalarmyists preparing an area for explosions, 1932?   23
4. Construction of a lock on the Belomor Canal, 1932   24
5. Nearing the completion of the construction of a lock on the Belomor Canal, 1932   24
6. Starting point of the Belomor Canal prior to the commencement of construction—confluence of Lake Onega and the Povenets River, 1931   26
7. Entrance to the Belomor Canal from Lake Onega, 1933   27
8. Entering the first lock on the Belomor Canal, 1933   27
9. View of the entrance to the Belomor Canal from the first lock, 1933   28
10. View of the entrance to the Belomor Canal from the first lock, 1993   29
11. Long-range view from the bridge of the second lock of the Povenets Steps, 1993   30
12. Hotel in Medvezhegorsk constructed for Stalin on the occasion of his visit to the Belomor Canal, 1933   31
13. Contemporary view of the hotel in Medvezhegorsk constructed for Stalin on the occasion of his visit to the Belomor Canal. The Belomor Canal Museum is housed on the first floor, far-right side, 1993   32
14. Door from a barracks of the Belomor Canal prison camp, Belomor Museum, Medvezhegorsk, Russia, 1993   33
15. Semyon Firin with members of the Soviet Writers Brigade to Belomor, August 1993   51
16. Copy of a page of the Belomor camp newspaper *Perekovka*   55

17. Ivan Nikolaevich Rusinov, Honored Artist of the USSR and actor in the Belomor camp theater, photographed in his Moscow apartment, July 1993   148
18. Front side of the Karelian Ministry of Internal Affairs file card for Fyodor Dostoevsky's grandson, Andrei Andreevich Dostoevsky, who was imprisoned on the Belomor Canal   186
19. Reverse side of Andrei Dostoevsky's Karelian MVD file card   187
20. First page of three-page excerpt, which contains editorial cuts and comments from the draft manuscript for chapter 4, "The Prisoners," in *The History of Construction*   221
21. Second page of three-page excerpt, which contains editorial cuts and comments, as well as Vs. Ivanov's name in the left margins, for the draft manuscript for chapter 4, "The Prisoners," in *The History of Construction*   222
22. Third page of three-page excerpt, which contains editorial cuts and comments, from the draft manuscript for chapter 4, "The Prisoners," in *The History of Construction*   223

Preface

The purpose of this study is to expxilore the construction of the Belomor Canal within the context of the literary works written to commemorate it. Foremost among these is *The History of the Construction of the Stalin White Sea–Baltic Canal,* a volume notorious in the annals of Russian literary history largely because of its topic—the construction of the White Sea–Baltic Canal (Belomor) through the use of forced labor. In reconstructing the history of the Belomor project and its attendant literary works, I hope to encourage a deeper understanding of the mechanisms at work in the development and implementation of Stalinist culture and to reopen the discussion of the Belomor incident.

When considered as a constellation of literary and historical events, Belomor makes an interesting case study in Stalinist policy and practice. Belomor marks the first construction project where the officially sanctioned program of political-social reforging—an idea that had only been theorized about prior to that time—was fully implemented. Although the public rhetoric about political-social reforging virtually disappeared after the 1930s, reforging itself continued—albeit less overtly—to influence cultural thought and policy throughout the existence of the Soviet Union. Moreover, Belomor continued to emphasize collective labor as the process through which the USSR would modernize and sovietize itself. As such, Belomor becomes a pivotal event in tracing the evolution of Soviet cultural policy and the politics of control.

Thanks to its interdisciplinary nature, this study will appeal to a variety of readers. The joining of a cultural-historical narrative with literary analysis will appeal to specialists in Soviet history and literary studies, as well as to generalists in the field of Soviet studies. Even those readers interested in transportation history will find useful new information. Finally, this study will appeal to readers who simply are interested in Soviet history and culture.

I would like to acknowledge the support and assistance of the people and institutions that enabled me to carry out the research for this book. Research in the summers of 1991–93 was made possible by a number of sources: summer research fellowships and a travel grant from the University of Kentucky Office of Research and Graduate Studies, three summer research grants from the American Council of Teachers of Russian. In addition, research was supported in part by a grant from the International Research and Exchanges Board (IREX), with funds provided by the National Endowment for the Humanities and the U.S. Department of State, which administers the Russian, Eurasian, and East European Research Program (Title VIII).

At the University of Kentucky I would like to thank the staff of the interlibrary loan department of King Library, as well as my colleagues Roger Anderson, Gerald Janecek, and Edward Lee, who will find evidence of their valuable comments throughout this book. Karen Petrone generously agreed to collect and transport what must have seemed like a ton of photocopied material from Russia.

My research in Russia was aided by scholars and friends, among them the staffs at the Russian National Library in St. Petersburg, the Russian State Archive of Literature and Art (RGALI), and the State Archive of the Russian Federation (GARF), especially Vladimir Kozlov, Deputy Director of the Archive; the filmmaker Vitaly Bronislavovich Mileiko; Irina Gennadievna Petukhova, Nina Ivanovna Os'kina, and Oleg Giorgievich Chistyakov at the State Archives of the Republic of Karelia; Sergei Koltyrin at the Belomor Canal Museum, Medvezhegorsk, Russia; Alla Iurievna Gorcheva of Moscow State University; Vladimir Pozniakov, Russian Academy of Sciences; Nadezhda Aleksandrovna Teplitskaia and Ivan Nikolaevich Rusinov. Special thanks to Nadezhda and Sergei Letemin.

Two additional people in Russia deserve special thanks: my adviser at the Gorky Institute of World Literature, the late Alisa Mikhailovna Kriukova, and Ivan Ivanovich Chukhin at the Karelian MVD. Without Ivan Ivanovich's help, it would have been impossible to complete this book.

In the United States, many people contributed to this project. Bill Wolf first alerted me to the Belomor files in GARF, and for that I am grateful. Jim Curtis was a constant and enthusiastic supporter, as were Valerie Nollan and Catherine Theimer Nepomnyashchy. At the University Press of Florida, thanks go to Meredith Babb, Alex Leader, Judy Goffman, and freelance copyeditor Jackie Brown for their patient assistance, insightful comments, and professional guidance. This project would not have proceeded without initial support and encouragement from Walda Metcalf, formerly of the University Press of Florida. The anonymous reviewers deserve thanks for their cogent comments and suggestions, which significantly contributed to enhancing this study; however, the ultimate responsibility for the book's content rests with the author. I appreciate the time and care with which Dick Gilbreath prepared the map for this book.

I gratefully acknowledge the support of the Ladika and Ruder families and my friends, especially Anna Bosch, Kathleen Dillon, Mary Nicholas, and Karen Ryan-Hayes. Anthony Dunaway was the best research assistant anyone could have. I am especially grateful to Amy Williamsen for her advice, astute commentary, and unfailing friendship. I regret that Steve Ruder and Veronica Ladika did not see the completion of the project. Two people constantly supported this project and never doubted its completion: my deepest gratitude to Igor Sopronenko and Mary Ruder.

Abbreviations

The Belomor project is discussed in historical sources and in this study with various acronyms that can confuse the reader. Note that *Belomor*, rather than the English translation, *White Sea*, will be used throughout this book. The following list attempts to clarify these acronyms, each of which reflects a particular aspect of the entire Belomor project.

* * *

BBK, *Belomorsko–Baltiiskii Kanal imeni Stalina*, is the official name of the Canal, translated as the Stalin White Sea–Baltic Canal. This study will use the shortened form Belomor Canal or the acronym BBK when referring to the Canal itself.

BBVP, *Belomorsko–Baltiiskii Vodnyi Put'*, translated as the White Sea–Baltic Waterway. This name denotes the entire Belomor waterway, of which the Canal is one part. Other segments include the Neva River and Lake Onega.

BelBaltLag, *Belomorsko–Baltiiskii Lager'*, translated as the Belomor–Baltic Prison Camp. This complex was established along the construction site to house inmates who built the Canal.

BBKK, *Belomorsko–Baltiiskii Kanal Kombinat*, translated as the Belomor–Baltic Canal Kombinat. This administrative body assumed the operation of the Canal upon its completion.

OGPU, forerunner of the KGB, the initials of which stand for the *Ob"edinennoe gosudarstvennoe politicheskoe upravlenie*. The English translation would be the Unified State Political Directorate.

MVD, *Ministerstvo vnutrennykh del*, the Ministry of Internal Affairs, supervises internal state security.

Istoriia stroitel'stva Belomorsko-Baltiiskogo Kanala imeni Stalina is the complete title of the Writers Brigade volume about the Belomor construction project, translated as *The History of the Construction of the Stalin White Sea–Baltic Canal*. Throughout this study the volume will be referred to as the Belomor volume or *The History of Construction*.

* * *

Unless otherwise noted, all translations from Russian are mine. The Library of Congress system of transliteration has been used except in those instances where the accepted spelling of a Russian word or name deviates from the LC system. In those cases, the popularly accepted form has been used. All citations in Russian from *The History of Construction* are taken from the 80,000 tirage edition, published in 1934. Any errors or inaccuracies are ultimately the responsibility of the author, who apologizes in advance for any inadvertent lapses in acknowledging the contributors to this project.

Constructing the Problem Historically and Theoretically

> The problem is that life is messy. Hindsight offers a clarity that escapes us while we muddle through the present. Done right, history reimmerses us into the messiness of the past. To understand what happened, we must confront the fears and confusion of the moment.
>
> Art Jester, book editor, *Lexington (Ky.) Herald-Leader*, 6 August 1995

During the bulk of its more than sixty-year existence, the Belomor Canal (an abbreviated version of its full name, the Stalin White Sea–Baltic Canal) remains a source of both fact and fiction. Rarely, if ever, has a major Soviet building project generated so much positive and negative press during and after its construction. The Belomor Canal, exalted in the 1930s by the Stalinist press and foreign observers, became a symbol of what was morally deplorable in Stalinism.

In spite of this troubling past, the whole Belomor episode provides much of interest to contemporary readers and scholars of Soviet literature, history, and culture. A great deal of this information has never been fully discussed or has been obscured by particular political or ethical positions vis-à-vis the forced labor brigades that built the Canal. A more productive approach reexamines the Belomor project and its attendant literary events to deepen our understanding of the mechanisms at work in life and literature during the early 1930s and throughout Stalinism.

To accomplish this task, Art Jester's words should be heeded. Only the clarity of hindsight brings into sharp relief what should have been and what could have been. Jester's comments "also suggest that hindsight can distort, by providing a kind of false clarity."[1] To project everything we know from hindsight onto the Belomor project prevents us from delving into precisely the "messiness" of the past of which Jester speaks and provides us with an incomplete picture of the Belomor event. In exploring this "messiness" the hope is that some sense of that era can be brought to life. "It's the immersion in the enthusiasm of the era that allows us to understand, not twenty/

twenty hindsight, where good and bad are so easily distinguishable."[2] We know what Belomor means within the context of our current era; we need to know what Belomor meant within the context of its *own* era.

For the first time in English, this study introduces the Belomor (hi)story in its many forms and reconstructs the literary history of a historical, political, social, and, most important to this discussion, literary event. To accomplish this, in chapter 1, I open with the reconstruction of the history of the construction of the Belomor Canal. Then I reconstruct the literary history behind the writing of the most famous account of the Canal's construction, *The History of the Construction of the Stalin White Sea–Baltic Canal* (*Istoriia stroitel'stva Belomorsko-Baltiiskogo Kanala imeni Stalina*). In so doing it will describe one kind of literary production in the early 1930s and the increasing state control over it.

Within the context that these discussions provide, I attempt in chapter 3 to reconstruct how a Soviet Writers Brigade wrote *The History of Construction*. Next the other literary responses to Belomor that support and oppose the presentation of the construction project in *The History of Construction* are analyzed with an eye toward examining all the literary responses as a totality of reaction to the Belomor event. In chapter 5, I link the thematic strands that underpin the whole discussion and offer some suggestions as to how Belomor still shapes Russian thought and perception as well as our own perceptions of that period. I will show that Belomor has much relevance even in the late twentieth century.

The Belomor story is by necessity a work in progress, in part because we still do not have access to all pertinent archival information. But the materials presented here attempt as thoroughly as currently possible to document and narrate the Belomor episode and its literary manifestations. This book strives to open, not close, the long-dormant discussion of Belomor.

I have woven certain themes into the fabric of the narrative and linked the historical event with the literary works surrounding it. Foremost among these themes is the program of *perekovka,* best rendered into English as *reforging;* yet the term connotes much more than remelding something into a new form. Implicit in perekovka is the philosophy that it is possible through forced labor and ideological conditioning to create "new" people, in this case, new Soviet people, who embody the ideology and spirit of their age and who personify the Soviet Union in action and deed. The multivalent application of perekovka to all levels of society makes the Belomor project unique, for it was the first project to formally introduce and, more important, institutionalize, reforging. Even though perekovka would be deemphasized later in official Soviet rhetoric, the mechanism for it and the ideas behind it persisted and arguably still persist, within and outside the former Soviet Union. This process of perekovka raises a critical question: Can people really be remade? The thematic thread of perekovka illuminates the struggle between building the new Soviet society and dismantling that which came before it. This idea strikes at the heart of the impulse behind reforging and underpins the whole discussion of collective authorship and literary production.

Therefore, no discussion of reforging would be complete without a parallel analysis of collective authorship and its function within that system. Like perekovka, collective action (certainly not a new concept in the Russian context) provided the pretext for undertaking the Belomor literary and construction projects and reveals itself as a method through which reforging in the literary sphere can succeed.

It also will be argued that contemporary literature from the Belomor period can help us understand this event. In my analysis, I follow a less traditional approach to the literary texts surrounding Belomor in order to get at the "messy" history behind the event. In my discussion, literary works function similarly to the historical documents that help to reconstruct the history of the Belomor project. In avoiding a more traditional historical approach, my analysis, like its main subject of discussion, *The History of Construction,* is a hybrid work. The ambiguities and uncertainties that mark the Belomor project require an approach that tries to clarify them in an effort to reach at least one kind of truth about Belomor.

These themes support a feature that permeates this entire study: Belomor, as construction project and literary event, is characterized by a wide range of seemingly antithetical phenomena. These include enthusiasm versus atrocities, sincere goodwill versus cynicism, energy versus exhaustion, self-destruction versus self-preservation, scorn and envy of the West versus a desperate hunger for a dazzling achievement to impress the West.[3] While these juxtapositions illustrate precisely the "messiness" inherent in the Belomor event, they also capture the tension that infused not only the Belomor project but countless other events in the Soviet context. As such, Belomor can be viewed as a microcosm of Soviet Russia.

Belomor in Context

A sizeable body of historical and literary criticism dedicated to this period already exists. The pioneering work of historian Sheila Fitzpatrick, who first challenged the "totalitarian model" interpretation of Stalinism, helped recast the discussion of the 1930s. Fitzpatrick's fundamental premise that Stalinism and Stalinist culture were not necessarily the products of a single dictate from above but rather the result of a complex interplay among various social levels and power bases underscores the action/reaction dynamic so important to contemporary analyses of the period. Fitzpatrick's work has engendered other historical accounts that contribute to the ongoing reevaluation of Stalinist history and culture.

For example, we know much about what happened not only at Belomor but also at other camps and construction sites, thanks to the rich and ever-expanding memoir literature about the period, as well as to scholarly studies that have benefitted from newly available archival materials. Among them, Stephen Kotkin's massively complete study of Magnitogorsk and Anne Rassweiler's thorough examination of Dneprostroi pioneered the examination of Stalinist construction projects and their historical, social, economic, and political ramifications. Michael Jakobson's pivotal work, *Origins of the GULag,* traces the development of the GULag and its shift from a traditional system of punishment to a system of forced labor designed to benefit the state.[4] My study is indebted to these works.

My study also owes much to the body of work that has preceded it on Stalinist literature, culture, and its attendant artistic canon, socialist realism. Foremost among them is Katerina Clark's work, especially her study *The Soviet Novel: History as Ritual,* and related articles. What Fitzpatrick did for history, Clark did for literature; her study remains the seminal work on socialist realist novels, the mainstay genre of Stalinism. In it Clark reshapes the discussion of socialist realist novels by arguing that they are a reworking of largely early twentieth-century traditions (Brooks, 974), especially given their reliance on "master plots," a critical framework Clark devised (à la Vladimir Propp's study of folktales) to look at the novels in a fresh light. In Clark's analysis, writers manipulated the supposedly fixed socialist realist canon while creating a novelistic mytho-history of Soviet life that generally supported the political ideology. To Clark, Soviet literature under Stalin was not a static process; but as she notes, "the only thing that was absolutely new about Socialist Realism was the term itself" (Clark 1985, 29). Moreover, in her 1978 article "Little Heroes and Big Deeds: Literature Responds to the First Five-Year Plan," Clark was the first literary scholar to formally discuss *The History of Construction.* Her work urges us to rethink traditionally held notions about Stalinist literature that maintained there was nothing of interest in boring Soviet production novels.

Evidence of the ongoing struggle to define and analyze Stalinist culture and socialist realism obtains in the spate of older and more recent studies devoted to this theme. Herman Ermolaev's *Soviet Literary Theories 1917–1934* stands as the pioneering work on socialist realism. Regine Robin's *Socialist Realism: An Impossible Aesthetic* stands as a counterpoint to Boris Groys's *The Total Art of Stalinism*. While Robin follows a more traditional approach in tracing the roots of socialist realism to nineteenth-century realism, Groys argues that socialist realism and, consequently, Stalinist culture are really the extension of avant-garde theory to its most extreme practice. Socialist realism actually achieved that which the avant-garde only attempted to do—create a new aesthetic for art in all its forms, thereby breaking from the traditions that preceded it. Other scholars, among them Thomas Lahusen and Evgeny Dobrenko, assert that just as Stalinist political/social/economic policy did not uniformly emanate from above, so, too, was Stalinist literature molded by a variety of factors only partly determined from above. In effect, the socialist realist canon was not fixed but could be manipulated to suit the agenda of whoever was applying it. Even Igor Golomshtock's seminal work *Totalitarian Art*, which includes extensive discussions of socialist realism and Soviet art, affirms that Stalinist culture was consistently reshaping itself, evolving to fit the demands of a particular period and mandate.

The thread that links all these studies is the contention that Stalinist culture and its nascent cultural canon, socialist realism, were dynamic, organic systems that did not operate unidirectionally. Rather, they responded to the shifts and pressures of time, place, and creator. This conviction differs markedly from earlier examinations of the system, which argued for a fixed model determined by edicts from above. Just as our approach to Stalinist history has been revised (in a positive sense), so, too, has our approach to Stalinist culture and socialist realism. This study is a direct outgrowth of that shift in thinking.

Similarly, Andrew Wachtel's recent work on Russian/Soviet writers and their passion for history, *An Obsession with History*, pushes the analytical envelope even further. The "obsession" Soviet writers seemed to have with history was not a new phenomenon; as Wachtel argues, the stance of writer as historian has a long precedent throughout Russian literature. So it should be neither a surprise nor an anomaly that we again encounter this phenomenon in the context of the Belomor episode. Within this framework, then, the Belomor project merits a closer examination because it illustrates the dynamic nature of Stalinist culture and its desire to create its own history, a history judged by technological achievement and economic progress.

Previous Scholarship on Belomor

Up to this time, critics and scholars have devoted to the Belomor project few critical analyses, and these frequently are inaccurate or address only one aspect of Belomor. For example, Soviet sources from the 1930s focus almost exclusively on the social and economic ramifications of the Belomor Canal's construction. Even the most recent source on the Belomor project, Ivan Chukhin's book *Kanaloarmeitsy* (Canalarmyists), 1990, considers the historical, economic, social, and ethical questions implicit in the Belomor project to the exclusion of cultural and literary issues. More important, Chukhin thoroughly documents and explores the use of forced labor in harsh climatic conditions to build a canal that was probably unnecessary. This more traditional position closely echoes the scant Western treatments of Belomor that focus most pointedly on the issue of forced labor, to wit Jakobson's analysis.

Discussions of Belomor's attendant cultural phenomena limit themselves to treatments of the forced labor question and its presentation in literature. Most striking among these, of course, is Alexander Solzhenitsyn's scathing condemnation of the attempt by selected Soviet writers to document the history of the Belomor project in *The History of Construction*.[5]

My analysis challenges these earlier treatments and suggests that Belomor is not just another forced labor project, the likes of which were to be repeated throughout most of Soviet history. Belomor is unique in that it was the Soviet experiment par excellence; however, for most of its existence, it has been a taboo topic, in spite of the fact that its image was and still is found everywhere in the former Soviet Union: on packs of the most famous and widely smoked *papirosy*, filterless cigarettes with a pungent aroma. Everyone knows the Belomor Canal exists, but few people talk about it. In part, this silence derived from the process of de-Stalinization, during which anything remotely connected to Joseph Stalin was expunged from libraries, streets, buildings, and to some extent people's memories. As with many difficult events in Soviet history, to admit publicly that Belomor existed and that it had been built by forced labor, a fact generally acknowledged in private, was to imply Stalinist excess. And an admission of excess suggested a failure in the Soviet system.

Moreover, because so much information was still classified and unattainable prior to perestroika, little data could be solidly documented through archival materials and personal reminiscences. For all the efforts of Stalin, his minions, and Soviet writers to make Belomor unforgettable, the burden of secrecy and the Stalinist control of information managed to undo almost completely the wildly enthusiastic public pronouncements that greeted the completion of the Canal in 1933.

No sooner had perestroika commenced than did a small body of information about the construction of Belomor begin to appear. Two of the best memoirs were written by Russian intellectuals imprisoned at Belomor according to Article 58 of the Soviet penal code. In *Life (Zhizn')*, the philosopher A. F. Losev relies on fictional genres such as novellas and short stories to recount his personal experiences, while in *From Thoughts about the Past (Iz dum o bylom)* the renowned ethnographer N. P. Antsiferov records his experience as his nonfictional recollections of past events.

While it would be possible to devote an entire study to the memoirs about Belomor and the camp experience, I have chosen to omit a more detailed discussion of the memoir literature surrounding Belomor in favor of those literary works written concurrently with the project. Unlike the recent memoir literature, the synchronicity of the Belomor project with its attendant literary texts affords the rare opportunity to examine an historical event as it was perceived in its own era, to immerse us, as it were, in that time. The power of memory that propels memoirs sometimes distorts events in a subjective way that dilutes the power of the recollection and detracts from the spirit of the moment. Fictional or metafictional works about the Belomor experience tend to be overlooked in favor of memoir literature. Readers often privilege memoir literature; they regard it as the bearer of truth about an occurrence and ignore the insights that fictional accounts can provide. Memoirs contribute one truth among a *number* of truths that can be distilled from a particular event. As a result, we can discover another kind of truth in the nonmemoir literary works about Belomor.

Documentary literature, also a valuable resource for information about Belomor, does not come under close scrutiny in this study. All of it was written and gathered long after the construction of the Belomor Canal. As such, these materials benefitted from the advantage of hindsight and did not capture, as did literary sources, the Belomor event as it was unfolding. The almanac *The GULag in Karelia: A Collection of Documents and Materials, 1930–1941* (*GULag v Karelii, Sbornik dokumentov i materialov 1930–1941*) substantiates the establishment and administration of the GULag system in Karelia prior to World War II. The compilers, scholars, and staff of the Karelian State Archives rely not only on memoirs but also on official documents culled from those archives. As such, they lay bare much of the internal workings of the GULag administration, as well as illuminate inmate life. In addition, the almanac *Links*, which contains scattered references to Belomor, remains a rich repository for various documents and memoirs on camp life. Even the dated (1947) *Forced Labor in Soviet Russia* by David J. Dallin and Boris I. Nicolaevsky provides some of the earliest documentation for the excesses of the Belomor prison regime. These documentary sources are treated not as texts unto themselves but as material that supports the conclusions that can be drawn from the literary texts. Nonetheless, all this information—books, memoirs, articles, archival materials, films—continues to deepen our understanding of the Belomor project, while grounding that understanding in factual evidence.

The Writer as Historian

While scholars have discovered rich resources in these documentary materials, they have ignored or dismissed the literary works produced contemporaneously with the Belomor project. Consequently, a promising group of texts generally has remained unexamined, thereby preventing a fuller critical evaluation of Belomor. To redress this omission, the present study contextualizes the poetic, novelistic, and dramatic representations of the Belomor project, focusing attention chiefly on *The History of Construction,* the premier literary work devoted to the Belomor Canal. Significantly, while portrayed by its authors as the verified truth about Belomor, the work represents a border genre that blends fact with a modicum of fiction to produce a work that falls cleanly into no specific genre classification. Therein lies its appeal. The literary sources offer, perhaps, the best "psychological immersion" into that time available to us.

Unique among the major construction projects of the 1930s, Belomor best displays the ever-increasing symbiotic relationship between Soviet literature and politics. In fact, public rhetoric about the Belomor project singularly publicized and applauded the use of forced labor on a major construction site. Because of the project's prominence, the Soviet state engaged some of the leading writers of the time to promote this agenda. My study is the first to reconstruct *writer motivation,* to try to comprehend this mechanism, and seeks to determine whether writers who participated completely compromised themselves or whether they actually believed in reforging.

To contextualize the Belomor episode, the literary works examined here are localized in time and place to afford us an opportunity to immerse ourselves in the era. They all focus on the actual construction of the Canal and were written and published in 1933–1934. (Although published in 1957, Mikhail Prishvin's novel *Osudareva doroga* [The Tsar's Road] is included because the initial drafts of and ideas for the novel were conceived and formulated in the 1930s.) These converging discourses include Nikolai Pogodin's popular play *Aristokraty* (The Aristocrats); poetry by Konstantine Simonov and Nikolai Kluyev; inmate writings, including poems, slogans, stories, and newspaper articles; and, most prominently, *The History of Construction*.

These texts create a mytho-history of an event that celebrated its sixtieth anniversary on 2 August 1993, a date that went almost unnoticed in Russia save for a three-minute televised report that aired a few days after the anniversary. What a remarkable difference sixty years made in the reception of an event that, at its inception, was heralded as one of the greatest achievements of the First Five-Year Plan. This change is not unexpected, considering the more pressing demands being made upon people daily in post–Soviet Russia. Because Western scholars are outside that milieu, we benefit from the distance, both in time and place, and can bring fresh interpretations to Belomor and the constellation of literary works around it. This study relies on previously unexamined and unavailable archival documents and pairs them with older, long-available texts, thereby guaranteeing a wider historical perspective from which to reassess the Belomor episode.

Preparing the Site

To understand this junction of historical event and literary interpretation, this study will "reconstruct" the history of the building of the Belomor Canal. This treatment provides the background against which subsequent literary interpretations of the Canal project can be judged.

In relying on previously unexamined archival documents, this study will also reconstruct the history of the writing of *The History of Construction* as a prelude to a detailed discussion of this collectively written volume. As the central text on the Belomor project, *The History of Construction* merits a full treatment because it was the account of Belomor against which all other literary and documentary accounts were measured. Even when taken in isolation, *The History of Construction* proves to be a problematic, although carefully crafted work that provokes a challenging question: Are we to read *The History of Construction* as literature or as history? Presumably the text can be read both ways, for its authors perhaps intentionally blurred the line between two distinct modes of discourse. We can locate *The History of Construction* on the compromised boundary between history and literature, a position that encourages a reconsideration of the function of history, literature, and the interplay between them in the Soviet context.

An in-depth examination of the Belomor incident also suggests how this event was both consistent with and deviated from cultural, literary, and political policy at the time. As with many cultural and literary phenomena of the early 1930s, the Belomor project illustrates most poignantly the struggle between building the new Soviet society and dismantling that which preceded it. Just as the period in which it was produced was contradictory and unsettled, so, too, was the Belomor volume and the Canal project itself.

Belomor was the pivotal event that focused the discussion and implementation of perekovka. As Jakobson recounts, Soviet penal policy at the beginning of the 1930s shifted decidedly toward the "labor reforms criminals" model. Officially, perekovka was regarded as the savior of thousands of erstwhile social reprobates who could be metamorphosed into productive members of society. But unofficially, convicts came to be viewed as cheap, infinite sources of labor who could be corralled into working on projects to which other workers could not be lured without force. While touted as sound penal philosophy, in fact, the practice of reforging underpinned a system of inmate labor exploited for economic gain that did little to reform hardened criminals and frequently killed or ruined political prisoners in the process. The program of perekovka was widely promulgated during the first half of the 1930s, and no other event emblematized, applauded, and amplified its successes and excesses as well as Belomor.

Moreover, the history of the writing of the Belomor volume bespeaks the overarching goal of reforging Soviet literature as well as Soviet society. Reforging as a system had ramifications far beyond the prison camp; the Belomor project promoted reforging as a class-neutral, society-building process. Those Soviet writers who assumed the task of writing Soviet history, i.e., the Belomor volume, embodied and advanced this goal.

While the practice of literary figures writing history is neither an unexpected nor new phenomenon, the assumption of such an important nation-defining task precisely by writers speaks to broader issues: the nature and interplay of history and history writing in that society, and the pitfalls of a program that enjoins those who most successfully create fictional worlds to be the arbiters of supposed historical fact and truth.

To assist in this inquiry, the theoretical work of Hayden White will be applied to the discussion. White has asserted that the writing of history is essentially a literary act because the historian employs many of the same devices to organize and present the facts that an "imaginative" writer commonly uses to produce a fictional narrative. White's assertion proves equally applicable to *The History of Construction*, in which the roles are reversed but the premise remains the same. In fact, the Belomor volume tangibly bears out White's contention that historical and literary discourses frequently overlap, yield to, or invade each other, and the product of those boundary transgressions is often a hybrid.

This dynamic accentuates the importance of the Belomor project and hints at one of the earliest shifts within Soviet society and literature, from a system that permitted multiple voices and points of view to one that insisted on one voice, one point of view. While unofficially the multiplicity of points of view continued to exist, Belomor demonstrates how the notions of uniformity and collectivism, achieved through reforging, were institutionalized and legitimized. The introduction to Belomor that this study provides, as well as the heretofore unrevealed archival documents and personal recollections it includes, initiates a discussion of Belomor that is long overdue.

1
Reconstructing the (F)Actual History of the Belomor Canal

> The White Sea–Baltic Canal will go down in history as more than a school of the newest technology of hydroconstruction. It will also go down in history as a school of massive reeducation, of the remaking of people led astray from the path of labor by capitalism.
> *Leningradskaia Pravda*, 29 June 1933, 1

> It [the Belomor Canal] is shallow and narrow.
> Joseph Stalin

The Stalin White Sea–Baltic Canal (hereafter the Belomor Canal or BBK) was built in only twenty months. It is 227 kilometers (155 miles) long, longer than either the Panama Canal or the Suez Canal. Yet Belomor's lack of grandeur startles the observer. In some places only 20–25 meters (about 60 feet) deep and 30 meters (about 80 feet) wide, it hardly looks majestic to the contemporary viewer. In fact, were it not for the sign "Entrance Strictly Forbidden" on the gate leading to the first lock, one would never know that the Canal stretched beyond a line of birch trees planted along its raised embankment.

The abundant rhetoric about the Canal in contemporary newspapers, literary works, and speeches implies the reverse. Those who supervised the waterway's construction described it: "The bravery of comrade Stalin's idea concerning the White Sea–Baltic Canal's construction is evident not only in the very fact of the creation of this hydrotechnological giant, whose construction was only a dream for centuries, but also in the fact that it became a reality only under Soviet power (Firin, 11). Members of the Writers Brigade sent to the Canal waxed lyrical about its construction. Vera Inber wrote:

> At a never seen before pace,
> In a period of time legendarily small,
> On the strongest base of diabase,[1]

Was built the Belomor Canal.
And seeing these cliffs you don't know
What is more tenacious,
The spirit or the granite?
What is more outstanding,
The power of the Canal
Or of those who supervise it. (Insarov, 66)

Even many of the prisoner-workers who built the Canal joined in the praise heaped on the project; they filled the pages of the camp newspaper, *Perekovka*, with poems, stories, and testimonials dedicated to the BBK. To wit, the last stanza of a poem by Vladimir Lidin, "And our report will inform Moscow / of the production line of shock-work of the brigades / The Great Waterway will be ready for the country / on time!"[2]

As we would expect, the official Soviet rhetoric created a myth of the history of construction based on the premise that the capitalist system could never accomplish such a feat. Only the methods and philosophy of Communism could ensure success. Consequently, only Stalin, as the true guardian of Marxist-Leninist ideology, would be able to inspire workers to complete such an enormous task. "The White Sea–Baltic Canal is glaring proof of the correctness of the politics of our party, which has capped the First Five-Year Plan with grandiose success under the leadership of comrade Stalin, to whom belongs the initiative to create the Canal" (*Ogonyek*, 5 June 1933). Missing from all the reports and accounts of the project are data on the loss of life, health, ecological balance, and quality of life; however, the purposely omitted data should not obscure the fact that the construction of the Belomor Canal was met with enthusiasm by many of the workers who built it, the writers who documented it, and the readers who read that documentation. Many people genuinely believed that the Canal was an achievement worthy of the praise it garnered and viewed the program of reforging as a success.

Yet, as one of the epigraphs to this chapter notes, the very architect of the plan—Stalin—was not pleased with the results of the construction, an unexpected reaction from the person who reputedly initiated the Canal project. As the ensuing discussion illustrates, the construction of the Belomor Canal was a building feat unparalled for its time, although Stalin did not appreciate it as such.

A refutation of the myths about Belomor is possible only if we reconstitute the history of this construction project prior to the time when Stalin co-opted it as his own. Here we have in mind not only the Stalinist myth of Belomor that conveniently ignored key details concerning the actual living conditions and loss of life on the Canal but also subsequent myths, which argued that Belomor should be perceived only as an embarassment, a pointless moral violation for which there could be no excuse. Therefore, this historical "pre"-text provides factual material and addresses the questions as to why the Canal was built and how it was used to strengthen Soviet (that is, Stalin's) power and create a paradigm for the program of perekovka.

Historical (F)Acts

Archival sources and print material note one of the first references to a canal-like waterway in this region in the fifteenth century. Both A. S. Insarov and I. Isakov mention the movement of Novgorodians along a primitive waterway, but Insarov marks that movement in the fifteenth century, while Isakov places it in the sixteenth. To complicate matters further, among archival documents in the writer Sergei Alymov's file there is a narrative that places the first attempt to use the path of the future Belomor Canal in 1264. This date cannot be verified based on the extant references, but it could indicate the first attempt to establish a route that predates the Canal.[3]

Novgorodian *ushkuiniki* (fourteenth- and fifteenth-century armed retinues charged with seizing land and trading or robbing along Volga trade routes) reached Soroka from Lake Onega along a course that started at the Povenets River, continued through the system of waterways situated between Soroka and Lake Onega, including Lake Vyg, and reached the northern outlet of the Vyg River at Soroka (see fig. 1). These ushkuiniki hauled their barges through this difficult terrain to expand their commercial domain.

This territory, known today as the Autonomous Republic of Karelia, is situated in the northwest corner of the Russian republic. Once a part of Finland and still bearing the marks of its Finnish heritage, the area is rich in lakes, rivers, rocky cliffs, and moss-covered ravines. The path through this region, from Povenets to Sumskii Posad, was well traversed by religious faithful en route to the sacred Solovetsky Monastery in the White Sea (Chukhin, 8). In fact, as the Russian Orthodox *raskol* (schism) spread throughout Russia, an increasing number of Old Believers sought refuge in the rough terrain of northern Karelia.

In the most general terms, the sobriquet Old Believers (*starovery*) came to mean religious faithful and their churches that opposed ritual and doctrinal reforms adopted by the Russian Orthodox Church in the seventeenth century. Old Believers considered themselves both the practitioners and defenders of the traditional, and therefore most authentic, religious rites in

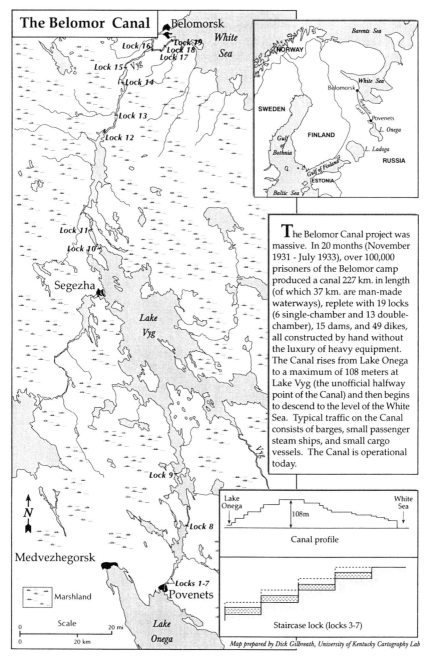

1. Map of the Belomor Canal, including all of its locks. The Canal is also illustrated in relation to its location in Russia and Scandinavia. Map designed by Dick Gilbreath, director of cartography, University of Kentucky Cartography Lab.

Russian Orthodoxy—for example, making the sign of the cross with two fingers instead of with three. They opposed any reforms in church doctrine and liturgy, viewing changes as heretical. Their fervent and vocal opposition to church reform resulted in their oppression, banishment, or self-imposed exile to remote areas of Russia—thus their exodus to Karelia. They settled there (as in other places) because of its remoteness, lack of settlements, and close proximity to the Solovetsky Monastery. Fur trapping, fishing, logging, and mining promised them self-sufficiency as well. When the construction of the Belomor Canal began in late 1931, Old Believers still inhabited areas that became the route for the Canal.

The next known attempt to traverse the difficult terrain between Lake Onega and Soroka to the north was circa 1555 or 1566, with 1566 appearing in the majority of sources. (The differing dates simply could be a copying error in the documents.) On 3 August 1566 the Englishmen Thomas Sowen and John Spark launched three boats at Soroka, loaded them with their goods, and journeyed south to Novgorod to sell their wares.[4]

The most notable attempt to exploit the Karelian north was mounted under Peter the Great in 1702, when workers hauled two frigates from the White Sea in the north to Lake Onega in the south. Dubbed "The Tsar's Road," this path was designed to enhance the tsar's defenses during his conflicts with the Swedes. He personally supervised this enterprise, having decided to expedite the movement of ships built in the north to defend St. Petersburg in the south.[5] The then-current route required sailing around Scandinavia and entering St. Petersburg through the Baltic Sea. However, Peter did not pursue an actual construction project that would have established a northern route and thereby reduced the travel time between Arkhangelsk and St. Petersburg.

The idea of a White Sea–Baltic waterway was revisited in the nineteenth century. At least fifteen attempts were made to initiate a canal project, but various difficulties arose that prevented any of them from reaching fruition. As early as 1800 the Englishman Armstrong and the Petrozavodsk merchant Zhdanov (no first names given) surveyed the area to ascertain if such a project was feasible. Whether the plan failed to be endorsed by the tsarist government or was abandoned by its initiators is unclear; the project was not pursued. Tsarist administrations throughout the nineteenth century returned to the project. The merchant Antonov's son (no name given) launched a plan in 1824 to develop such a waterway, and he brought White Sea fish to St. Petersburg as proof of the necessity for and viability of such a venture. Another project, proposed in 1832, was supported by the department of the navy. An expedition was organized to resurvey and reanalyze the possibility of constructing a waterway through Karelia, but the Directorate of Waterways dismissed the plan as "inconvenient and outdated" (B. Lepin, 9). In 1835 a plan was suggested to Count Benkendorf, but again the project was determined to be unimportant and "not deserving attention" (ibid.).

Throughout the second half of the nineteenth century, ten attempts were made to revive the idea of building a northern waterway; each time the project was ignored, abandoned, or rejected. In 1858 Arandarenko (no first name given), the governor of Arkhangelsk, delivered a speech about the feasibility and need for such a link, and even Alexander II became interested. However, the project was rejected as being too expensive. In 1868 a group of private investors initiated geological and hydrological surveys of the area to ascertain the feasibility of building a canal and organized an investment group to provide financing for the project. The plan was then submitted to the government for its approval. In 1870 the *Olonetskaia guberniia* (province) supported the project, the cost of which was estimated to be twelve million rubles (Chukhin, 9). In 1874 the Olonetskaia guberniia presented to the government a petition reaffirming its support. Although this plan was approved, by 1875 the group of investors could not reach any agreement, so the investment group dissolved, and the project was abandoned once again.

At the same time another group of businessmen, Akhsharumov and Co., presented a plan that was approved by the proper authorities but still did not proceed. This same scenario was repeated, even though the local authorities supported such a project, various surveys and expeditions were undertaken to examine the feasibility of the project, and the technical expertise was available to accomplish the task. Perhaps the most important reason why plans for building a canal were set aside at the end of the nineteenth century was the government's emphasis on building the Murmansk railroad. In 1895 plans for a canal were postponed until a decision was made about the train, with the result that the railway was built but the canal was not.

Interest in a canal project did not diminish, even with the construction of a land route that connected St. Petersburg with the far north. Repeatedly, scientists, businessmen, and government officials returned to the issue. From 1889 to 1906 Professor V. E. Timonov (first name and patronymic not specifically identified in the sources) intensively studied the idea and was the first to propose a complete water system to connect the White and Baltic Seas, of which the Belomor Canal would be one component (Isakov [b], 146). From 1908 to 1910 the government impaneled another commission to examine the Belomor question. The commission concluded that a canal would be useful, but their recommendation was not strong enough to implement the plan.[6]

With the outbreak of World War I, Russia again found itself unable to use its Baltic Sea access. The issue of building the Belomor Canal resurfaced. In fact, during World War I the merchant Volkov (no first name given), with the help of the forestry department, offered to build the Canal using his own money. That same agency later refused his request.[7] In addition, in 1915, at the 9th Congress of Industrialists and Merchants, the engineer Tokarsky (no first name given) delivered a speech about the absolute necessity of building the White Sea–Baltic waterway (ibid., 147).

The last prerevolutionary attempt to build a canal came in 1916, when the chairman of the Naval League, Beklemishev (no first name or patronymic given), approached the general staff of the navy with a proposal that argued for the necessity of building a waterway. Attached to his request was data that outlined how it was to be built; he even provided specific plans for the system of locks to be used. This proposal was also dismissed.

In light of these attempts to undertake the construction of both the Belomor Canal and the larger White Sea–Baltic waterway, certain patterns emerge. First, there was no lack of local interest in the project. In fact, most of the attempts to implement a canal project originated in Arkhangelsk or Karelia and were supported by both the government and private businessmen of the region; the economic importance of such a waterway was not lost on them. The construction of the Murmansk railroad at the end of the nineteenth and beginning of the twentieth centuries filled the immediate need for a transportation link. Nevertheless, businessmen in Karelia were interested in transporting raw materials to market, and a large waterway would serve to supplement the railroad.

A northern waterway would serve strategic purposes as well. Peter the Great's wars with the Swedes and World War I demonstrated that Russia needed an alternate naval route in the event that the sea route through the Baltic was inaccessible. However, given the Baltic route's extended period of accessibility and considering that the northern waterway would be frozen and unusable for at least six months out of the year, the need for constructing the northern waterway seemed questionable.

Undoubtedly the overriding reason for not building a canal prior to 1917 was financial. Estimates of the projected cost ranged from 3.5 to 12 million rubles. If the government was engaged in the large tasks of building railroads and industrialization, then such an expenditure for a waterway with no guarantee of success would have seemed exorbitant. With the outbreak of World War I, financial concerns intensified, although none of the sources previously cited suggest why the government did not accept Volkov's offer to build the canal with his own money in 1910; perhaps other projects were considered higher priorities or the government did not favor the private ownership of a strategically important waterway. No single, clear, defining reason emerges for not building the canal, especially given the numerous attempts to initiate the project and the varying degrees of support each attempt drew.

In addition, the Soviet sources cited do not evenhandedly discuss the tsarist approaches to the Belomor project. Rather, they are laced with exaggeration and bravado. Hyperbolic expressions like "buried in a sea of paper" or "drowned by the bureaucracy," while fitting nautical images and arguably apt metaphors for the tsarist bureaucracy, do not reveal the reasons for the prerevolutionary government's reluctance to build the Belomor Canal.

Of course, Soviet sources claim that the true reason was the inability of the capitalist system to design and implement such a project. Only Communist ideology, under the direction of the Bolsheviks, could make the plans for the Belomor canal a reality. Such a position, however, does not consider that the tsarist government had the expertise and scientific knowledge to complete the project. While the true motivations for not building a canal prior to 1917 remain unclear, one thing is obvious: Soviet power exploited prerevolutionary Russia's inability to build a Belomor waterway as a counterpoint to the successful completion of the project under Stalin. Such a juxtaposition had important ramifications not only for the completion of the Canal but also for all the cultural and political activities that emerged from it.

The Belomor Canal in Soviet History

The Soviet government addressed the Belomor question as early as 1918. An expedition was organized under the supervision of one Professor Shokal'sky, but because of protracted preparation and the onset of the civil war, the trip failed to take place (ibid., 148). Another expedition, in 1922, was successful, but the results were not seriously considered until 1929, when the construction of the Belomor Canal was included in the First Five-Year Plan.

Stalin's correspondence with Viacheslav Molotov confirms the support for the Belomor project at the highest levels of government. As he states in his letter, "I'm told that Rykov and Kviring want to squelch the matter of the northern canal, contrary to the Politburo's decisions. They should be taken down a peg or two and given a slap on the wrists. Yes, the financial plan has to be cut as much as possible, but it's a crime to squelch this matter" (*Stalin's Letters*, 212). In a note he later contends that, "I think it's possible to build to Onega. As for the northern section of the canal, we should limit ourselves to surveying for now; I have in mind relying mainly on GPU [i.e., prisoners. Trans.]. At the same time we must assign someone to calculate yet again the expenses in building this first [southern CR] section. 20 million plus 70 million. Too much" (ibid.).

Stalin based his comments on the Politburo's resolution of 5 May 1930 that approved construction of the complete Belomor Canal, which stated in part that "Calculations for the construction plan for the southern section [Leningrad to Lake Onega, CR] of the canal should be based on the following requirements: (1) Construction work on this canal section (from Leningrad to Lake Onega) should start at the beginning of the next economic year and be completed within two years.... The Commissariat of Transport with the participation of the armed forces and the OGPU [the Unified State Political Directorate, forerunner of the KGB] should be charged with conducting a geological survey for the digging of the northern canal section (from Lake Onega to the White Sea)" (ibid.). The translators and editors of the Stalin-Molotov correspondence note the following from archival materials: "On 5 October 1930, the Politburo told the OGPU that it should be guided by the decision of 5 May 1930, and the question of appropriations for the Baltic–White Sea Canal should be put off until consideration of the target figures for 1931 was completed" (ibid.). From the Canal project's inception, the Party joined forces with the OGPU to pursue it.

Finally, on 18 February 1931, the Council of Labor and Defense of the Soviet Union decreed that the Belomor Canal was to be built. Responsibility for construction was handed over to the OGPU. No sooner had the decree been issued than the OGPU began to incarcerate the engineers who would draw up the designs for the Canal. These engineers were arrested as "saboteurs" and "wreckers" who purposely intended to ruin the Soviet state through shoddy engineering practices. (How ironic that they then were entrusted with the strategically important task of designing the Belomor Canal!) In reality, the arrested engineers included some of the best and brightest specialists trained in tsarist technical institutes and academies.

Throughout the spring and summer of 1931, engineers were brought to Moscow and put under house arrest in the construction bureau located on the top floor of a building behind the OGPU headquarters on Liubianka Square (the building with a *gastronom* [food store] on the first floor). The engineers worked, ate, and slept in one large room. In November 1931, when the plans were complete, the engineers, along with the first contingent of workers who would actually build the Canal, were shipped by rail to Medvezh'ia gora (Bear Mountain, hereafter cited as Medvezhegorsk), on the northern shore of Lake Onega. Given what little they had to work with in terms of materials, the engineers who designed the Belomor Canal achieved significant engineering accomplishments by designing gates, locks, and operating mechanisms that, while made out of wood, initially withstood the stress and destructive force of the water. Thus the construction of the Belomor Canal commenced.

Under the direction of OGPU officer Semyon Firin the *Belomor-baltiiskii lager'* (camp) maintained its administrative offices in Medvezhegorsk. Firin reported directly to Matvei Berman, head of the entire GULag system and a frequent visitor to the Canal construction site. Construction materials would be obtained from areas surrounding the building site so that little, if any, cost was incurred to cover the transport of materials. It was decreed that the Canal was to be built using only those materials readily at hand: wood, granite, peat, and dirt; some cement would eventually be used, but for the most part, the natural wealth of Karelia was to be exploited to its fullest. This was the cheapest way to construct the Canal. Labor—slave labor—would be supplied by the Belomor GULag. This plan coincided perfectly with the OGPU's goal, which can be summed up best: "Quickly. Sturdily. Cheaply. Less metal, less cement, not a single kopeck of foreign currency, more lumber" (Insarov, 55).

As a result of this policy, work on the Canal was carried out by almost primitive methods. Wheelbarrows, pickaxes, horses, wooden pulleys, and assorted other equipment, often engineered on the spot, were the basic tools of construction. During the course of the entire enterprise canal workers used 15,000 horses, 70,000 wheelbarrows, and detonated 4.5 million explosions. In addition, if all the lumber used had been laid end to end it would have covered half the distance around the globe. Cement totaling 390 cubic meters was used, and reservoirs, built during the construction of the Canal, held 7.1 million cubic meters of water, enough to quench the thirst of the world's population for seven years (Chukhin, 103).

As with many large waterway projects, this enormous quantity of water was, in part, responsible for the flooding of various homesteads along the Canal. The most dramatic deluge occurred in Lake Vyg, where countless formerly inhabited islands were flooded to make the Lake more navigable. All told, scores of people lost their homes, gardens, and, sometimes their lives. Among them were mostly Old Believers, who had thought that they had successfully evaded persecution by moving to Karelia. Even cemeteries were flooded, and anecdotes describe caskets floating in the Canal as a result of islands being inundated, an image that recalls events in Alexander Pushkin's narrative poem "The Bronze Horseman" (1833) and ties the Belomor episode to the long tradition of narratives that addressed the Russian north. No figures are available for the monetary amount of property damage, although the damage done at Belomor is probably equal to or surpassed by other projects such as the Tennessee Valley Authority, the Aswan dam, or the more recent plan to dam China's Yellow River.

From Medvezhegorsk, prisoners embarked on a journey by foot to Povenets, a distance of twenty miles, and points farther. Prisoner convoys included common criminals as well as sizeable complements of political prisoners. When the first shipment of laborers arrived in Medvezhegorsk and began their march to Povenets, they stepped into a forest almost untouched by human hands (see fig. 6). No barracks had been built to accommodate them, no buildings had been constructed to begin the project. If the prisoners wanted to sleep under cover they were responsible for building their own shelters. In this manner temporary barracks were dug out of the earth to provide lodging for the first workers on the Canal.

The orchestra conductor Leopold Teplitsky was in one of the first convoys to march to the construction site. Fortuitously, Teplitsky's widow, Nadezhda Aleksandrovna Teplitskaia, still lives in Petrozavodsk and graciously agreed to be interviewed.[8] Initially trained at the St. Petersburg Conservatory as a pianist, Teplitsky was forced to abandon the instrument because of a physical impairment in his hands. He then trained as a conductor and debuted at the Marynsky Theater in St. Petersburg. A promoter of American jazz and show music (he was a fan of George Gershwin) in the Soviet Union, Teplitsky performed with his Russian jazz band in Philadelphia in the late 1920s. Teplitsky's arrest most likely resulted from his passion for jazz and his sojourn in America.

According to his widow, Teplitsky's Belomor convoy departed in late fall 1931, and while they were in transit the OGPU guards systematically took away any warm clothes the prisoners had with them. If they wanted to sleep, they had to fell trees and build their own barracks. When the time came to bathe, the most fortunate place in line was the last one, since those who bathed first were required to stand in the cold with little or no clothing and wait while the rest of the convoy took their turns bathing. Only when the last man had washed could the convoy continue. Countless prisoners at the front of the line fell ill and died. The OGPU could afford to be so careless with its workforce because of the ease with which they could replace prisoners. There was no paucity of labor because the OGPU contin-

2. Canalarmyists hauling away soil from the construction site of a dike, 1932. Most of the work on the Canal was carried out by hand, including the transport of millions of tons of rock and dirt from the site. Used by permission of Ivan Chukhin.

3. Canalarmyists preparing an area for explosions, 1932[?]. Teams of camp inmates were responsible for driving chisels into solid rock to provide slots in which to insert sticks of dynamite for explosions. These work brigades were the deadliest on the Canal. Used by permission of Ivan Chukhin.

4. Construction of a lock on the Belomor Canal, 1932. Originally all locks on the Canal were constructed from wood and peat, with as little cement as possible. Used by permission of the Karelian State Archive, Petrozavodsk, Russia.

5. Nearing the completion of the construction of a lock on the Belomor Canal, 1932. Used by permission of the Karelian State Archive, Petrozavodsk, Russia.

ued to arrest common criminals and politicals in increasing numbers to meet the demand of the Canal project. (Both Jakobson's and Solzhenitsyn's contentions about the economic basis of the GULag system are borne out by this practice.)

Teplitsky himself survived his term on Belomor. He was freed thanks to his success as a shock-worker. (A shock-worker [*udarnik*] performed unbelievable labor feats that demonstrated an ability to exert oneself far beyond what could be humanly expected of a worker—record production in record time.) After his release from Belomor in 1933 he taught at the local music school and became the conductor of the Petrozavodsk State Symphony Orchestra, a post he maintained until his retirement. He died in 1965.

Teplitsky's canal biography, as narrated by his wife, typifies the personal histories of a significant portion of the prisoner population that worked on the Canal. While the workforce was divided between common criminals (*ugolovniki*) and political prisoners (sentenced under various paragraphs of article 58 of the Soviet criminal code), among the political prisoners were some of the best and brightest the Soviet intelligentsia had to offer. Aside from Teplitsky, the philosopher A. Losev, the ethnographer N. Antsiferov, the futurist poet Igor Terent'ev, and the literary critic/historian Dmitry Likhachev were among the members of the intelligentsia who served time in the Belomor camp. (Likhachev was transferred from Solovki to Belomor but was released shortly after his transfer. He worked on the Canal, achieved the status of shock-worker, was released early from the camp, and returned home on 8 August 1932, having served four years in the GULag.)[9] Many survived their incarcerations and recent memoir literature vividly captures how their Belomor experiences marked them.[10]

Considering that winter had already arrived in Karelia when the Belomor construction project commenced, the physical conditions were not ideal. (Figures 2–11 illustrate the entrance to the Canal before construction began and after the first lock at Povenets had been completed and the Canal opened.) In snow and cold, with few tools and materials, the prisoners began to dig the Canal. Work continued through the winter, with an increasing number of prisoners shipped to various locations along the way. Although a system of natural lakes and rivers already marked out a potential route, intensive, often fatal, labor was required to make the Canal a reality. From 1931 to 1933, more than 126,000 prisoners were transported to the Belomor project, of whom 12,484 received immediate release from prison as a result of their labor on the Canal, 59,516 were granted reduced sentences, and large numbers were not released but shipped to other construction sites such as the Moscow–Volga Canal and the Baikal-Amur railroad (BAM) (ibid., 209). Countless others died or escaped. Based on archival records in the Karelian MVD, Chukhin estimates that at least 10,000 prisoners tried to escape, although the figure is probably higher (ibid., 189).

The entire enterprise was entrusted to the OGPU, which supervised the construction project with great vigor. As recounted in *The History of Construction,* "According to Stalin's suggestion, the Party authorized the OGPU to take charge of the construction project" (69). Some accounts claim only thirty-seven OGPU guards were employed to patrol over 100,000 inmates; however, it is improbable that the number of guards remained that low, especially since the OGPU recruited guards from among the inmate population. In addition, escapes were commonplace, even in such dire physical conditions. Chukhin suggests more guards were needed and deployed. He cites a document about a particular work brigade that notes: "The number of guards according to the state of and corresponding to the number of in-

6. Confluence of Lake Onega and the Povenets River, starting point of the Belomor Canal prior to the commencement of construction, 1931. The territory, comprised of marshes, bogs, steep, rocky cliffs, and mostly coniferous forests was largely untouched by human hands when the construction of the Canal commenced in late 1931. Used by permission of the Karelian State Archive, Petrozavodsk, Russia.

7. Entrance to the Belomor Canal from Lake Onega, 1933. The obelisk was designed and built by camp inmates. Used by permission of the Karelian State Archive, Petrozavodsk, Russia.

8. Entering the first lock on the Belomor Canal, 1933. Notice the images of Stalin and Yagoda. Used by permission of the Karelian State Archive, Petrozavodsk, Russia.

9. View of the entrance to the Belomor Canal from the first lock, 1933. The wooden buildings that were constructed along the Canal route served as administrative offices and living quarters for administrative personnel. Used by permission of the Karelian State Archive, Petrozavodsk, Russia.

mates: *zeks* [an acronym for *zakliuchiennie,* prisoners] 1869, guards 81 is insufficient. It is imperative to increase the guard to 100 persons" (Chukhin, 58).

Aside from the officially reported inaccuracies about the actual number of guards in service at the Belomor camp, the practice of *tufta,* or inflating labor and production records, detracted from the mythic representations of Belomor. In practical terms, prisoners engaged in tufta whenever they overestimated or consciously overreported the amount of work they had accomplished. Tufta was most apparent when work brigades competed against each other for prizes and awards. To gain the advantage, brigade leaders would claim that their group had overfulfilled the plan of work by 200 percent instead of 100 percent, or they would boast that they had greater surpluses of a particular building material or had poured a larger amount of cement than they had in reality. Tufta became such a problem at Belomor that the camp administration initiated an anti-tufta campaign designed to find and punish the perpetrators of tufta: *tuftachi.* According to Firin, those engaging in tufta were class enemies and were to be treated as such (*History of Construction* [hereafter, *HC*], 376–388). But tufta was

10. View of the entrance to the Belomor Canal from the first lock, 1993. The wooden structures visible in figure 9 are no longer standing, nor are the obelisk and images of Stalin and Yagoda that decorated the entrance to the Canal in the 1930s. Used by permission of Igor V. Sopronenko.

so pervasive that it continued to plague the construction project up to its completion in 1933. In the words of a camp ditty, "Without tufta and ammonial, there would be no Canal" (Chukhin, 135). (*Ammonial* probably refers to ammonium nitrate, a common ingredient in explosives.)

As Chukhin argues, however, the tufta campaign pitted common criminals against political prisoners, with the politicals unfairly shouldering much of the blame for tufta (136). Charges of tufta against engineers, for example, were by law tantamount to wrecking and sabotage. Political crimes included anything that threatened the security of the state—treason, sabotage, wrecking, and other supposed terrorist acts. The problem was that practically anything, from mistakenly dropping a hammer to writing a letter to one's wife about poor work conditions, could be subsumed under the rubric of political crimes. Thus, the law was loosely interpreted so as to afford the courts and the government the broadest latitude in arresting so-called state enemies.

With the threat of lengthened sentences hanging over politicals and with the promise of reduced sentences, conjugal visits, and additional rations for

11. View of the Povenets Steps in the distance from the bridge of the second lock, 1993. The Povenets Steps, locks 3–7, succeeded one another exactly like steps on a staircase. Used by permission of Igor V. Sopronenko.

those prisoners who overfulfilled their work plans, the impetus to produce was intense. Yet the practice of tufta was not limited to the Belomor project and reappeared at other projects. Arguably tufta, despite all the official propaganda against it, continued to flourish throughout the entire Soviet period.

Reports of tufta aside, in point of fact, for its time the Belomor Canal project was massive. In twenty months the prisoners of the Belomor camp produced a canal 227 kilometers in length (of which 37 kilometers are man-made waterways), replete with nineteen locks (six single-chamber and thirteen double-chamber), fifteen dams, and forty-nine dikes, all constructed by hand without the luxury of heavy equipment (see figs. 4–11). The Canal rises from Lake Onega to a maximum of 108 meters at Lake Vyg (the unofficial halfway point) and then begins to descend to the level of the White Sea. In addition, because a section of the Murmansk railroad was located in an area that was to be flooded according to the construction plans, canal workers moved 182 kilometers of the rail line. Trains were already running on new tracks by June 1933 (*Leningradskaia Pravda*, 27 June 1933, 4). The inmates even constructed a hotel in Medvezhegorsk to accommodate Stalin on his visit to Belomor in July 1933. The hotel, still standing, now houses the Belomor Canal Museum, which commemorates the inmate experience at Belomor (see figs. 12–14).

Sources cite three dates that mark the official completion and opening of the

Belomor Canal. Some propaganda pieces note May 1933; however, this was the anticipated date of completion. In fact, the Belomor Canal was officially completed on 20 June 1933, approximately a month later than the original projection. The steamship *Chekist* was the first vessel to sail through, in June 1933. Its name was most appropriate, since Chekists were responsible for the construction of the Canal. (OGPU agents were called Chekists, after the original acronym of their organization, the Cheka, the "Extraordinary Committee" [*Chrezvychainaia kommissiia*].) The third date, over a month later on 2 August 1933, marks the official opening of the Canal.

In early June 1933 the government dispatched a commission to Belomor to certify that the Canal was operational. Members of the commission traversed the Canal on the steamship *Sevastopol*. According to one report, the commis-

12. Hotel constructed in Medvezhegorsk by Belomor camp inmates for Stalin on the occasion of his visit to the Belomor Canal, 1933. The "tower" that graces the front of the hotel contained an atrium on the top floor that, during Stalin's visit, was decorated with potted plants and was especially designed to provide him with a view of the entrance to the Canal from the front windows. Used by permission of the Karelian State Archive, Petrozavodsk, Russia.

13. Contemporary view of the hotel constructed in Medvezhegorsk for Stalin on the occasion of his visit to the Belomor Canal. The Belomor Canal Museum is housed on the first floor, far right side. After the building was closed as a hotel, it served as a school for orphans, then became the Belomor Canal Museum in 1992. It is devoted to documenting the Belomor camp experience during Canal construction. Used by permission of Igor V. Sopronenko.

sion, having navigated the locks on the Povenets Steps several times, found that "the system of locks performed fantastically well, and instead of fifty minutes, the whole process lasted less than half an hour" (*Izvestiia*, 26 June 1933, 4). This achievement is especially remarkable because the Povenets Steps are a series of locks, numbers Three through Seven, that are built like a staircase on water. Each lock represents one step up or down the staircase, depending on the direction in which the vessel is sailing. The view north from the second lock confirms this design because each succeeding lock is visible beyond its predecessor, thereby creating the effect of a staircase. (See fig. 11.)

In mid-July 1933 Joseph Stalin officially toured the Canal in the steamship *Anokhin*. Joining him on this voyage were Klim Voroshilov, Politburo member and Stalin's Minister of Defense, and Sergei Kirov, Politburo member and Leningrad Communist Party Chief. According to a biographical chronicle, Stalin arrived in Leningrad with Voroshilov on 18 July 1933, joined Kirov, and immediately embarked for Belomor. From 18 to 25 July

14. Door from a barracks of the Belomor Canal prison camp, Belomor Canal Museum, Medvezhegorsk, Russia, 1993. It was found by the museum organizers in the woods bordering each side of the Canal during one of their searches for remnants of the Belomor camp. Used by permission of Igor V. Sopronenko.

the trio sailed through the Canal to "get acquainted" with the various hydrotechnical innovations employed in its construction. Having traversed the entire length, they arrived in Soroka to meet with the Soviet northern fleet and to tour a submarine. They proceeded to Murmansk to view the port and polar bay and then returned to Moscow (Stalin, *Works*, 414–15).

The irony of Stalin's visit to the Belomor Canal stems from the fact that, having endorsed its construction from the first felled tree, when he finally saw the completed project, Stalin found it to be inadequate: "According to eyewitness accounts, having completed his excursion along the Belomor Canal, Stalin noted with dissatisfaction, '[it's] shallow and narrow'" (Chukhin, 18). Stalin's exact words are reported to have been, "A senseless undertaking, of no use to anyone" (ibid.). Presumably Stalin, neither an engineer nor a sailor, envisioned the Belomor Canal as an entity much larger than it actually was and had no sense of proportion when the plans for the Canal were approved.

The Belomor Canal was officially opened on 2 August 1933, to much fanfare. All the major papers provided front-page coverage of the event.

Articles featured the edicts of the Communist Party Central Committee, which listed those Chekists and canal workers who had received commendations and reduced or commuted sentences. In addition, the official opening of the Canal prompted the organization of a Writers Brigade, comprised of 120 Soviet writers, who traveled to Belomor in mid-August. Like Stalin and his entourage, they sailed the entire Canal so as to acquaint themselves not only with the various technological innovations, but also with the "canalarmyists." The joining of the Russian word *kanal* with a noun derived from the word *armiia* (army)—*armeets* (one who is part of the army)—produced the sobriquet *canalarmyists* (*kanaloarmeitsy*), which was first coined by Lazar Kogan, head of the Belomor construction project. The term injects a military metaphor into the Belomor event, for it underscores the purported battles against nature, undesirable ideologies, and each other in which the canal workers were engaged. As a result, both the project and its workers became linked with the prevailing rhetoric of the time that exhorted Soviet citizens to fight internal and external enemies in order to make the Soviet Union a world power. The builders of the Canal emerge on the "frontlines" of this battle, an enterprise for which many believed it was not worth fighting.

Reportedly a total of 111,000 people passed through the Belomor Canal during this first, shortened shipping season—workers, writers, and tourists (Insarov, 20). Added to all this fanfare was the reality that the Belomor Canal had, in fact, dramatically reduced the travel time between Leningrad and Arkhangelsk. Prior to Belomor's existence, a typical sea trip between the two cities took twenty days and covered 2,840 nautical miles. After the completion of the Canal, this trip was reduced to 674 miles, easily covered in eight to ten days (Insarov, 142; *Leningradskaia Pravda*, 23 June 1933, 1). The passenger steamship *Karl Marx* began to offer regular runs through the Belomor Canal to serve people who needed to reach the northern or southern points on the route (*Pravda*, 29 June 1933, 1). Even the Arctic Institute took advantage of the shortened route to send an expedition to the island of Novaia Zemlia (New Land) (ibid.). Recent anecdotal evidence suggests that tourist cruises are now sailing through the Canal as well. One of these trips, scheduled for late summer 1997, included a visit to Goritsy and the Kiril-Beloozersk Monastery. The Belomor Canal was mentioned in the trip literature as the "Volga/Baltic Canal" (S&S Festival Tours '97, brochure).

Given these facts, the Soviet press was accurate to a certain extent: The construction of the Belomor Canal truly was a feat equal to, if not more impressive than, the Suez Canal and the Panama Canal. The Suez, 189 kilometers long, took fifteen years to build and was constructed without locks. The Panama Canal, 64 kilometers in length, took thirty-three years to build and includes locks; at the height of its construction, the Panama Canal project employed 40,000 workers, many of whom suffered from a variety of maladies, including yellow fever and malaria. Both the Suez and Panama Canal projects were not without their losses of human life.

In terms of usefulness, however, both the Panama Canal and the Suez Canal outperformed Belomor and continue to do so. This record stems in part from the fact that the Belomor Canal was closed for most of World War II because of the destruction wrought upon it by the Finns and Germans. Repairs were completed in 1946, after which it was reopened. Since that time it has been renovated (and periodically closed) in each of the decades since the postwar reconstruction. Eventually most of the wooden structures were replaced with metal, and all mechanical functions were electrified and automated. The wooden walls and floor of the first lock are the last wooden components on the Canal and are scheduled to be replaced soon.

Contrary to the persistent myth of heavy usage, even today the Belomor waterway operates approximately six months out of the year, and while open might handle only six ships per day (frequently that number is smaller). This assessment is based on a conversation with the operator of the first lock on the Canal. He revealed that during the shipping season long hours pass before a ship sails through, largely because the locks are too narrow and shallow for most seagoing vessels.[11] In contrast, the Suez Canal handles fifty to sixty ships a day. And the Panama Canal, even with declining use, handles at least 10,000 transits per year. While the locations of both of these canals encourage heavier usage, the Belomor Canal, from the first day of operation, serviced a lightly traveled area.

Comparative statistics suggest that the Belomor Canal was never as heavily used as its contemporary sources would have us believe. Granted, in its early days the Canal seems to have been used frequently. Insarov cites a figure of 16,700 ships that passed through Belomor during the shortened shipping season in 1933 (20). Indeed, lumber products have been and continue to be transported along Belomor.

The economy exercised by the OGPU in building the Canal was evident in the total cost of construction, 101,316,611 in 1933 rubles as compared with $83 million for the Suez Canal and $336,650,000 for the Panama Canal. (This would be $17,468,381, according to present exchange rates $1.00 to 5.8 rubles [per the 1997 currency reform] and $60,789,966, according to pre-perestroika exchange rates of approximately $0.60 to one ruble.) Arguably, this monetary gain was lost in other ways when we consider the Canal project's effect on local inhabitants, project participants, and generations of Soviet citizens. While it did provide a route through which the riches of Karelia could be exported, there were environmental costs, which have yet to be documented, including the reshaping of the landscape, the erosion of arable soil, and the destruction of fish and animal habitats. Many of these scars have already healed, but undoubtedly at the time the destruction was felt acutely. The emotional cost was paid by those who suffered during the construction of the Canal. Psychologically, perhaps the greatest effect was the enduring, albeit subtle, presence of the mentality of perekovka. Many other effects cannot be and have not been measured fully. However, after being reconstructed four times since World War II, the Canal still operates, and those working on it consider its existence vital to Karelia and the Russian north as a trading, strategic, and navigational route.

Nonetheless, this situation begs the question of why the Canal was actually built. One then-contemporary commentator noted that the project was significant for a number of reasons: it was a source of pride for Soviet technology, it was important for the economy of the entire country, it was significant for the cultural and domestic development of the Soviet north, and it strengthened the defensive capabilities of the country (ibid., 18).

Note, however, that Soviet sources from the 1930s rarely mention the strategic function of the Belomor Canal and almost uniformly focus on the economic benefits of the waterway to Karelia in particular and to the Soviet Union as a whole. This position is not unexpected, since the Belomor Canal project was included in the First Five-Year Plan and was lauded as the beginning of the Soviet Union's attempt to modernize and expand its system of waterways to enhance and exploit the economic possibilities of the country. Any strategic functions would have been undisclosed state secrets in order to preserve the integrity of national security. In fact, the plans for the Belomor Canal originally were top secret because of this strategic function; only when authorities recognized the true propaganda value of the Canal project was its existence publicized.

The most complete current analysis of why the Canal was built, Ivan Chukhin's *Canalarmyists*, echoes the sentiments of the 1930s but expands on the actual motivations for the project. Chukhin notes economic, defensive, and political reasons for constructing the Canal precisely at that time. As he argues, economically the Belomor Canal would enable the Soviet Union to accomplish two goals. First, Karelia, rich in natural resources including timber, minerals, and furs, could be exploited more fully with the presence of a route through which raw materials could be transported out of the region. Second, the Belomor route significantly reduced the travel time between Leningrad and the northern ports (Chukhin, 18–19).

In terms of defensive purposes, Chukhin cites two main concerns. In many places the border at that time with Finland was perilously close to Leningrad and Murmansk. It posed a military threat to the USSR's security, especially given that a pro-Fascist government had assumed power in Finland. In addition, the USSR needed to develop a northern fleet that would be able both to defend the northern borders and to sail out to the Atlantic should the Baltic fleet be prevented from doing so. Chukhin points out, "That the construction of the BBVP was initially kept secret and the first caravan of ships that passed through the Canal was military speaks to the importance of the military function" (21). Submarines were shipped through the Canal on barges prior to and during the early part of World War II, until the waterway was rendered unusable by German bombers.

As for the political motives for building the Canal, the present history concurs with Chukhin and posits two (Chukhin, 22–25). One, the successful completion of the Canal would serve as a rich source of propaganda for the new Soviet state. What could not be accomplished under the tsarist regime could be accomplished under Soviet power and would affirm Stalin's leadership, foresight, and intelligence. This is precisely the tack taken by the Soviet press and contemporary tellers of the Belomor tale. Two, through the successful construction of Belomor, the OGPU and the entire Soviet government would be able to justify the use of slave labor to construct not only the Canal but other large-scale building projects as well. Under the guise of perekovka the OGPU argued that corrective labor could and would remake criminals and enemies of the state into productive, skilled members of Soviet society and would continue to contribute to socialist construction. According to this thinking, reforging justified the exploitation of an essentially unpaid labor force that frequently worked simply to survive. These political motivations, however deplorable and unpalatable to contemporary critics, were applauded as yet another example of the new society that Soviet power was able to create thanks to the Communist Party and the careful guidance of the OGPU.

This discussion might intimate that Chukhin is the only source worth consulting in regard to the reasons that underpinned the construction of the Belomor Canal. While David J. Dallin and Boris I. Nicolaevsky in their book *Forced Labor in Soviet Russia* note the strategic importance of the

Belomor Canal, they do not focus exclusively on the Belomor project as Chukhin does. In relying on previously inaccessible MVD archival files, Chukhin has succeeded in reconstructing the history of the Belomor project from a political and social perspective.

His greatest service in reconstructing this history, though, has been to document the atrocities and injustices perpetrated against the forced-labor workforce that built the Canal in the name of the state. In this respect Chukhin surpasses even Alexander Solzhenitsyn in the documentation and discussion of the absurdity of the Belomor project from the point of view of the prisoners. Chukhin's meticulous attention to the details of the project and the copious inclusion of original documents in the narrative mark his work as the first relatively full account of the Belomor GULag—from administrative decrees to inmate reminiscences. Since its publication, other memoirs have appeared that further substantiate Chukhin's argument. But in spite of the inclusiveness of his account, Chukhin bypasses the cultural, literary, and manifestly historical issues that the Belomor construction project raises, the topics that the present study addresses.

Given the abundant rhetoric in Soviet newspapers of the time and the public energy and enthusiasm that large-scale construction projects generated in the early 1930s, it is no wonder that the Belomor project was touted as a premiere example of Soviet economic policy and Stalinist ideology. The use of forced labor, promoted through the program of perekovka, was viewed positively. The public embraced the Canal project as yet another way by which the Soviet Union demonstrated its technological advancement and expertise. Providing the public with accurate details about Belomor was not a government priority. Instead, as with other large construction projects, the government exploited the event as an opportunity to propagandize for and legitimize the regime.

Indeed, all officially sanctioned contemporary accounts of Belomor contributed to the myth-making and rhetoric common to Stalinist journalism and literature, but none did so more enthusiastically or generated such intense scrutiny as *The History of Construction*.

2
Mythmaking and Mythbreaking
The (Hi)Story behind *The History of the Construction of the Stalin White Sea–Baltic Canal*

> [I'm] like a dog: I understand everything, yet am silent.
> Maksim Gorky, from the notebook *For Notes about the Solovetsky Camps of the OGPU*

> Notwithstanding all the objective reasons and circumstances, subjective [reasons]—the measure of the personality of every writer, his personal moral and artistic strength—played no small role. On this "subjective" ground, literary conformism, the readiness to accommodate oneself to ideological tasks and aesthetic norms, was widespread.
> Vyacheslav Vozdvizhensky

> And here I confirm that the work on the creation of the history of the Belomor Canal in one of the literary brigades is, and will be for me, one of the best days of my creative life.
> Vsevolod Ivanov, speech to the First Congress of the Writers Union

> I am convinced that in order to judge the history of our native culture, a feeling of human goodwill, not the destructive "clarification of relations," is absolutely necessary. Only the sense of an inner duty before others gives one the right to judge oneself as well as reality. Yet can one judge? First and foremost, one must understand.
> Tamara Ivanova, widow of Vsevolod Ivanov

Tamara Ivanova's admonition to understand rather than to judge underpins the following discussion, for if we are to reconstruct the dynamic that produced the Belomor volume, we must suspend our belief in a system measured in black and white, pluses and minuses. Each epigraph to this chapter testifies to the complicated processes that circumscribed Soviet literary life, especially in the 1930s.

Gorky's more private admission of his obedience and submission contrasts sharply with his public image as chief literary propagator of the Soviet cause but is consistent with his problematic biography. Ivanov's energetic pronouncement about his work on the Belomor volume appears almost too enthusiastic, given the reality of the project. The critic Vyacheslav Vozdvizhensky perceptively describes the objective and subjective parameters that demarcate writer motivation and action in the 1930s, yet at the same time he outlines precisely the dilemma that many writers faced. These apparent contradictions, when coupled with Ivanova's inclination to reconcile personal action with historical reality, define exactly the conflicting opinions that shape any discussion of writer motivation and literary event in the 1930s.

The conflict intensifies when we apply these statements to the Belomor project, because it is the event that brings into sharpest relief the complex symbiosis of motivation and action. Within the Belomor context all of these contentions ring true, a fact that supports rather than contradicts the actual unfolding of events and enables us to begin to understand the pressures and circumstances that compelled writers to participate in the project, even if those reasons initially seem implausible or baffling. It is impossible to appreciate how *The History of Construction* was written, without first grasping the events that preceded its creation.

To that end, this chapter will detail how the Writers Brigade was organized, who participated, and what conclusions we can draw from this process. Even more important, the following discussion will debunk many of the myths that have surrounded the Writers Brigade and its participants for more than sixty years. In so doing, the mythmaking that characterized the Belomor episode and provided the glue that held the Belomor volume together should become more obvious and open to critical inquiry.

Establishing the Parameters

Assorted newspaper articles as well as literary works in different genres attempted to capture the essence of the construction of the Belomor Canal. Neither the boundaries separating fiction from nonfiction, nor the physical boundaries that separated writers outside the Belomor prison camp from those within limited the variety of written responses to Belomor. Nor were they limited in time, as Prishvin's novel *The Tsar's Road* and recent memoir literature attest.

Among these literary responses *The History of the Construction of the Stalin White Sea–Baltic Canal* stands as one of the more unique and problematic documents produced during prewar Stalinism. Promoted as the official history of the Belomor Canal project, this literary work, more than any other fictional or nonfictional account about the Canal, attempted to document both the history of the project and the personal histories of those who built it.

The process through which work on *The History of Construction* was organized is as complicated as the text itself. Numerous myths, fallacies, and omissions have marked the discussion of its production. Moreover, readers and critics have never fully understood how this text came into being. Who conceived the idea to produce a collectively written "history" of the construction of the Belomor Canal? Who formed the Writers Brigade that traveled to the Canal and served as the group from which the authors of the *History* were drawn? How did the Brigade operate? What motivated writers to participate in an enterprise that sought to praise and immortalize an event that was organized by the OGPU and carried out on the backs of prison camp laborers, many of whom were unjustly imprisoned? Never have readers of the Belomor *History* been apprised of all the facts and details behind the writing of this controversial volume.

Those readers were, and still are, firmly divided into two groups. For those who supported Soviet power and socialist construction, the Belomor *History* reads as a glorious tribute to the Soviet system and especially to Stalin and the OGPU. Supporters of the Canal project firmly believed that it could have been constructed only under Stalin, for no one else had the foresight and sheer force of will to complete it.

For those who despised or were disillusioned by Soviet power, the Belomor volume represents everything deplorable in the Soviet system. The most stinging criticisms were heaped on the 120 writers who participated in the Brigade, thirty-five of whom produced *The History of Construction*. As with most writers who continued to publish during the 1930s, those who visited Belomor were universally condemned by Soviet opponents of the system as well as by Western scholars for participating in such a clearly manipulated and artificial journey.

The recent polemic between Vsevolod Ivanov's widow, Tamara, and Vozdvizhensky testifies to the fact that even after sixty years the Belomor Canal volume still incites strong feelings in those who encounter it. As the quotations cited at the beginning of this chapter suggest, Tamara Ivanova, who visited the Belomor Canal on the Writers Brigade with her husband, advocates a more moderate approach to the Belomor episode. Vozdvizhensky, however, believes that the writers who participated in the Belomor project should be held accountable for their actions. As he argues, the particular circumstances surrounding the Belomor project should not exempt participants from moral and ethical censure. Moreover, Alexander Solzhenitsyn registers the strongest condemnation, in his discussion of the Belomor volume in his *GULag Archipelago*. Consistent with his position throughout his work, Solzhenitsyn condemns anyone who participated in such an enterprise, regardless of his or her personal or political concerns.

Recently it has become clear that the more we learn about Stalinism, the more we realize that it is impossible, and often unproductive, to classify events and actions in purely black-and-white terms. The history of *The History of Construction* is no exception, for close examination of it reveals much about literary life, perekovka, and controlled cultural production in Soviet society. Arguably, the Belomor project as well as the Belomor volume provided further explication of a model for action and policy that could very possibly trace its roots back to the proto–socialist realist models of Chernyshevsky and others. In fact, the Belomor episode illustrates two sides of the same coin, life shaping art. How the Belomor Canal was constructed bore directly on how the Belomor volume was written. But as soon as the Belomor volume was published, art began to shape life, based on the models for reforging and other positive behaviors that the book outlined.[1] Within these historical and cultural contexts, we can unravel the myths and reassemble the facts of the production of the "official" history of the Belomor Canal.

While this process in itself amounts to a history within a history, the goal differs. Rather than judging the moral underpinnings of the compilation and creation of the Belomor volume, this presentation discusses the facts of the project so as to capture the diversity of experience and motivation among writers who participated. In addition, the ensuing narrative organizes, for the first time, the progression of events and intentions that culminated in the publication of *The History of Construction*. Questions of style, narrative method, theme, and function will be reserved for the following chapter.

Organizing Production

It is difficult to document the precise moment when the idea for *The History of Construction* was born, but it is possible to posit a likely genesis. The Soviet writer Kornelly Zelinsky contends that a meeting at Maksim Gorky's house on 19 October 1932 included Party writers who met to discuss Soviet literature with Stalin, Politburo members Viacheslav Molotov (the Head of the Council of People's Commissars) and Klim Voroshilov (the minister of defense). Clearly the distinction between Party and non-Party writers was being made well in advance of future developments, and even though non-Party writers were afforded the opportunity to speak at the First Congress of the Writers Union in 1934, the stenographic notes for that congress recorded Party affiliation or the lack of it for every participant. Already in 1932, Party writers were benefiting from their political connections.

A week later, according to Zelinsky, who was present at this meeting on

26 October 1932, individual Soviet writers were summoned to a gathering at Gorky's home to discuss the state of Soviet literature. Zelinsky classified some of these writers as non-Party, although he did not specify which ones he had in mind. Unbeknownst to them, Stalin, Voroshilov, Molotov, and Lazar Kaganovich (Politburo and Party Central Committee member and Stalin's confidant) were to be in attendance. The writers included M. Sholokhov, Vs. Ivanov, A. Fadeev, V. Kataev, L. Leonov, L. Seifullina, A. Afinogenov, P. Pavlenko, N. Nikitin, S. Marshak, Yu. German, V. Ermilov, V. Gerasimov, L. Nikulin, F. Berezovsky, F. Gladkov, F. Panferov, V. Lugovsky, E. Bagritsky, K. Zelinsky, M. Chumandrin, A. Surkov, G. Kats, N. Nakoryazov, N. Ognev, E. Gabrilovich, A. Malyshkin, Yu. Libedinsky, Sh. Soslani, V. Kirpotin, L. Subotsky, V. Bakhmet'ev, M. Kolosov, V. Il'enkov, L. Averbakh, I. Makarov, V. Kirshon, V. Zazubrin, G. Nikiforov, I. Razin, M. Kol'tsov, P. Kryuchkov (Gorky's personal secretary), G. Tsypin, I. Gronsky, P. Postishev. The last eleven writers, beginning with Averbakh and ending with Postishev, participated in the meeting but were later repressed during the Stalinist purges.[2]

The archives reveal that Zelinsky recorded his impressions of the 26 October meeting and rewrote his narrative four times in the 1960s. While sometimes he deleted an occasional word or phrase, he did not edit each successive variant significantly and the list of participants he included remained the same. In the foreword to the last variant in 1966, Zelinsky stated, "In publishing this information that has long since become an historical document [his description of the meeting], I want to close with the words of V. I. Lenin from a letter to S. Varga: 'We need complete and truthful information. But the truth must not depend on those whom it must serve.' In my opinion, these words of Lenin should be the slogan for the publication of any historical documents."[3] There is no proof that Zelinsky ever published his notes, but his sense of the history of the moment, his willingness to present his memoirs as historical text, and sense of responsibility to report the truth emphasize a predisposition to assume the mantle of history writer as a legitimate part of a writer's responsibilities.

More important, Zelinsky understood the need to document Stalin's pronouncement and the list of participants. It was as if Zelinsky felt compelled to expose the mechanisms of literature that operated in the 1930s, while alluding to the contradiction that the meeting with Stalin underscored: Participation in the literary mainstream did not insure salvation from the Stalinist terror. Moreover, by naming names, especially the names of formerly repressed writers, Zelinsky broke a taboo that had existed since the 1930s, dissolved during the late 1950s, yet persisted into the 1960s:

Prior to Stalin's death it was taboo to identify publicly those who had been repressed.

Zelinsky himself embodied the contradiction of the time. Although an avowed constructivist early in his career, he joined the Brigade and participated in the Belomor writing project, having abandoned constructivism in 1930. His career as a literary theorist continued well into the 1960s, but we sense in his reminiscences a need to set the record straight, to do as Lenin bade—present the truth for truth's sake, not to serve special interests. The fact that Zelinsky cited Lenin, arguably not a lover or preservationist of truth, to justify his recollections should not diminish what Zelinsky revealed or even his attempt to reveal it; thanks to him we have an instructive record of the interplay between political intent and literary action.

As Zelinsky narrates, throughout the evening Stalin and the writers discussed the direction of Soviet literature. At one point in the proceedings, Gorky is reported to have said, "Here is the Belomor Canal. This is already a change in the geography [of the USSR]. Yes. Writers have also written a fair number of books. Among them there are some good ones. But there are also many bad ones. . . . Now we need to talk about how together we can create Soviet literature, a literature worthy of the great fifteenth [anniversary of the revolution]."[4] The creation of a truly Soviet literature remained for Gorky the driving force behind all his literary work—in his own writing, his editorial work, and in his patronage of young writers. Had anyone other than Gorky sounded the call to create a literature worthy of the legacy of the revolution, the pronouncement would have seemed shallow and ungenuine. But given Gorky's commitment to the development of a truly authentic Soviet literature, his remarks remain consistent with his approach to it.

As the conversation continued, Stalin began to speak, uttering one of his most famous statements regarding Soviet writers: "Your tanks won't be worth anything if the souls in them are [made of] clay. No. The production of souls is more important than the production of tanks. . . . Here someone correctly said that a writer must not sit still, that a writer must know the life of the country. And that is correct. Man is *remade* [italics added] by life itself. But you, too, will assist in *remaking* [italics added] his soul. This is important, the production of human souls. That's why I raise my glass to writers, to the engineers of the human soul."[5] On the heels of this speech, the screenwriter and author Evgeny Gabrilovich, also present at the meeting, noted that Stalin himself suggested that the writers tour the Belomor Canal.[6]

When analyzed closely, Stalin's remarks on the role of the Soviet writer outline, point for point, the approach the authors followed in the writing of *The History of Construction*. All the key ideas resonate—production, not only in industry but, most pertinent to our discussion, in literature as well; the seminal notion of perekovka, the idea that the most intimate, essential part of a person, one's soul, can be remade; the notion that precisely *writers*, not politicians or economists, will accomplish this task. This program forms a continuum with the already well-documented place the writer has always enjoyed in Russian and Soviet life as the bearer of truth whom readers trusted and revered. As Andrew Wachtel has persuasively argued, writers, thanks in part to this special social status, came to view themselves as fitter than professional historians to be historians.[7] This attitude certainly obtains in the Belomor volume.

It is no accident that the convergence of these ideas, including Gorky's plan to create a new literature worthy of Soviet achievements since the revolution, occurred precisely at this moment. As the Soviet writer Alexander Avdeenko notes regarding the Belomor volume, "Gorky's dream was fulfilled—actually having issued the call to assemble writers under one roof and convince them of the necessity of unity.... True proletarians and fellow travelers. Litfrontists and Lefists. Perevalists and Litpostists. Con-structivists and Lokafovists. Kuznetsists and the Serapion Brothers. Sympathizers and Partial-sympathizers" (13). As the First Five-Year Plan continued to unfold, collectivization gained momentum and the literary factions that Avdeenko lists were officially dissolved because of the April 1932 decree that created the Union of Writers. In fact, at the time many writers viewed the liquidation of RAPP (Russian Association of Proletarian Writers), too, as a liberation; however, viewed in retrospect, everything seemed to point to the increasing control and consolidation of all segments of Soviet life.

In order to expedite government programs, the populace needed to believe that such measures were crucial to the success of the Soviet state. The key was to achieve this end without the public realizing that they were supporting increased limitations over their lives. The mandate could be achieved, though, if it was camouflaged as a great project to create a "new" society. Hence the rhetoric and program of perekovka—not only would people be reshaped into new Soviet men and women, but literature, economics, even nature would become Soviet, too. What better example to illustrate this point than the Belomor Canal construction project, an endeavor that sought to remake the Karelian landscape as well as to reforge the canal workers, Soviet writers, and the literature they produced?

Moreover, rapid industrialization and mechanization, two hallmarks of the First Five-Year Plan, shaped the metaphors of the time and linked the Belomor Canal project to the larger goal, that of *reforging* the Soviet Union from a supposedly backward agrarian nation to an economic and industrial superpower. It is no accident that Stalin's phrase "engineers of human souls" turned on this industrial metaphor. Every construction project, every collective farming endeavor, every element of the First Five-Year Plan strove to remake the Soviet Union. The abundant rhetoric that agitated for and applauded intense industrial development also sought to mobilize Soviet citizens into action. How could it be wrong to contribute to the country's efforts at industrialization? And how could any project, dependent on forced labor or otherwise, detract from the speedy improvement of the Soviet industrial base, thereby molding the USSR into a competitive world power?[8]

These were heady times in the Soviet Union, when intense rhetoric ignited the fervor of many citizens. It became seemingly acceptable not only to participate in a construction project but also to publicly aggrandize it as long as it was for the ultimate good of the state. In the face of explosive economic development, especially in a country that had suffered through revolution, civil war, and famine, it seemed appropriate to advertise successes.

That much of this rhetoric overstated many Soviet agricultural and industrial achievements goes to the heart of the Belomor issue. Within the industrial metaphor it was possible to legitimize any measure, extreme or otherwise, as long as it moved the USSR toward a dominant position. The epitome of overstated success and positive results came to be *The History of Construction*. Within this context it becomes easier to understand how writers could embrace, or seem to embrace, this event so enthusiastically. To participate in a writing project like the Belomor project, to engage oneself in the process of building a new state was, for many writers, a matter of adjusting to the times and finding a way to contribute. Of course this is only one part, albeit a significant one, of the question of writer motivation and participation in the Belomor project. But this defining metaphor helps us realize how writer participation was not only possible but not unexpected as well, given the circumstances.

As Clark also suggests, there were other compelling reasons why writers participated in the Belomor project: Some were genuinely inspired to participate, such as Ivanov and Avdeenko. Others, among them Victor Shklovsky, had personal agendas that reflected either an interest in preserving their own careers or in aiding, perhaps even saving, someone else. No matter what a writer's agenda, the collaboration of these writers to produce the

Belomor volume concentrated all the goals of the First Five-Year Plan within one event. This was an era of great ferment, activity, and change. It is no small wonder, then, that the Belomor Canal project emerged as a pivotal event that prompted such intense publicity and literary reaction (Clark(a), 192–99).

It would be a mistake to think that the Belomor endeavor was unique because the Writers Brigade was sent to the Canal to describe its success. On the contrary, brigades were being organized and sent throughout the Soviet Union to document and praise industrialization, collectivization, and mechanization. Writers' groups traveled to the Donbas, Magnitogorsk, auto plants, steel works, collective farms—any place where people were reforging the Soviet Union and the Soviet Union was reforging people.[9] Literary activity mirrored industrial production as the rhetoric demonstrates. Writers engaged in "production," worked in "brigades," and became "engineers," all terms that bound literary work to the dominant industrial metaphor (ibid., 194–96).

The peculiarity of Belomor stems from the fact that no other brigade successfully produced a work of literature that was literally *collectively written* and no other brigade *publicly* documented an event where forced labor enabled the project to succeed. This combination of intent and event marked Belomor as the first project of its kind. As such, it epitomized the very ideas about which Stalin spoke that evening in 1932—society needed to be reforged, and writers were enlisted to achieve that goal. (Note that in his comments Stalin says "you will help," not "you should help" or "you are encouraged to help." This was a command, not an invitation.) Given this situation, it is not difficult to see both how *The History of Construction* came to be written and why this text is so problematic: It advocates and applauds the remaking of Russian society into a Soviet Stalinist society.

The Brigade to Belomor

On 17 August 1933 a group of Soviet writers assembled in one of the halls of the Organizing Committee of the Organization of Soviet Writers in Moscow. The group included not only some of the most popular writers of the time—Valentin Kataev, Ilf and Petrov, Alexey Tolstoy—but also young writers such as Alexander Avdeenko, as well as writers from the Ukrainian, Belorussian and Uzbek republics, and Karelia. This group totaled approximately 120 writers; a complete list has been impossible to document. Appendix I provides the most complete list based on names culled from newspaper articles, archives, memoirs, and other sources. How these writers were chosen or who specifically chose them cannot be documented, although it is clear that Gorky personally invited at least one writer, Avdeenko, to join the Brigade.

Organized by the editorial board of the publishing house The History of Factories and Plants, the Writers Brigade left Moscow the evening of 17 August on a week-long journey to the Belomor Canal. Prior to their departure, however, the writers were treated to a pre-trip orientation at which Semyon Firin, the head of the Belomor prison camp and the Writers Brigade's escort through the Canal, supplied information about Belomor. According to one newspaper account of the event, "Firin's description [of the Canal] instilled in the travelers unusual energy and provoked enormous curiosity. Everyone hurried to the train. The seats in the train cars were occupied an hour and a half ahead of the departure time" (*Literaturnaia gazeta*, 29 August 1933, 4). The enthusiasm with which all the writers greeted the trip has not been thoroughly documented, nor can we accept without question that all the writers made a quick dash to the train. Ivan Chukhin has determined that the archives of the former KGB contain presently inaccessible files that would undoubtedly reveal much about actual writer response to enlistment in the Belomor Brigade. The file titles "Testimonials of Soviet Writers about the Belomor Canal" and "Agent Notes on Soviet Writers in the Belomor Brigade" tempt with the promise that they contain more complete, accurate information. (As an aside, Vitaly Shentalinsky's recent work *Arrested Voices: Resurrecting the Disappeared Writers of the Soviet Regime* has opened the door, as it were, of the KGB archives for literary scholars; it is hoped that the Belomor files will eventually enjoy such accessibility.)

A good deal of enthusiasm was evident among some of the writers, including Avdeenko, who, as a very young writer, was thrilled to be included in the group. In his recollections of the event Avdeenko, writing with the hindsight of over fifty years, noted, "From the minute we became guests of the Chekists, complete communism began for us. We eat and drink on demand, we pay for nothing. Smoked sausages. Cheeses. Caviar. Fruit. Chocolate. Wines. Cognac. And this in a year of famine!" (Avdeenko (b), 11). We can interpret Avdeenko's comments as the observations of someone who was excited by the opportunity to eat and drink whatever he wanted. Arguably, the tenor of Avdeenko's recollections, when taken in toto with his statement that "complete communism began for us" injects some irony into the passage. He is startled by his own naïveté and gullibility more than fifty years after the fact. Gabrilovich notes that for whatever reasons, the writers imbibed heartily throughout the excursion: "The writers got drunk."[10]

After their orientation program, the Moscow contingent of the Writers Brigade boarded buses and departed from the Writers' Hall to the Leningrad train station, where they occupied four train cars for the overnight ride to Leningrad. In Leningrad local writers, including Mikhail Zoshchenko and Mikhail Kozakov, joined the Moscow contingent. Finally, the entire group departed for Medvezhegorsk (*Literaturnaia gazeta*, 4). From there they boarded the steamship *Anokhin* and embarked on their weeklong excursion through the Canal, beginning with the first lock at the confluence of the Povenets River and Lake Onega, and ending with the final lock at the entrance to the White Sea at Soroka. Their specific itinerary included the following stops:

17 August 1933

1. Moscow-Leningrad. In Leningrad, dinner in the dining room of the House of Writers and an assembly of Leningrad writers.
2. Leningrad-Medgora. In Medgora, a tour of the camp.
3. From Medgora to Povenets on the steamship *Anokhin*, ascent along the Povenets Steps, and a tour of the mechanism of the ninth lock.
4. Passage through Lake Vyg on the steamship *Anokhin*, including a stop at the Nadvoitsy dam with a tour of the Nadvoitsy lock's gates.
5. Tour of the Shavansky lock.
6. Tour of the Tungunsky lock.
7. Tour of the Sosnavetsky lock.
8. Exit into the White Sea.
9. Return trip on the steamship *Anokhin* to Povenets.
10. From Povenets to Medgora, and the train to Leningrad and Moscow.[11]

Shortly after the Brigade's trip to Belomor, an account of the journey, entitled "Six Days," appeared in *The Literary Gazette*. Penned by V. Reg, this account includes seventeen numbered paragraphs, each of which details a particular site, incident, or idea encountered on the writers' voyage through the Canal (*Literaturnaia gazeta*, 4).

Throughout their journey the writers were supposed to be provided with opportunities to meet the canalarmyists. Although the Brigade enjoyed performances of the inmate-staffed camp theater, most meetings with canal workers were tightly controlled, with the writers only seeing the Belomor inmate-workers from afar. "The life of [the inmates] was observed by the artists indirectly, not straying far from the steamship" (Vozdvizhensky, 180). Tamara Ivanova confirms the fact that they were being presented with a sanitized version of camp life: "They showed what were for me personally, even then, obviously 'Potemkin Villages'" (Ivanova, 6).[12] As Gabrilovich testifies, "This was a structure, as it became clear, built on bones. . . . Everything was cleaned up."[13]

Those inmates with whom the writers had contact were common criminals and not political prisoners. Oddly Gabrilovich maintains that there were no contacts with any of the prisoners; however, Ivanova contradicts this assertion and notes that the Brigade met with common criminals imprisoned at the Canal. She adds that even though every participant in the Brigade knew there were "falsely arrested [prisoners]," the OGPU "never showed us a single political prisoner" (ibid.).

The writers' excursion along the Belomor Canal was carefully planned and manipulated. Participants repeatedly note that they rarely strayed far from the steamship, and the only real camp they viewed was the one in Medvezhegorsk (technically not even on the Canal). Moreover, all extant photographs of the writers on the Canal depict them with the camp administration, the Chekists in charge of construction—Firin, Uspensky, and others (see fig. 15). In spite of the fact that camps littered the entire length of the Canal and construction of the Canal had officially ceased, some prisoners were still in those camps when the writers traversed the waterway.

According to *The History of Construction* the writers supposedly had access to a large number of OGPU documents and the camp newspaper, *Perekovka;* however, this does not reflect the experience of those writers who produced chapters in *The History of Construction* on the engineers who designed the Canal. In this case the authors either sent written questions to the engineers or interviewed them two to three months after the Writers Brigade. The archival files of Sergei Budantsev confirm this practice. His personal papers include the questions submitted to the engineers, a written reponse to his questions, which the engineer Orest V. Vyazemsky signed and dated, as well as the transcript of a meeting between six Brigade writers (Budantsev, Shklovsky, Berzina, Rykachev, Zelinsky, and Averbakh) and the chief engineer of the Belomor project, Nikolai I. Khrustalev.[14]

As a result of all these circumstances, the mythicization of the Belomor Canal was encouraged from the first moments of the writers' journey through Belomor—from the luxurious food and drink available only to them to the sanitized Belomor construction site. The population at large, especially those suffering from the famine, and the inmates at Belomor enjoyed none of the delicacies bestowed upon the writers. The OGPU per-

15. Semyon Firin with members of the Soviet Writers Brigade to Belomor, August 1933. Firin is in the center, in the dark uniform with medals on his chest. Some other writers pictured are Vera Inber (at the left, seated, with beret); Boris Lapin (directly behind her); and Vsevolod Ivanov (with glasses, standing behind Firin). Used by permission of the Karelian State Archive, Petrozavodsk, Russia.

petuated the myth of plenty by treating the writers to such lavish fare. Consistent with its practices, the OGPU controlled not only the project but all information about it as well. From the very first moments, the writers' experience at Belomor was manipulated mostly through half-truths and outright lies, a key factor that could threaten the integrity of *The History of Construction* as an historical document, if we perceive it as such. How, then, can an accurate history emerge from a foundation constructed largely of untruths?

Critical to our understanding of the Belomor paradigm is the fact that writers either perceived or were deceived by these untruths. Some bent the truth about Belomor in exchange for the benefits that they would receive for their duplicity. Others chose to compromise on the issue of truth in exchange for the opportunity to write and simply to survive or to save someone else from the Stalinist terror. Still others accepted the Belomor paradigm as gospel truth and proceeded to record it as such. These distinctly individual attitudes toward the Belomor project, stated publicly or privately, complicate any interpretation of the *History*. Consequently, the condemnation leveled against those who participated might not be justified in some cases, a fact to which some of their motives, reconstructed in this study, testify. In fact, subsequent reader and critical response to the participation of writers in the Belomor Brigade has fostered myths not only about their journey along the Canal but also about the actual authors of *The History of Construction*.

120 Individual Journeys

While we cannot fully document the reasons behind each writer's participation in the Belomor Brigade, archival materials and personal reminiscences help reconstruct, at least in part, some of their motivations for joining the Belomor project. Such reconstructions are especially revealing when they pertain to those brigade members who actually wrote *The History of Construction*. Even among those thirty-six writers, it has been almost impossible to discern the reasons for participation in all but a few of them. However, those few are some of the more famous participants in the enterprise.

Contrary to the lore of Belomor, not everyone who took part in the writing of the Belomor volume participated in the Writers Brigade. Conversely, not everyone who participated in the Brigade collaborated on the volume. Moreover some writers refused altogether to participate in the Writers Brigade, while others wanted to but were denied. This wide range of response not only suggests the selective nature of the gathering of the Brigade, but also points to the writers' diverse moral and political positions.

If we begin with the last profile delineated in the previous paragraph, we find a clear juxtaposition of intent and belief. Reportedly Mikhail Bulgakov was asked to join the Brigade but refused. As his wife, Elena Bulgakova, noted in her diary, "In the evening the American journalist Lyons with his astronomical satellite—Zhukhovitsky . . . Zhukhovitsky at supper: 'You aren't doing the right thing, Mikhail Afanasievich, not the right thing! You should be going with some brigade to some factory or to the Belomor Canal. You should take along those fine fellows who, all the same, can't write, but who could carry your suitcases.' . . . 'I'm not the right person to go to the Belomor Canal—I won't go to Malakhovka, because I'm tired'" (Bulgakova, 51).

In contrast, Mikhail Prishvin, who wanted to participate in writing the history of Belomor, was refused. The reasons for this refusal are undocumented; however, the Russian filmmaker V. B. Mileiko, who produced the most recent documentary film on Belomor, *Kanal imeni Stalina* (The Stalin Canal), reports that while researching his film, he discovered that Bulgakov had been invited to participate in the Brigade and Prishvin had not. Mileiko's documentation is based on interviews and numerous personal conversations he conducted for the film, rather than on any written record. Mileiko claims that Prishvin already had prepared a text to contribute, but it was declined, an ironic turn of events since no other writer knew the area in which the Belomor Canal was being built as well as did Prishvin.[15] It is possible that the experiences of other writers would also reflect those of Bulgakov or Prishvin, but sources neither reveal their identities nor suggest their motives.

Those writers who participated in the Brigade but did not collaborate on the Belomor volume—or the reverse, those who helped write the volume, but were not part of the Brigade—are somewhat easier to document. Because we have the list of contributors provided on the second page of the *History of Construction*, we might be tempted to assume that everyone on the list took part in both projects—Brigade and volume. Yet this information misleads the reader. Gorky, although the organizer of the Brigade, did not participate in the actual trip to Belomor. Instead he spearheaded the journey to Belomor and was one of the editors of the volume and the force behind the entire History of Factories and Plants series. In writing about Gorky's instigation of this project, Lazar Fleishman notes that "the first, impressive success of Gorky in [his] post as chairman of the *Orgkomitet* [ORGanizing COMMITtee of the Writers Union]—[was] the organization of a group trip of writers to the Belomor Canal. . . . The Brigade was by no means comprised of strictly inveterate hack writers—leading writers were in it (A. N. Tolstoy, M. Zoshchenko, Vs. Ivanov, V. Kataev, V. Lidin, A. Malyshkin, V. Shklovsky, D.P. Mirsky, K. Zelinsky, etc.)" (135–36). Contrary to the information that Fleishman provides about the Brigade to Belomor, he incorrectly includes Shklovsky as a Brigade participant. According to Shklovsky's daughter, Varvara Viktorovna Shklovskaia-Kordi, Shklovsky did not participate in the Brigade but traveled to Belomor independently.[16] As the discussion in this chapter will illustrate, documents in Shklovsky's personal archival file support her statements.

Gorky's participation in writing *The History of Construction* consisted of organizing the actual writing, editing submissions, and providing the framing essays in the Belomor volume: the introduction, entitled "The Truth of Socialism," and the conclusion, "First Experience." Gorky's public pronouncements about Belomor were frequent. We find references to the project in the essay "About hills and hummocks" in articles in the

Literaturnaia gazeta and in his correspondence. In "About hills and hummocks" (1933) Gorky complains that "not a single one of them [Soviet writers] lamented the fact that he had not spent time on the construction site of the White Sea–Baltic Canal" ("About hills and hummocks," 276). As we know, Gorky visited and wrote positively about the Solovki camp in the White Sea, and his devotion to and support of the Belomor project cannot be denied. Vozdvizhensky argues, "Of course today, from our safe and well-informed distance, to blame Gorky for everything is easy to do. But to vindicate/excuse [him] is impermissible" (180). While Vozdvizhensky's position might seem too strident to some, it highlights Gorky's paradoxical literary biography; however, as the quotation cited at the beginning of this chapter suggests, Gorky knew and understood more than he could admit publicly and proceeded to support the state and Stalin in spite of an inner acknowledgement of the truth.

Besides Gorky, Sergei Alymov (1892–1948), one of the most prolific contributors to the Belomor volume, physically could not have participated in the Writers Brigade because he was an inmate in the Belomor camp. For his activities in the revolutionary movement, he was exiled to Siberia in 1911 but escaped abroad in the same year. Anecdotal information suggests that Alymov fled to Harbin, China, where he published his first collection of poems in 1920. Prior to his internment in Belomor, he had published poems and was famous for the song "Over Hills and Dales" (Avdeenko (b), 16). As it turns out, however, Alymov did not author this song. P. S. Parfenov actually wrote the words even though they had been attributed to Alymov for over thirty years.[17] He returned to the Soviet Union from Harbin in 1926 (*Modern Encyclopedia,* v. 1, 141). He was promptly arrested (probably because he was considered a traitor and spy having spent the October Revolution not in Russia but in China) and sent to Solovki.

After his stint in Solovki, Alymov was moved to the Belomor project, where he became the editor of the camp newspaper, *Perekovka,* and the driving force behind the development of the literary talent of the camp inmates (fig. 16). In fact, the documents in Alymov's archival file are, for the most part, his own original poems, songs, plays, and articles about Belomor, as well as many examples of inmate literary production—songs, poems, articles—and their letters to him as the editor of the newspaper. It could be argued that Alymov was one of the most popular figures on the Canal project, if not the most popular, for the canal workers named him the "poet of the great construction project."[18] As editor of the newspaper *Perekovka,* Alymov was, at least officially, an enthusiastic promulgator of the program of perekovka, although his special status as inmate-writer casts an ironic pall over this enthusiasm. His songs, poems, and plays applauded the remaking of criminals into active participants in socialist construction. The scholar Alla Gorcheva, who has researched extensively the newspapers at Belomor and other camps, believes Alymov was one of the most flagrant perpetrators of the myth of reforging. She holds him responsible for much of the disinformation that filled the pages of *Perekovka*.[19]

As a counterpoint to this position, when members of the Writers Brigade encountered the revered Alymov at Belomor, his reaction bespoke a different attitude. As Avdeenko recounts, when a group of writers happened upon Alymov in one of the barracks, they jocularly spoke to him and asked Firin, who was accompanying them, for Alymov's early release. To this question Firin replied that Alymov's term had already been shortened and that he would be returning to Moscow. After Firin left, the writer Aleksander Bezymensky asked Alymov, "Seryozha, how did you end up here?" In reply, "the Canal-soldier Alymov waved his hand, burst into tears and climbed on to the top bunk" (Avdeenko (b), 16–17). Certainly humiliation

16. Copy of a page from *Perekovka*, the Belomor camp newspaper, featuring a photograph of Yagoda on the front page. Photographed from a display at the Belomor Canal Museum. Used by permission of Igor V. Sopronenko.

before one's peers would evoke such a strong reaction. Given the trauma of the situation, the unexpected meeting of his colleagues in such unpleasant, em-barrassing conditions could have provoked his emotions. Or he could also have been plagued by guilt or a sense of failure or isolation.

Alymov finally returned to Moscow after the completion of the Canal and continued to write; he became one of the Soviet Union's most revered and popular songwriters. Many of his songs were and still are considered classics of Soviet popular music, including "Song about Russia," "Vasya-Vasilek," "Trails and Byways," "The Garden Flowers in Springtime Are Grand," and the war songs "Baltic Glory" and "The Song of the Marines." Alymov's unceasing and staunchly pro-Soviet stance while at Belomor and afterward did not diminish with time and experience. Within the context of the war, his devotion to his homeland in the face of the German threat overrode any other sentiments, and his patriotism here is understandable. With regard to his Belomor experience, any combination of sentiment could have motivated Alymov to be faithful to the Soviet cause: blind faith, cynicism, self-delusion, fear, even a willingness to compromise to save his own life. No matter what motivated him, his unquestioning support of the Soviet system has earned him harsh criticism for being a malleable puppet of state power.

In contrast to Alymov, Victor Shklovsky was not at all moved to participate in the Belomor project because he supported the program of perekovka. Given the facts of Shklovsky's biography, perekovka represented the antithesis of everything that he believed in at the beginning and end of his career.

Victor Shklovsky, literary theoretician, scholar, and writer (1893–1984), was one of three sons born into a mathematician's family. After studying philology at the University of Petrograd, Shklovsky launched his literary career by cofounding the OPOYAZ (Society for the Study of Poetic Language) in 1916, a group that evolved into the formalists. The formalists were leading literary theoreticians who supported the independent value and status of art. They believed it was more important to study the literary text in and of itself rather than the author who wrote it. Central to formalist thought was a focus on language and its use in literature. As Shklovsky claimed, a literary work is the sum of its devices. In addition to his work with the formalists, he also aligned himself with the Serapion Brothers, a group of independent writers who included Mikhail Zoshchenko, and with LEF (the Left Front of Art), a group of futurist poets. Shklovsky spent 1922 and 1923 in Berlin and published two novels there, *Zoo: or, Letters not about Love* and *A Sentimental Journey*. While Shklovsky officially distanced himself from formalism by the late twenties and early thirties, many of its theories remained ingrained in and were attributable to him throughout his career.

As a literary theorist, Shklovsky is best known for his seminal work *On the Theory of Prose* (1929). In this work Shklovsky sets forth the idea that form dominates content in literature. To achieve form, the writer employs a variety of devices to create the text. These devices, not conscious authorial design, motivate the development of character and plot. When we read any of Shklovsky's work—novels, literary treatises, newspaper articles, film reviews—we observe his theory put into practice. In his own writing Shklovsky favored short paragraphs, disjointed trains of thought, and verbal leaps from one topic to another. The work seems disorganized, even chaotic, although there is always a thematic or structural thread that unites the narrative.

Shklovsky's approach seems even more appropriate when we consider his work in film. Both a critic and screenwriter, he embraced the techniques of modern Soviet cinema, especially those espoused by the famous Soviet film director Sergei Eisenstein. Eisenstein's theory of montage appealed to Shklovsky's artistic sensibilities and was consonant with the way he produced his prose works, be they novels or critical essays. What captivated Shklovsky about montage, as Eisenstein practiced it, was the ability to quickly shift scene and atmosphere and to defy the expected logic of the piece, as well as to break down and reassemble the constituent parts of a work so as to create a new whole, and as a result, a new effect.

One of Shklovsky's key contributions to literary theory, *ostranenie*, the act of making the commonplace strange and therefore new, operated in film as well. In all his work, he demonstrated that he embraced many of the tenets of modernist thought, even in his contributions to the Belomor volume (see chapter 3). As such he is best remembered as one of the most influential formalists as well as a writer of imagination and originality. While his work during Stalinism might have veered from his original path, he strove to produce original, creative work, no matter in which era he worked. This adaptability or, perhaps more precisely, his ability to choose which personal and professional battles to fight, reveals itself in his participation in the Belomor project.

In fact, Victor Shklovsky did not participate in the Writers Brigade but instead made a personal trip to Belomor in October 1932 with a definite goal in mind: to assist in the release of his older brother, Vladimir, from the Belomor camp—ultimately a successful undertaking. As his daughter, Varvara, recounts, Shklovsky had earlier succeeded in obtaining his brother's release from Solovki. Vladimir was a lexicographer who was fluent in many languages and compiled dictionaries. Arrested as a conspirator in a supposed plot to send secret information to foreign governments through a dictionary that he had compiled, he eventually perished in 1937 after he was arrested a third time; on this occasion Victor could not save him. Shklovsky's trip to Belomor is well documented in archival materials and served as the impetus for actively participating in the writing and editing of the Belomor volume.[20]

Shklovsky traveled to the Belomor site 6–10 October 1932 on a business trip for the journal *Pogranichnik* (The Border Guard). While at the Canal he visited various construction sites, met with prisoners, talked with L. Kogan, head of the Belomor construction project, and collected materials from which he would later produce stories, sketches, and a screenplay (in collaboration with Vera Inber). While at the Canal, Shklovsky is reported to have responded to an OGPU officer's question "How do you feel here [on Belomor]?" with the quip: "Like a live silver fox in a fur store."[21]

Whatever his subsequent pronouncements about Belomor, Shklovsky's comment captures the situation fully; however, his understanding of the situation did not prevent him from contributing to the Belomor volume, since he viewed his participation as the "price he had to pay for his brother's life."[22] It could be argued that Shklovsky went beyond what was expected of him by writing not only short stories but also a screenplay, as well as actively editing and assembling the Belomor volume. In January 1934 he spoke to a group of writers in Leningrad "about the work of the writers' collective on the volume about the Belomorstroi."[23] He also described writing the Belomor volume in a number of publications. In fact, on all levels he visibly and actively participated in the Belomor event, although always with the ulterior motive to free his brother.

We might be tempted to judge Shklovsky's actions as suspect, contradictory, or even deplorable. Yet to do so addresses them on only one level. Instead, his situation and response suggest that the mechanisms of control were increasingly moving into place, thereby prompting contradictory responses from writers. While these responses probably do not conform to contemporary conceptions of how writers should have responded to increasing Stalinist control, they nonetheless intimate that, for some writers, finding the path of least resistance and personal reward was difficult and antithetical. As Daniil Danin notes in an article commemorating Shklovsky's one hundredth birthday: "And he sinned against his deepest convictions. And he yielded to pressure from the authorities. And he performed unforgiveable deeds. (Like the mockery of Meyerhold's "The Inspector

General" or his leading authorship in the apologetic book about the Belomor Canal.) But I do not feel that I have the right to be his judge. . . . In our turbulent days here and there the forgotten, or conversely, unforgettable faults and sins of everyone sinless of Shklovsky's generation—from Akhmatova to Zoshchenko—are newly made public" (*Literaturnaia gazeta*, 6). Danin then lists the literary compromises that the most revered and popular Soviet writers made in response to the demands the state imposed on them. As he implies, while no one is blameless, neither are contemporary critics in a fair position to judge those choices made during a most peculiar and frightening time.

In contrast to Shklovsky, Alexander Avdeenko was a fledgling writer when he journeyed along the Belomor Canal. At the time, participation in such an excursion was considered a great honor, especially if, as in Avdeenko's case, one was invited to participate by Gorky himself. As Avdeenko relates, he was beside himself with wonder at being in the company of such great Soviet writers as Kataev and Zoshchenko. To think that someone of such humble proletarian beginnings would be invited to join some of the most esteemed writers of the Soviet literary establishment! The tremendous success of Avdeenko's first book, *I Love* (1935), makes his participation less surprising than the author himself is willing to admit, and its popularity probably had everything to do with his inclusion in the Brigade. Avdeenko notes, "That's how I got to the top of the hill and my life took off. A shock-worker, called to literature! And I immediately fell into the ranks of writers worthy of great honor" (Avdeenko (b), 8).

The great honor to which Avdeenko refers, of course, is his inclusion in the Writers Brigade to Belomor. For him this is especially important because he epitomized the new breed of writer, common worker turned literary figure. Avdeenko was living the proletarian dream. Having grown up in the provinces and worked in a factory, he was "discovered" thanks to his inaugural work, *I Love*. For a worker from humble beginnings this attention and privilege meant everything. Avdeenko adds, "I could hardly wait until the evening. What wasn't I afraid of. I thought—at the very last minute they'll drop me from the list. Or I'll be late for the departure. I won't see something, I won't hear something, something important will pass me by" (ibid., 9). With all the vigor of a novice writer, he approached his trip to Belomor, not with critical eyes and a jaded perspective, but with the energy and enthusiasm of a young man about to join a prestigious and privileged club.

As fate would have it, Avdeenko was the compartment mate of the literary critic Il'ya Selivanovsky and Prince Dmitry Mirsky, who suffered a peculiar fate at the hands of the Stalinist system in spite of his participation in the Belomor Brigade. In recounting his journey to Belomor with Mirsky and Selivanovsky, Avdeenko reveals his youthful naïveté. When Selivanovsky and Mirsky recite poetry to each other—the verses of Pushkin, Lermontov, Homer—he is entranced and enthralled by their ability to remember centuries of verse by heart. "The ability of my fellow travelers to hold in their memories lines created by poets of every nation and every era was for me incomprehensible. I was amazed and depressed" (ibid., 12).

When Mirsky determines that Avdeenko is from the Donbas, an area with which Mirsky is familiar, he engages the younger man in conversation. Their exchange accentuates Avdeenko's youthful zest for things Soviet. In discussing the Donbas, Mirsky fails to mention the *sotsgorod,* the "socialist city," a purported model of socialist society and planning. When Avdeenko calls him on this point, Mirsky responds, "I didn't forget [about the *sotsgorod*]. The real sotsgorod, my dear man, has yet to be built. But even now, without a real sotsgorod, barrack-laden Magnitka is the greatest city on the earth. It is great because of the enthusiasm of the working class" (ibid.). When Avdeenko wonders to himself, "For whom is he saying all that? Whom is he enlightening?" he reveals his complete lack of understanding, not only of Mirsky's position but of the increasingly tenuous situation in which many Soviet writers, including Avdeenko himself, were to soon find themselves (ibid.). Moreover, Avdeenko's smug comment "Whom is he enlightening?" bespeaks his own self-confidence and certainty in the workers' revolution, the development of Soviet power, and his knowledge of both.

In his account of the trip to Belomor, Avdeenko consistently elaborates on the often subtle apprehension of the situation by some of the writers participating in the Brigade. Most obviously, the lavish, elegant dinners that the OGPU provided for the writers contrasted sharply with the daily menu for the canal workers. Instead of caviar, sausages and chicken Kiev, the canalarmyist dinner consisted of 1.2 kilos of cabbage soup, 300 grams of kasha with meat, 75 grams of fish cutlets with sauce and 100 grams of cabbage pies per person (ibid., 15). Having feasted on the OGPU-provided delicacies, Avdeenko's remark that "given the hunger of that time, the canal workers eat well" might seem to smack of ignorance, had it not been for the severe famine that swept through many areas of the USSR. By providing the detailed menu he, perhaps unwittingly, underscores the contrast between the luxurious and bountiful food and drink available to the writers on their trip and the poor fare of the canal builders. While glorified as heroes of socialist construction and reforging, the canal workers survived on meager rations, made even more meager by the fact that they, unlike the writers, were engaged in intense physical labor daily. But at least they had rations, in stark contrast to the millions of starving Soviet citizens in Ukraine and elsewhere.

Avdeenko's narrative description of the trip includes telling moments that imply some of the writers in the Brigade understood and passively acknowledged the harsh reality of the Belomor project. Consider, for example, the exchange between Prince Mirsky and Semyon Firin. To Mirsky's question "Were there mistakes, accounting errors?" Firin responded, "Of course, there were, as in any new undertaking." When Mirsky probed further, "How much did it cost the government?" Firin noted, "I don't remember the exact figure. . . . But I can assure you, comrades, that much less was spent [on this project] than by, say, Ferdinand de Lesseps on the Suez Canal. Or by the motley bunch of swindlers on the construction of the Panama [Canal]. And we expended significantly fewer hours of manpower." In response to this explanation, Mirsky posed the question, "And through which means was the cost of the BBK successfully reduced?" Firin responded, "Through a sharply curtailed construction period. Through the good organization of labor. Through the enthusiasm of the canal workers, the enthusiasm called forth by the fact that the prisoners were presented with the opportunity to participate fully in this grandiose construction project." When Mirsky prodded further, "And probably because of free labor?" Firin, unflinchingly and in full propagandistic mode, replied, "Yes, of course. People serving out their punishments do not receive a salary. That's the way it's been for the longest time in the entire civilized world. Do you have any other questions?"

Undaunted, Mirsky continued, "And what was the idea behind the secrecy? Why was the project, the heroic epic of the canalsoldiers, hidden from the people and from the whole world for two years?" Again Firin countered, "Strictly speaking, Belomorstroi was not secret in the literal sense of that word. It simply was not written about in the papers nor talked about on the radio." Mirsky asked the question, "And why?" to which Firin responded, "Comrade Stalin wisely advised us up to the last minute to display a maximum of modesty. The fewer the words, the bigger the deed. That's how we proceeded. And now, when the canal already is in operation, we show the world our pride, which is justified. The end is the best reward." When Mirsky asked whether or not the canalworkers were aware of Stalin's presence when he visited the Canal, Firin replied that they were not and that the Chekists made sure it stayed that way, to which Mirsky rejoined, "Comrade Stalin didn't want to call the attention of the canalsoldiers to himself so as not to tear them away from their work?" (ibid., 18). This exchange left those who witnessed it fidgeting in discomfort; Avdeenko felt somewhat guilty, as if he were responsible for Mirsky's disconcerting questions.

The discomfort that probing questions evoked reemerges in another exchange, this time between Firin and Valentin Kataev. To Kataev's question "Tell us, Semyon Grigorievich, did the canal soldiers often get sick?" Firin replied, "It happened. It couldn't be otherwise. A man isn't [made of] iron." Kataev continued, "And did some die?" Firin responded, "That happened. We are all mortal." Kataev's final question "And why haven't we seen a single cemetery on the banks of the Canal?" drew the sharp retort from Firin, "Because there's no place here for them," at which point "the happy and hospitable Firin grew stern and walked away" (ibid., 20).

Actually, there are numerous reasons for having no cemeteries along the Canal. Workers were buried in unmarked graves or in marked graves deep in the forest. As Solzhenitsyn notes in *GULag Archipelago,* sometimes bodies were mixed into the concrete poured at some of the locks and dams or they were simply left frozen in the snow, only to reappear after the spring thaw, at which point the corpses could be seen floating in the Canal (Solzhenitsyn [b], 99). From the official point of view there was no reason to blacken the success of the OGPU and the project by formally and publicly admitting that such atrocities had occurred, considering that the Writers Brigade traveled to the Canal to document the success and glory of the Belomor project. While this exchange underscores that the "truth" the OGPU provided to the Writers Brigade was a selective truth, and not the whole truth, it also demonstrates that many of the writers were insightful enough to realize the OGPU's intent.

Avdeenko himself was to discover this reality as a result of subsequent events, but at the time he participated in the Belomor Brigade, the distinctions among truths, half-truths, and outright lies were still not clear to him. It would not be far-fetched to conclude (although probably impossible to document fully) that other participants echoed Kataev's and Mirsky's opinions. Not every writer accepted without question or suspicion the official pronouncements about Belomor. In this regard, Avdeenko, with all his naïveté, youth, and revolutionary zeal, provides the perfect foil to Mirsky's more critical and more accurate reading of events and of Belomor in particular.

After Mirsky questioned Firin, an exchange that produced a great deal of discomfort for all concerned, he continued the same line of conversation with Avdeenko. Mirsky correctly assumed that the young man did not agree with him, but for Mirsky there were more critical issues that neither Firin nor the other writers would or could discuss. Having ascertained that Avdeenko disagreed with his line of questioning, Mirsky proceeded to explain why he posed such questions. According to Avdeenko, Mirsky believed in Lenin and supported much of what was happening, but he was convinced that Lenin would not approve of much that had occurred since his death. Mirsky commented to Avdeenko, "And the saddest thing is that I clearly see shortcomings, blunders, mistakes, negligence, and sometimes arbitrariness; but your eyes, accustomed to the large and small defects, don't notice them. . . . For example, you look at the Canal only as a great wonder and you don't see the other side" (ibid., 18). Avdeenko was too young and inexperienced to "see the other side" and disapproved of Mirsky's whole line of thinking. When Mirsky suggested that the writers were seeing only part of the whole picture, Avdeenko was incredulous. When Mirsky said, "Here at every step there are hidden secrets. Under every dam. Under every lock. In the fate and work of every canalsoldier. If fate were to conveniently make me younger and assign me to your enviable position as a young writer, you know what I would do? I would write a story 'The Secret of the Three Letters'" (ibid.). Mirsky proposed a story that would reveal the real truth behind the three-letter acronym for the Belomorsko–Baltiiskii Kanal—BBK.

That Avdeenko disbelieved Mirsky is not unexpected, especially given the time and atmosphere in which Avdeenko was raised. He grew up and matured during the revolution and civil war. His consciousness was defined by postrevolutionary life and thought. The opposite was true for Mirsky—a prince from one of Russia's oldest families, who fled Russia after the October Revolution, only to return in the hope of rebuilding his life in his homeland. When Avdeenko incredulously questioned Mirsky's judgment, when he wondered that it could even be possible for the Belomor Canal to be anything but what they had seen, Mirsky replied, "It can be, my dear, it can be. People are capable of creating not only wonders, but all sorts of cunning traps for their own brothers as well as for themselves. Throughout human history anything has been possible. More often than not the great human calamities have started from the good intentions and assurances of the powerful of this world" (ibid.). Mirsky and Avdeenko's conversation highlights the gap between them—a gap based on experience, generation, even class. The exchange also suggests who merits and does not merit reforging. Mirsky, the product of another generation, another class, and different experiences, is much less likely to be reforgeable but is a prime candidate for implementing reforging. Avdeenko's profile suits the reforging process perfectly, but he does not need it, for he already exemplifies the "new Soviet man."

More succinctly than any other commentator on the Belomor project, Mirsky, while still at the Canal, revealed his complete comprehension and suspicion of the Belomor project's true significance. No doubt other writers on the Brigade shared his sentiments. Perhaps in hindsight even Avdeenko shared Mirsky's opinions, for it is Avdeenko who quotes Mirsky extensively in his recollections of the Belomor episode. Most important to this discussion is the inherent conflict in Mirsky's actions. On the one hand, he understood what was happening, questioned it, and spoke out about it. On the other hand, he participated in writing *The History of Construction*. What motivated someone of Mirsky's stature and background to participate in a project that he obviously knew to be false and brutal? To condemn Mirsky on the basis of his participation in such a project, especially if we consider his personal history and his commitment to and love of Russian culture and literature (he was the author of arguably the best concise history of Russian literature), might seem unwarranted, given the very clear evidence that he understood Belomor. Was his participation the personal compromise he had to make in an attempt to assure his survival? Perhaps Mirsky believed or tried to believe that Belomor held the promise of being what it was supposed to be rather than what it turned out to be. Participation in the Writers Brigade did not, could not, necessarily imply that one embraced wholeheartedly what Belomor was intended to symbolize.

For all of Avdeenko's unwavering support of the Belomor project, he did not contribute to the volume, while Mirsky did; however, this did not prevent Avdeenko from contributing in other ways. After Belomor, Avdeenko was sent to the Moscow–Volga Canal construction site to recount the ongoing success of socialist construction and, as a consequence, of perekovka. While Avdeenko posed as a Chekist, replete with a uniform and the telltale raspberry epaulettes and trim, his Moscow-Volga experience turned out to be less than inspiring. Just as Mirsky and Kataev had incurred Firin's wrath at Belomor for their importunate questions, so, too, did Avdeenko at Moscow-Volga. Such a twist of fate was not uncommon in literary biographies throughout the 1930s.

The irony of Avdeenko's participation in the Belomor Writers Brigade, one played out in the lives of many writers who participated not only in the Brigade but also in the collectively written *History of Construction*, was that participation in the Belomor project did not insulate writers from future repression and execution. In Avdeenko's case, his downfall came not in the form of imprisonment in one of Stalin's camps, a fate he constantly feared. Instead, Avdeenko was denied the privilege of being published, a much less harsh fate than that suffered by many of his peers but a crushing blow all the same, especially (if we are to believe Avdeenko's sentiment in retelling these episodes) for a writer from the working class who was totally dedicated not only to the Soviet regime and socialist ideology but to Stalin himself as well. Arguably, the rise and fall of Avdeenko during prewar Stalinism typifies the frequently arbitrary way in which writers were controlled throughout this period.

In short, Avdeenko supposedly had erred egregiously in two distinct and familiar ways: He had been friends with people who, as it turned out, were actually "enemies of the people," and he wrote what came to be labeled "anti-Soviet" works. Among Avdeenko's contacts were supposed "state enemies" such as Sergo Ordzhonikidze (at the time minister of heavy industry, a Party and Politburo member, and Stalin's Georgian crony), with whom Avdeenko conversed regarding his soon-to-be published novel *Fate*; Gvakharija (first name not given), the head of the Makeevka Metallurgical Factory; Vsevolod Meyerhold (the famed theater director) and his wife, to whom he gave a lift from the train depot to the Makeevka theater. Two of these three contacts were established in Avdeenko's hometown of Makeevka. Added to these less than desirable contacts were Avdeenko's unpublished novel, *I Am the State*, and his film, *The Law of Life*, released in 1940 and immediately pulled from distribution. Critics publicly and privately branded Avdeenko an enemy of the state who had betrayed his working-class roots by associating with other class enemies—all of the people noted above. His latest novel failed to portray "accurately" the life of a Donbas miner. The film slandered Soviet youth by supposedly depicting a medical institute graduation party as a drunken orgy.

For these indiscretions, Avdeenko was removed from his house in Makeevka, his apartment in Moscow, the Union of Writers, the staff of *Pravda*, and the Communist Party of the USSR. In addition to these demotions, Avdeenko was condemned publicly in *Pravda* and *Literaturnaia gazeta*, as well as privately by the likes of Andrei Zhdanov, Nikolai Pogodin, Aleksander Fadeev, V. Kataev, and last, but certainly not least, comrade Stalin himself. Kataev and Pogodin participated in the Belomor Brigade with Avdeenko but, perhaps not so incredibly, had nothing positive to say about him at this most critical moment. In addition, Fadeev lived in the same apartment building in Moscow as did Avdeenko—their sons were friends. This relationship did not prevent Fadeev from turning on him when necessary. Paradoxically, Stalin, while condemning Avdeenko in 1940, personally rehabilitated him during the war in 1943. But the most poignant irony is the fact that Avdeenko was assigned to cover Stalin's funeral for Soviet radio and as a special correspondent for *Ogonyek*. As Avdeenko notes, "I was amazed that they *trusted* precisely me to cover Stalin's funeral" (ibid., 129).

This brief digression to divulge some of the details of Avdeenko's personal biography underscores the arbitrariness that often marked literary life as well as much of Soviet life in the 1930s. This is not to suggest that programs, doctrines, ideologies were ignored or used perfunctorily. Anyone familiar with the history of Stalinism in the 1930s knows that this period is marked by a mix of rigid adherence to rules and programs on the one hand, and arbitrary, frequently coincidental or chance occurrences, on the other. The topic on which this book focuses—the construction of the Belomor Canal—exemplifies the implementation of ideology and dogma in Soviet life. What resonates in Avdeenko's participation in the Belomor project and subsequent difficulties at the hands of the literary establishment is that for him, as for Mirsky, Budantsev, Zoshchenko, and others, participation in an officially sanctioned, fervently pro-Soviet project did not, and probably could not, ensure being exempted from personal and professional misfortune and, in Budantsev's case, from a politically motivated death. While these writers could not have known this in advance, it was as if the original horror of Belomor was revisited in small doses upon those who so diligently described and praised it.

The dispensation of these small doses of horror hints at a number of explanations as to why they occurred. Most important, that a writer could later suffer in spite of participation in an officially sanctioned project speaks to the capricious nature of literary life in the 1930s. It was impossible to predict one's personal fate, which meant that any attempt to mitigate it could produce equally positive and negative results. There was a risk involved when a writer attempted to gauge the political landscape as a measure for literary activity.

That there was such a high probability of negative outcomes suggests that, at least in the early 1930s, there was no fixed government policy that provided guidelines for behavior. Both Katerina Clark and Sheila Fitzpatrick note this phenomenon. They argue that the period of the First Five-Year Plan generated more instability than stability in the literary world. As a result, the search for ways to participate in literary life and to capture in literature what was happening throughout the Soviet Union prompted more confusion than consensus. Only after the Second Five-Year Plan commenced in 1933 was there a real movement to consolidate and codify literary groups and activities.[24]

If there was no fixed, undoubtedly unstated code of behavior for writers, then the potential for falling victim to changing political demands increased. What was acceptable in 1933 might not be acceptable in 1937. History has proven that this was the case. Moreover, a documented shift in literary heroes did occur with the onset of the Second Five-Year Plan. Katerina Clark and Karen Petrone note the shift in emphasis in the mid-thirties from "little heroes" with big deeds to "big heroes" with big deeds.

Clark and Petrone each argue that literary heroes changed markedly in the mid-thirties. Whereas in the early 1930s literature applauded the masses, the comman man who worked tirelessly to strengthen Soviet power through large building projects, from the mid-thirties on, the positive hero, a single powerful arbiter of truth and ability, commanded the reader's and writer's attention. With the formulation of the positive hero, the little man no longer mattered. In his stead appeared individual heroes who, thanks in part to their own personal characteristics and their development within the Soviet system, achieved great feats for the Soviet Union. The working masses, the collective, functioned as the background against which this new hero operated. Collective responsibility and success gave way to individual achievement.[25]

Thus, as the ideology adjusted to fit the political demands of the time, so, too, did the literary paradigm. That this shift was possible at all portended the likelihood of the unstable fates of many writers. As we have seen, this outcome did not bode well for a variety of writers, whether or not they made the calculated risk to adjust their literary practice in accordance with the prevailing political situation.

Related to this shift is the notion concerning which writers were suited to reforging and which were not. Consider Mirsky and Avdeenko. We would expect Avdeenko to participate in writing the Belomor volume because he was already a believer; he supported the Soviet system and represented the "new" Soviet writer—a worker who, based on his proletarian experiences, becomes a writer. But he did not participate in writing the Belomor volume. Mirsky, the least likely participant because of his political views, contributed to the volume.

This unlikely turn of events could imply that the system was already producing "new Soviet men" by itself, without any additional help from projects such as the Belomor Brigade and volume. Avdeenko embodied the type who emerged from the system naturally. In contrast, Mirsky represented the prime candidate for reforging, and if his shift in thinking and practice was successful, it would serve as a model for others to follow. This outcome suggests that reforging was designed not so much for those who were already being molded by the system as for those who were the products of a previous system. Perhaps the success or failure of one's process of reforging also determined one's ultimate fate.

That the nightmare of Belomor seemed to revisit certain writers might simply be the result of a moral equation that harks back to a basic law of physics: For every action there is an equal and opposite reaction. If we apply this law to literary activities, it becomes clear that for many writers, later tribulations and difficulties emerged as simple reactions to their participation in such a horrific project. While this contention might initially seem to smack of high-minded moralism, there is something to be said for the thought that every action is repaid in kind. If this is true, then each attempt to praise the Belomor project could well have been met with an equal dose of poetic justice. No matter which explanation seems most plausible, there often tended to be an uncanny relationship between participation in Belomor and one's fate at the hands of the very system that sanctioned the project.

With this information in mind, we can approach the final category of inclusion: those writers who participated both in the Writers Brigade and in the creation of the Belomor volume. Although Prince Mirsky falls into this category, the following portraits of Sergei Budantsev, Boris Lapin, and Mikhail Zoshchenko emerge as fuller examples of the process through which writers negotiated their work on the Belomor project within the context of their own literary biography. While these three literary figures initially were chosen for inclusion in this discussion based on the extensive documentable evidence of their participation, the selection has been fortuitous. The writers share the common bond of participation, but their unique literary interests yield insights into three distinct approaches to a literary career, especially in the 1930s.

Three Sides of the Same Triangle

The writers who participated both in the Writers Brigade and in the writing of the Belomor volume represent an interesting mix of (1) authors still widely esteemed in Western criticism, (2) authors generally unknown to Western criticism, and (3) authors considered morally compromised mouthpieces of the state. This trio of writers, often diametrically opposed in their literary methods and political inclinations, reaffirms the often confusing and complicated nature of literary life in the early 1930s.

While it would be desirable to assess the participation of every writer in the Belomor Brigade and its subsequent written history, this task is impossible, because archival sources and personal reminiscences reveal only part of the story behind the attitudes, impressions, and motivations of those writers. Moreover, the veracity of the sources that do exist, as well as the various attendant issues that reminiscences raise, make the task of reconstructing writers' responses to Belomor even more difficult.

The three writers highlighted here are not the only interesting cases, but they have turned out to be the most thoroughly documentable among the group of fascinating and famous personalities in Soviet literature who contributed to the Belomor project. Moreover, a quick overview reveals that, as was the case with those writers discussed previously—Avdeenko, Shklovsky, Mirsky, and Alymov—a writer's fate was not necessarily contingent upon or influenced by his or her participation in the Belomor project.

Valentin Kataev and Bruno Jasensky, arguably supporters of Soviet power, participated in both the Writers Brigade and the Belomor volume yet shared quite different fates. Jasenky perished during Stalin's terror, while Kataev continued his career for another forty years. An established Soviet writer like Alexei Tolstoy, for example, participated and suffered no documentable dire consequences. Evgeny Gabrilovich, who, along with Boris Lapin, was drawn to constructivist and expressionist poetry in the early twenties, also collaborated on the volume. As we know, Gabrilovich became one of the Soviet Union's leading screenwriters. Vera Inber, always a faithful friend of the state, not only helped write the Canal volume but also edited it and, with Shklovsky, collaborated on a screenplay about Belomor. Her successful career continued long after completion of the Belomor project. Considered in hindsight, participation in the Belomor project could conceivably have meant nothing or everything in the personal fortunes of a writer.

In addition to the problems encountered in trying to reconstruct writer motivation in the Canal project, we confront the added problem of inconsistencies in source materials. While Avdeenko wrote about Mirsky and the Belomor episode almost sixty years after the fact in the atmosphere of perestroika, information about Budantsev and his activities is accessible only by examining his papers—manuscripts and letters—in Russian archives. Information about Lapin is scant and derives mostly from the recollections of his father-in-law, Ilya Erenburg and Lapin's widow, Irina Erenburg. Regarding Zoshchenko, we are faced with a mix of critical literature and actual authorial responses. While none of the sources, including the writers' biographies that follow, is without some drawbacks, when we consider the whole constellation of subjective interpretations of Belomor, both actual and literary, a fuller understanding of the event and of its ramifications for Soviet literary history emerges.

The writers profiled below—Budantsev, Lapin, and Zoshchenko—participated both in the Belomor Writers Brigade and in the writers collective of *The History of Construction*. Little else except their shared participation in these two projects links them closely. While no one raises questions about Budantsev's or Lapin's participation in the Belomor episode, Zoshchenko's role proves much more problematic and difficult to accept. Each case illustrates how the demands of the time, personal motivation, and the atmosphere of the moment combined to produce literary responses that might have been unheard of in another period. The following discussion neither supports nor condemns each writer's position. Instead, it tries to elucidate why each man participated and what this participation says, not just about the individual, but also about the time in which he was working.

Sergei Budantsev

In this group of writers, only Sergei Budantsev falls cleanly within the category of ardent supporter of the Soviet regime, because of his other activities and ideas, all of which were devoted to applauding the system. Aside from these official activities, however, little is known about his personal life. He was born in 1896 into an intellectual family. He entered Moscow State University, but did not finish because of the onset of World War I. Subsequently, he worked as a correspondent for various newspapers. Budantsev was arrested in 1938, and later died in a prison camp. He was rehabilitated in 1956.

Budantsev's archival materials confirm one fact: He did not foresee his arrest and imminent death at the hands of the very Stalinist system that he had so vigorously supported in his literary works. His archival file reveals that he was responsible for the idea of producing a volume entitled *The Great Waterways of the USSR*, which was to be published in 1937 in honor of the twentieth anniversary of the October Revolution. Similar to *The History of Construction*, Budantsev's *Great Waterways* was to be a collectively authored work; each participating writer would be responsible for profiling one waterway, either natural or man-made, that comprised the great water transportation system of the Soviet Union. While no such volume actually exists, Budantsev had drawn up extensive plans for it and had even contracted writers to produce their respective entries for the collection. Archival records indicate that Budantsev had received manuscripts from a number of participants and had paid the collaborators for their submissions as well. The proposed contributors to the volume included V. Lidin, K. Paustovsky, B. Pilnyak, and I. Sokolov-Mikitov.[26]

Presumably the *Great Waterways* project was initially accepted for publication, but it is highly likely that the whole project was scrapped after Budantsev's arrest, although no documents confirm this belief. The only proof that the project did not reach fruition is that not a single copy can be found in any of the main Russian libraries or archival holdings. While it is possible to conjecture that the book was published in such a small print run as to have disappeared shortly after publication, this scenario seems unlikely. In all probability, the project was never completed simply because Budantsev was not there to complete it; he had been arrested and killed by the very regime he sought to honor.

Despite the paucity of biographical information about Budantsev, it is possible to reconstruct at least his literary and political leanings based on the materials in his archival file. The most interesting documents that illustrate Budantsev's commitment to the Soviet regime and the Belomor project are his letter to Stalin and his narrative description of the Belomor volume and its significance for Soviet literature.

It is not clear whether Budantsev ever sent his letter, dated 1934, to Stalin. (Since Budantsev cites the Seventeenth Party Congress in the opening lines of his letter, it is possible to infer that the letter was written in late 1933 or, more likely, early 1934, prior to the Party Congress at the end of January.) In this letter, Budantsev expounds four main themes that repeatedly underpin the entire Belomor episode: (1) the importance and achievement of the building of the Canal, (2) the uniqueness of the collectively authored volume that narrates the history of Belomor, (3) the reforging powers of hard labor, and (4) the unquestionable wisdom and foresight of the Communist Party, most fully embodied in Stalin. This letter, like many other documents of the time, is laden with the aggrandizing rhetoric of pro-Soviet propaganda. The tone and ritualized discourse should not cloud our reading either of the intent of Budantsev's letter or of the fervor it conveys. Documents reveal, in so much as it is possible, that Budantsev's fervor did not diminish after the construction of the Belomor Canal but continued and deepened, as evidenced by his work on the collection *Great Waterways of the USSR*.

The laudatory way in which Budantsev writes about the Belomor Canal project in his letter to Stalin bears directly on our discussion. As he notes, "One of the greatest achievements in the accomplished socialist plan is the White Sea–Baltic Canal. Beyond its connections with the general process of socialist construction, the White Sea–Baltic Canal stands as a technically brave structure that mightily challenges the first-class canals of the world. . . . But the instructiveness of Belomorstroi lies in the fact that it cannot be perceived outside of this connection. The White Sea–Baltic Waterway is the result of the intense creative battle of the Communist Party and the OGPU."²⁷ Insofar as Budantsev sets up the Belomor Canal as a rival to any of the great canals in the world (although the comparison is not completely valid), he also argues that "the Belomor construction project is worthy of history." As a result, the Belomor project can be successfully appropriated as the topic of *The History of Construction,* especially since that volume is "the first authentic collective work in the entire existence of literature that is dedicated to the victory of socialism in our country, the approaching liquidation of [all] classes, the triumph of the socialist principle of labor" (ibid.) Like the official pronouncements about Belomor, both the Canal itself and its attendant volume support and legitimate the whole project. As Budantsev argues, it exemplifies the principles of socialist construction achieved through collective socialist labor and the guidance of the Party.

In writing about how *The History of Construction* was actually produced, Budantsev notes in the letter that "the writers were given concrete material about the saboteurs, contrarevolutionaries, kulaks, strident recidivists, about their past, about their paths to improvement.... Work on the book called forth new, as yet untitled forms of collaboration. The book is being created in [an atmosphere] of constant mutual criticism, of collective help for each other. The book grows with each day. But each day the authors grow as well."²⁸ Not unexpectedly, Budantsev praises the collective writing process and, like Shklovsky, alludes to the inherent process of mutual self-criticism that marked the writing of the volume and made its creation all the more collective.

When he describes the writing of the Belomor volume, Budantsev admits that "we, a group of non-Party writers, are writing the history of the BeloMorStroi. We are writing it in constant creative contact with Communist writers, organizers and Chekists."²⁹ That Budantsev emphasizes his non-Party status as early as 1934 speaks to his confidence in the safety of that status; one did not have to be a member of the Communist Party in order to be an active participant in socialist construction. Moreover, Budantsev's admission of his non-Party status makes his enthusiastic, supportive pronouncements about the Belomor project simultaneously striking and suspect. They are striking for their fervor yet beg the question: If Budantsev so strongly supported the Belomor project and, therefore, socialist construction, why did he not become a member of the Party? At the same time, might it not be possible to conclude that Budantsev's zeal for Belomor and its associated ideological program was meant to compensate for his non-Party status? Unfortunately, it is impossible to answer these tantalizing questions satisfactorily based on the information available. Budantsev's literary biography, like those of many of his contemporaries, is a complicated blend of personal agenda and public response.

Lest it be thought that Budantsev's energetic support of the Belomor project can be detected only in his letter to Stalin, other documents in Budantsev's file further support both his ideas and actions. In an untitled and unpublished article, he notes, "No one among us, the authors of the book about the Belomor Canal, will forget our work on it. Somehow, for the first time, we discovered the joy of joint labor. The enthusiasm with which we received already prepared sections of material grew and, finally, when the book was already edited, it reached the level of ecstasy. Yet independently of this surge of enthusiasm the discovery itself of the possibility to think and write jointly enriched all the participants immensely."[30]

Budantsev's intended audience for this article remains a mystery, yet the enthusiasm for collective authorship is unmistakable. Collaborative authorship could be inherently rewarding despite the subject matter. More important, this article echoes the pronouncements of both Victor Shklovsky and Vsevolod Ivanov about the nature of collective authorship in the Belomor project and its effects on the practitioners of it. Such rapturous regard for collective authorship does not, of course, imply that all writers within and outside the Belomor project uniformly embraced such a method with the same relish as Budantsev and others.

Evidence among Budantsev's papers suggests that the Belomor volume was not written entirely as was depicted in the press. In the press, as well as in *The History of Construction* itself, the members of the Writers Brigade consistently noted their conversations with the canalworkers and OGPU personnel at the Belomor construction site. Budantsev's recollections indicate a slightly different scenario in which those writers assigned to profile certain key figures in the construction project—the engineers N. I. Khrustalev, O.V. Vyazemsky, and K. M. Zubrik, among others—submitted written questions to the subjects of their reports. In turn, the respondents first replied in writing. Then, if possible, the writers met personally with the subjects of the profiles so as to clarify biographical, technical, or construction details.

Indeed, some of the material for *The History of Construction* was collected after the fact. To a certain extent this was due to the early release of several engineers. In particular, Orest Vyazemsky was arrested in December 1930 and was rewarded with an early release in November 1932. Archival documents indicate that Budantsev sent Vyazemsky a questionnaire on 26

September 1933, to which Vyazemsky responded in writing on 8 October 1933. These dates are significant because they fall one to two months after the writers' trip to Belomor.

Budantsev, along with Shklovsky and other Brigade writers, interviewed Nikolai Khrustalev, the chief engineer of Belomor, on 1 December 1933. According to the stenographic notes for that meeting, the writers interviewed Khrustalev for almost three hours about construction methods and engineering designs for the Canal. The writers' questions are surprisingly technical, suggesting that they familiarized themselves with the topic before posing the questions or that someone with technical expertise helped them draft the questions. The writers also attempted to verify information about events and people at the Belomor site, as well as confirming what they already knew. (The interview is marked by writers frequently saying "I've heard that . . . " or "Informed comrades have told me. . . .")[31] This fact indicates that the writers did not have the opportunity to speak to Khrustalev on the Belomor Canal, and in December 1933 Khrustalev was already working on the construction of the Moscow–Volga Canal and the Writers Brigade was feverishly trying to complete the *History of Construction* in time for the Seventeenth Party Congress in January 1934.

That the writers in the Belomor Brigade did not interview many of the Belomor canalworkers during their visit to the Canal is not remarkable. First, by August 1933 many of the workers who had built it had already been shipped to the Moscow–Volga Canal construction site or to the Baikal–Amur railroad project. Second, some workers and engineers had gained early prison releases for themselves as a reward for their intense shock-work. Third and perhaps most important, the writers' journey to Belomor, for all its pomp and circumstance, was a Potemkin Village journey. The writers *did not* witness the actual construction of the Canal, nor did they converse freely with the canalworkers, who only watched as the Writers Brigade sailed by.

No matter the method through which the Writers Brigade gathered material for *The History of Construction,* it is clear from Budantsev's account that he demonstrated his enthusiastic support for the project whenever possible. That there are inherent contradictions in Budantsev's presentation of his efforts as well as in his ultimate fate at the hands of the very state he sought so furiously to defend underscores the complicated tangle of literary life and practice in the 1930s. While it is impossible to delineate unequivocally Budantsev's motivations for working on the Belomor volume, it is safe to conclude that much of his fervor was genuine, even if misplaced. The intensity of Budantsev's belief, at least judging from the limited archival documents available, is best captured in this quotation from the draft of his chapter on the Belomor Canal in the proposed *Great Waterways* collection: "The Canal was named after that person on whose initiative this construction project was started, the person who proved to the whole world the power of socialist labor that created this gigantic structure and reformed people—it was named after comrade Stalin."[32] Budantsev directly links the construction of the Canal with Stalin personally, thereby reinforcing the belief or perhaps contributing to the myth that without Stalin the Belomor Canal never would have been built.

Boris Lapin

Although unknown to most present-day scholars of Soviet literature, Moscow-born Boris Matveevich Lapin (1905–1941) was a popular, well-respected writer during his lifetime. Lapin, a doctor's son, began his career in 1921 when he enrolled in the Briusov Institute of Literature. His first book of verse, a constructivist collection entitled *The Lightning Man,* was published in 1922. By the mid-twenties he had shifted from poetry to prose and began to write newspaper articles and documentary pieces that described the border regions of the new Soviet state. Frequently operating under the pseudonym "the border guard" (*pogranichnik*), Lapin chronicled his adventures from the Pacific Ocean to the Caucasus. As two of Lapin's Soviet biographers note, "Lapin unexpectedly decid[ed] that his path to literature would flow through the impassable cliffs of the Pamirs, through the arid steppes of Central Asia, through the snow-covered tundra of Chukotia. In his twenty-fifth year he was already an author, a newspaper reporter and a sketch writer" (Protasova and Temkina, 4).

An inveterate traveler and adventurer, Lapin roamed the most exotic regions of the Soviet Union. He worked in a fur-processing plant in Chukotia, helped take the census in the Pamirs, journeyed on foot through Central Asia, learned to fly—the list of his exploits seems endless. Lapin also served as a war correspondent in the Japanese-Mongolian war in the late thirties. In World War II, both Lapin and his chief collaborator, Zakhar Khatsrevin, volunteered for service as war correspondents for *Krasnaya zvezda* (The Red Star). They were killed in 1941 outside of Kiev. According to their colleague Lev Slavin, Khatsrevin suffered an unusually severe epileptic fit and was unable to move. Lapin, committed to his friend until the end, would not leave Khatsrevin behind as the Germans surrounded Kiev. Eyewitnesses reported that Lapin, slight in physical stature, was trying to carry Khatsrevin on his back but made little progress and finally sought a protected place to rest. It was the last time either writer was seen alive.

In spite of his untimely death, Lapin enjoyed a successful and active career. Not only was he a poet, journalist, and prose writer; he also wrote screenplays, some of which were eventually made into films, among them *My Name Is Sukhe Bator*. Although a member neither of the Communist Party nor of the Union of Writers, he participated in the first Writers' Congress in 1934. In 1939 he served on the editorial board of the journal *Molodaia gvardiia* [The Young Guard]. Throughout his career he never seemed to suffer any recriminations for his literary activity, although not all of his work in the thirties falls clearly under the rubric of socialist realism, nor can all of his work be considered totally and uniformly supportive of the USSR. Added to all these activities, of course, is Lapin's participation in both the Belomor Brigade and volume.

Lest it seem that Lapin was unaware of the increasing terror during the 1930s, the recollections of Ilya Erenburg, Lapin's father-in-law, attest to the contrary. (Lapin had married Erenburg's daughter Irina in 1933.) Ehrenburg recalled one conversation: "Throughout half the night she [Irina] and Lapin told us about all that had happened: an avalanche of names, and after each the single neologism: 'taken' [arrested]. I was very agitated and at every name asked: 'But why him?' Lapin tried to think of explanations: Pilnyak had been to Japan, Tretiakov often met with foreign writers.... Lapin advised me with a rueful smile: 'Don't ask anyone. And if someone starts talking about it, just shut up.'... Lapin added: 'They often arrest the wives and put the children in homes.'... Contrary to Lapin's advice I asked the whereabouts of this or that person" (Erenburg, 190–91). Irina Erenburg supports her father's reminiscences and stresses that she and Lapin were aware of what was happening, especially in the late 1930s.[33]

Lapin's character references ring uniformly positive. Ilya Erenburg recollected, "Whenever I think of Boris Lapin, I see a very modest man with nearsighted kindly eyes: He is sitting and writing, and books are all around, mountains of books, amazingly diverse—economic treatises on the markets of the Middle East, a Chinese grammar book, the verses of Persian poets, and the collected works of Schelling" (ibid., 5). Erenburg was favorably disposed to Lapin based on their personal relationship, but others recall Lapin in the same generous, positive way. Nowhere in biographical accounts of Lapin is there anything to cast aspersions on his reputation or character. These character assessments are bolstered by his attempt to save Khatsrevin's life.

While the recollections of Erenburg, Lev Slavin, and Gabrilovich, an early collaborator of Lapin's, might seem suspect because of their reputations and perceived ideological stance, it is noteworthy that Nadezhda

Mandelshtam mentions Lapin numerous times in both volumes of her memoirs. Many other writers are cited in Mandelshtam's memoirs, yet it is striking that a writer like Lapin, whose fame faded dramatically after his death and who is unknown to most contemporary readers, nevertheless merits recollection.

According to her, in 1922 "two young men who wanted to try their luck as private publishers asked [Osip Mandelshtam] to compile an anthology of Russian verse from the symbolists 'to the present day'. It started with Konevskoy and Dobroliubov and ended with Boris Lapin" (Mandelshtam, *Hope against Hope*, 237). She goes on to note that "he [Mandelshtam] very much liked two or three poems by Boris Lapin: one about 'stars in the windows of the Cheka,' and another beginning: 'As though nibbling the fingers of asters, Tril-Tral kissed the flowers!'" (ibid.). While the Mandelshtams were still living in Moscow, Lapin frequented their apartment. In *Hope Abandoned*, Nadezhda Mandelshtam notes that Lapin told Osip Mandelshtam about looping the loop in an airplane, among other stories about flying (135). Osip Mandelshtam later used some of the information he got from Lapin about flying in selected poems (ibid., 473). She also remembers that "Boris Lapin used to call on us with his typewriter and tap out some new poem on it. Once, I remember, he brought along with him a strip of film that we held up to the light and studied" (ibid., 540). Finally, Nadezhda Mandelshtam mentions that among the few books the Mandelshtams brought with them into their exile at Saratikha were volumes Lapin had given to Osip Mandelshtam before their departure. In describing their situation, she notes: "We were of course a little bored. M. had brought Dante, Khlebnikov, the one-volume Pushkin edited by Tomashevsky and also Shevchenko—which had been given to him at the last moment by Boris Lapin" (*Hope against Hope*, 357). This episode is dated 1937, which would mean that even at the height of the Mandelshtams' persecution Lapin remained a supporter.

These detailed personal recollections of Lapin demonstrate that his reputation as writer and individual seems to be quite positive; he was held in high esteem by most of his acquaintances, who included both praised and persecuted members of the Soviet literary elite, from Erenburg to Mandelshtam. Moreover, as Erenburg suggested, "Boris Lapin remained aloof from the mainstream of literary fame; instead he sought happiness through his work, his travels, books, his friends. He possessed a moral goodness which he never lost—he was a truthful person, and understood the meaning of loyalty" (Erenburg, 7). Lapin's contacts with the Mandelshtams and his relationship with his main co-author Khatsrevin attest to his loyalty and goodness.

Is it possible, however, to reconcile the glowing biography that these recollections construct with Lapin's participation not only in the Belomor Writers Brigade and volume but in the editing of the volume as well? After all, Lapin contributed the chapter "The Country and Its Enemies" (coauthored with G. Gauzner and L. Slavin) and the chapter "Comrades" (coauthored with six other writers, including Budantsev and Leopold Averbakh, both of whom subsequently perished during the Great Terror). Official pronouncements always included Lapin's name in the list of writers contributing to the Belomor volume. Shklovsky's public recollections of the Belomor project cite Lapin as one of the volume's main editors.

Solzhenitsyn also cites Lapin in the list of writers who participated in the Belomor project. Solzhenitsyn names fifteen of the thirty-six participants: "It would be only just, too, to preserve the names of the authors for the history of literature. Well, at least these: M. Gorky, Victor Shklovsky, Vsevolod Ivanov, Vera Inber, Valentin Kataev, Mikhail Zoshchenko, Lapin and Khatsrevin, L. Nikulin, Kornelly Zelinsky, Bruno Jasensky . . . Y. Gabrilovich, A. Tikhonov, Aleksei Tolstoy, K. Finn" (Solzhenitsyn [b], 82). For Solzhenitsyn, participation in such a volume is morally and ethically unforgivable, no matter what the writer's motivation or biographical peculiarities. However, by all accounts in Lapin's case, on balance there is nothing to suggest that Lapin was a morally bankrupt, unthinking writer or an opportunist.

Lapin's biography, perhaps more pointedly than the biographies of other writers who participated in the Belomor project, reinforces the notion that the process of creating one's literary life during prewar Stalinism was a much more complicated process than simply opting to support or condemn the regime. It is clear that life, in particular literary life, under Stalin was a constantly changing, frequently unpredictable process that necessitated reconfiguring one's existence and activities accordingly. This is not to suggest that it is possible to reconstruct completely a writer's motivations for participating in an event like the Belomor project. Instead, this discussion proposes that such a variety of intention and action supports a more unconventional, less prescriptive view of how morally deplorable and ethically questionable literary works came to be written.

To the question of why Lapin participated, we should respond that Lapin thought it was the appropriate thing to do at the time. Conversations with Irina Erenburg and the facts of Lapin's biography confirm that in this particular instance Lapin sought a compromise. In this regard, a compromise was a necessity, not a moral failure. By participating in the Belomor project so extensively, Lapin could secure for himself the "freedom" to pursue his other literary interests without serious repercussions. (Some of Lapin's stories from the late 1930s support this contention.) Or he could protect himself or others in exchange for his participation. His widow, Irina, simply stated that he had to; there was no other choice for him, given the situation. The quiet, unassuming Lapin wrote little about himself and left behind little evidence to answer our query definitively.

Mikhail Zoshchenko

To anyone familiar with Soviet literature, no writer would seem to have been a more unlikely participant in both the Writers Brigade and the Belomor volume than Mikhail Zoshchenko (1895–1958). Revered for his bitingly satirical vignettes of postrevolutionary Soviet life, Zoshchenko consistently wrote about the Soviet everyman in his own vernacular. One of the original members of the Serapion Brothers, Zoshchenko gained notoriety precisely because he did not conform, at least initially, to the demand for the inclusion of more ideological elements in literature. In fact, Zoshchenko consistently sought to follow his own path in literature, one that provided him with success and fame, but that also, thanks to that very fame, required him to concede some of his professional and personal autonomy.

Zoshchenko grew up in St. Petersburg, the son of a painter and an actress. Although he had matriculated in the law faculty of St. Petersburg University, World War I intervened and Zoshchenko volunteered for service. He served from 1915 to 1919, when he was demobilized for being physically unfit after having been wounded and gassed on the front. Zoshchenko's literary career commenced in 1920, when he began writing stories; he published his first book in 1921 and quickly became one of the best-loved Soviet writers.

Zoshchenko wrote short stories that cut to the very heart of Soviet reality in the 1920s. His satires pointed up the irritations of daily life for the average Soviet citizen. In so doing he was able to capture the essence of life in the twenties and poke fun at the bureaucracy and officialdom. No topic was sacred. Zoshchenko penned sketches about everything from the bathhouse to the housing shortage to philistinism. Much of the humor in his stories stems from his narrative method, which gives the narration over to a storyteller whose command of Russian is colloquial at best. The narrator engages the reader in the narrative using verbal ploys such as "I hear tell, comrades," that immediately weave a bond of familiarity between reader and storyteller. Zoshchenko's narrators use jargon, vulgar speech, malapropisms, and inappropriate stylistic elements (juridical or journalistic turns of phrase amid otherwise conversational speech). They interrupt their syntax with interjections of "I said," "he says," "they say," which can occur anywhere in the sentence. This combination of elements and personalized language came to be known as *skaz*, a device through which the author allows the narrator to speak in his own vernacular, even if it includes substandard or vulgar language, thus imbuing the story with truthfulness and authenticity. More important, Zoshchenko wrote the way people talked, thereby bridging the gap between literary form and reader reality.

An excellent example of Zoshchenko's method is the well-known story "The Bathhouse" (1924). The story opens with the lines: "I've heard, comrades, that bathhouses in America are mighty excellent. There, for example, a citizen can simply come, shed his clothes into a special box, then wash to his heart's content. He doesn't have a worry in the world, like having his things stolen or lost. He doesn't even bother with claim checks" (Zoshchenko, 289). In this concise opening Zoshchenko's narrator immediately establishes a rapport with his readers, creates a myth about American bathhouses, while, without uttering a word, he provides a complete picture of Soviet bathhouses that is the antithesis of everything in an American bathhouse: You can't wash to your heart's content, there are no special boxes for your clothes, and you need a claim check because your clothes can get lost or stolen.

The narrator proceeds to relate his recent adventure at a local bathhouse where he has to fight for a bucket with which to bathe, loses his claim check, which washes away while he bathes, and as a result loses his pants and his soap. As the narrator concludes, "I said: 'Fellow citizens, I can't spend my life getting dressed and undressed,' I said. 'This isn't show business. Why don't you give me at least what the soap cost?' They wouldn't. I didn't care any more. I went home without the soap. Of course, a curious reader may want to know—which bathhouse was that? Where is it? What's the address? Which bathhouse you ask? Any old bathhouse. Take your pick" (ibid., 291). In Zoshchenko's world the universality of the experience, not the specifics of time or place, occupies center stage.

Zoshchenko continued to write in the 1930s, but as we will see, the increasing pressure to create more mainstream Soviet stories took its toll on the author. His work in this period is a combination of more ideologically appropriate works and satirical works in the same vein as his writing from the twenties. Everyone knew Zoshchenko's stories and could recite favorite rejoinders from them, a phenomenon that survived even in the Belomor camp.

Zoshchenko participated in the Belomor project in two ways. First, he was a member of the writers contingent from Leningrad that joined writers from Moscow and other republics for the trip to the Canal. Second, he authored an entire chapter in the Belomor volume. His "The Story of One Reforging" is the only single-author chapter in the collection, aside from Gorky's introductory and concluding chapters. It details the life, exploits, and incarceration of Abraham Rottenburg, a thief and swindler, who was sentenced to Belomor. Zoshchenko portrayed him as a "social enemy," typical of the Soviet criminal element, a man who did not develop and mature in the Soviet system exclusively; like many prisoners, he was a victim of past excesses and thus a natural target for reforging. His attempts to reform his life through his hard labor on the Canal made him a new Soviet man, that product of the Belomor project second in importance only to the Canal itself.

In this chapter, Zoshchenko follows his typical device of allowing the chief protagonist to speak in his own voice, replete with its own verbal idiosyncrasies. Zoshchenko prefaces the tale of the protagonist, the reformed prisoner Rottenburg, with a few brief paragraphs that simultaneously introduce the ensuing narrative and serve to distance Zoshchenko from it. By having Rottenburg narrate his own tale, Zoshchenko displaces the bulk of the responsibility for narration from himself onto Rottenburg. Zoshchenko skillfully chooses this strategy because this displacement of narrative responsibility allows him to preserve his artistic integrity—the skaz style of structuring a narrative—while permitting him to avoid direct comment on the process of perekovka and the entire Belomor enterprise.

Upon closer examination, Zoshchenko's contribution to the Belomor project is paradoxical. In describing Zoshchenko's activities while sailing through the Canal, Evgeny Gabrilovich notes, "During the course of the trip everyone demanded to see Zoshchenko. . . . For the most part, Zoshchenko lay on his bunk in a black suit and didn't go out anywhere. When he did go out, there was a thunderous ovation."[34] This nonchalant, even morose attitude contrasts sharply with Tamara Ivanova's interpretation of Zoshchenko's enthusiasm for the project. As she notes, "I could not contain myself and asked Vsevolod [her husband] and Mikhail Mikhailovich Zoshchenko: Do you really not see that the performances of these 're-forged' criminals before your eyes are theatrical productions, that the cottages in the gardens with clean, sandy paths and flowers in the yard are only theatrical decorations? They answered me in all sincerity (they both believed in the possibility of the so-called 'reforging') that in order to re-educate a person, he first of all had to be placed in very good surroundings, completely dissimilar to those from which he had landed in the criminal world" (6). In addition, Ivanova proposes that Zoshchenko participated in the Belomor project "in the name of compassion, with a genuine desire to help people gain/find a human frame of mind" (ibid.).

Other considerations provide deeper insights into Zoshchenko's participation in the Belomor project. First, his account of Rottenburg's reforging was published not only in the Belomor volume. As the critic Anatoly Starkov notes, as early as September 1933 Zoshchenko wrote an article for *Literary Leningrad* bearing the title "Youth Restored" (the same title given to his then recently published short story). In this article, he relates his motivation for focusing precisely on a person like Rottenburg as opposed to the other inmates. Zoshchenko claims that:

> People who built their lives on idleness, deceit, theft, and murder interested me.
>
> I turned my full attention to those people and to their reeducation. I didn't want to be mistaken here. I'll tell the truth. I approached this matter skeptically, assuming that this famed reforging arose from a single, basic motive—from the desire to serve out one's sentence and to receive freedom or bonuses. I must say that I was mistaken on that general score. And I actually saw authentic restructuring, the real pride of the construction workers and the real change in the psychology of many comrades (now they can be called thusly) (Starkov, 139).

Zoshchenko then published an excerpt "from [his] new story about the Belomor Canal" in *Literary Leningrad* in December 1933, the full version of which appeared as an independent publication in early 1934 (ibid., 140).

Second, in spite of Gabrilovich's recollection of Zoshchenko's participation—staying in his cabin on his bunk with a morose expression on his face—Tamara Ivanova argues otherwise. She states that having heard the "moving" presentations by some of the criminal inmates of the Belomor camp, who, Ivanova adds, were doubtless very talented actors, Ivanov and Zoshchenko believed them, improbable as it might seem. "And the main thing [was that] they wanted to believe!" (Ivanova, 6).

There can be little doubt that, at least on some level, Zoshchenko actually believed in the reforging power of the Belomor experience. This is not to suggest that he completely complied with or accepted the encroaching system of control in Stalinist Russia. Yet his efforts to publish separately his contribution to the Belomor volume permit at least the conclusion that Zoshchenko, clearly in no way a hack writer, wrote for the Belomor volume with a modicum of honest commitment to and interest in the project. As

Ivanova also notes, "It is important to understand the political and moral atmosphere of those years, and then much becomes clear" (ibid.).

Third, the notion that Zoshchenko actually could have believed in what he wrote about Rottenburg is confirmed in Vladimir Bragin's discussion of Zoshchenko's contribution to the Belomor volume. As Bragin claims, "That's how Zoshchenko writes: he proposes three hypotheses to the reader, but then chooses the fourth, because the last idea—this is the main idea of 'Youth Restored', the writer was able to preserve the truth" (87).

Bragin reaches this conclusion on the basis of how Zoshchenko presents to the reader the possible reasons for Rottenburg's reformation. Zoshchenko notes in the story:

> Either Rottenburg, having passed through fire, water, and copper pipes, really changed his consciousness and really was reforged, having run into the correct system of reeducation.
>
> Or he engaged in new "speculation".
>
> Or he, being not a dumb person, and having analyzed everything, decided that the criminal world was really coming to an end and now a thief needed to retrain himself. And if that is so, then he did this not out of moral considerations, but out of necessity. I put forth these three propositions on the scales of my professional ability to figure people out. And I draw the conclusion that Rottenburg, thanks to a proper upbringing, changed his psychology and reeducated his consciousness and at the same time took into account the changes in our life. (ibid., 86)

As Bragin argues, rather than assuming that Zoshchenko wrote about Rottenburg simply to satisfy the demands of his participation in the Belomor project, it seems that in writing about Rottenburg, Zoshchenko continued to work out an idea that had most recently appeared in his story "Youth Restored." Instead of assuming, as critics have, that Zoshchenko wrote for the Belomor volume simply to please the authorities, Ivanova and Bragin both suggest that Zoshchenko used the Rottenburg story to pursue thematic and artistic goals that were important and attractive to him at that time. It is possible to conclude that Zoshchenko's participation in the Belomor project addressed a need that went beyond simple duty.

Key to understanding Zoshchenko's efforts in the Belomor project is a point that Tamara Ivanova stresses repeatedly in her discussion of her husband and Zoshchenko at Belomor. We need to understand the politics and atmosphere of the time in which Zoshchenko was writing. As Starkov points out, what Zoshchenko wrote about in 1933 he probably would not have written about in 1937. Starkov argues:

> It is possible to form a hypothesis about why Zoshchenko turned to the individual story of the life of "a famous international thief, freemason and adventurer," rather than to the fate of some other person who received a sentence for "political sabotage" or for disagreeing with Stalin's politics of the collectivization of the agricultural population of the country. I don't doubt that if Zoshchenko had had to decide this question for himself not in 1933, but say in 1937 or 1938, when it was impossible not to see even among his own circle that the cadres of the builders of structures like the Belomor Canal were filled for the most part with innocent people—Zoshchenko would hardly have written a similar work. He would have found in himself the courage to avoid the favorable tone in which the "Story of One Life" about the "reforging" of people in the conditions of the camp system of the GULag is spoken. (144)

Lest we forget, Zoshchenko, like many of his fellow travelers to Belomor, did not escape persecution at the hands of the system he had applauded in his contribution to the Belomor volume. The postwar persecution of Zoshchenko was severe and personally demoralizing. In 1946 Andrei Zhdanov, secretary of the Communist Party Central Committee and Party functionary, mounted a vicious and quite personal attack on Anna Akhmatova and Zoshchenko. Zhdanov publicly condemned both authors and subjected them to intense public scrutiny and persecution. His invective forced Zoshchenko to be expelled from the Union of Soviet Writers, and he never rebounded from this attack, resorting instead to translation work for the remainder of his career.[35]

As the cited examples demonstrate, partial or full compliance with the demands made on writers by the Belomor project did not exempt them from being victimized by the system they served. While it could be argued that writers did *not* have to participate in the Belomor Brigade and volume (witness the example of Bulgakov and others), logic would suggest that some benefit would accrue to those writers who did participate simply because they had complied with the demands placed on them. As we know, however, simple logic was not the operative mode during this period, nor did any benefits necessarily accrue from participation in officially sanctioned literary projects. Zoshchenko's biography proves this point only too well.

Meaning and Myth

Writer motivations for joining the Belomor project were distinct and varied; they depended on a writer's personal situation, ideological inclination, or artistic/professional concerns. Aside from this diversity of response, it is possible to propose other conclusions about this aspect of the Belomor episode.

The preceding analysis dispels many of the myths that have for many years swirled around the Belomor Writers Brigade and volume, even during those times when discussing the Belomor project was a taboo topic. As noted, Sergei Alymov and Victor Shklovsky did not participate in the Brigade. Nor was every participant a hack writer who complied with every state mandate. As archival materials prove, the Belomor volume was actually written by the writers to whom it is ascribed in its table of contents. Some of the best and brightest Soviet writers worked on the project, and this is perhaps still the fact most troubling to present-day readers and critics.

If we subscribe to the theory that something different, something fundamentally distinct from the Western tradition in method and application was being developed in Soviet literature and literary life in the 1930s, then how we perceive the Writers Brigade to Belomor and the resultant Belomor volume needs to be reassessed. Our reading of the Belomor volume could very well be altered, especially because the main issue here is not whether today's readers view the whole Belomor episode as morally deplorable. More than anything else, it is important to understand the situation and understand the writers, especially before condemning any of them. The compromises various writers struck, the shifts in behavior, and the lack of clear-cut explanations for their participation all underscore Art Jester's comment that life and history are messy. This concept gains full force when we realize that the confusing reality surrounding the composition of the Belomor volume was one in which some writers had the luxury to say no, while others, for whatever reasons, thought they could not. But by exploring the disorder of the past, we can appreciate better the predicament in which many people found themselves in the Stalinist period. On that basis we now understand who wrote the Belomor volume; the next step is to unravel how and why it was written.

3
Literary Text as Historical Narrative
The History of the Construction of the Stalin White Sea–Baltic Canal

> The Central Executive Committee of the USSR . . . authorizes the OGPU of the USSR to publish a monograph about the construction of the Stalin White Sea–Baltic Canal.
> *Pravda,* 5 August 1933

> The Belomor construction project is worthy of history.
> Sergei Budantsev

> The [volume] *Belomorstroi*—is one of the most monumental books of our epoch, one of the most significant historical works of world literature— consequently it shows in an attractive form how enormous social changes occurred in the psychology and consciousness of people, of the builders of the canal, and what an enormously positive influence these changes had in the matter of a more successful construction [project].
> *Kommunisticheskaia molodezh'* (Communist Youth) 34, no. 4, 60.

The monograph produced by the OGPU about the construction of the Belomor Canal was *The History of the Construction of the Stalin White Sea–Baltic Canal,* an impressive volume the first printing of which was embossed with a profile of Stalin on the cover. Produced under the auspices of the publishing series "The History of Factories and Plants," the Belomor *History* was issued three times. The first run of 4,000 copies was specially designated for the delegates to the Seventeenth Party Congress in January 1934. This Party Congress, titled the Congress of Victors in honor of the achievements of the First Five-Year Plan, provided the impetus to produce the Belomor *History* quickly—it was written and published in five months. According to newspaper accounts of the time, the second printing of 45,000 copies appeared six weeks after the first, with the final print run of 150,000 copies appearing later, sans embossed Stalin; this third printing was intended to "move forward into the masses, carrying the story of the wonders on the lakes of bleak Karelia" (Fin, 4). In actuality, the second and third printings of *The History of Construction* were 80,000 copies in 1934 and 30,000 in 1935; these figures are taken from actual print information on copies of the book. In addition, the format of the first printing consisted of large pages with two columns of typescript on each page, while the later two editions appeared in smaller format, without columns of typescript but with the same photographs accompanying the text. The Belomor volume was translated into English in 1935, although the translation does not coincide with the Russian original, either in the progression of the narrative or its division into chapters and sections.[1]

The text itself consists of fifteen chapters (perhaps one for each of the fifteen Soviet republics). All the editions contain a short bibliography that lists the works consulted, including the camp newspaper, *Perekovka*, OGPU documents, stenographic notes of conversations with camp inmates, and other assorted sources. The first edition, thanks to its special status, also includes a "list of technical words, jargon, and abbreviations" for the delegates to the Seventeenth Party Congress. Each edition contains a map that outlines the route, not only of the Belomor Canal but of the entire Belomor waterway as well.

Of the fifteen chapters in the volume, only three were not collectively written. These include the introduction and conclusion, both written by Maksim Gorky, and chapter 12, "The Story of One Reforging," penned by Mikhail Zoshchenko. The remaining twelve chapters resulted from the collective authorship of four to ten writers per chapter. In addition, the volume was produced under the collective editorship of Maksim Gorky, Leopold Averbakh—both active and established literary figures—and Semyon Firin, head of the Belomor prison camp. Thus the production of the volume united some of the best Soviet writers of the time with some of the highest members of the OGPU administration, a collaboration mandated by the Communist Party, as one of the epigraphs to this chapter notes. (See Appendix III for a list of the authors.)

The three editions of the Belomor volume differ minimally, except for the number of pages (410 for the first edition and 615 for the two subsequent editions) and the omission of Mikhail Kozakov's name in the list of contributors to the third edition. The reason for leaving out Kozakov's name is not clear; he might have been on the verge of being repressed, although nothing in his archival file indicates anything amiss. Indeed, all the manuscripts in his file demonstrate his support and enthusiasm for the Belomor project.[2]

This volume, a collaborative enterprise, even today frequently prompts critical reactions, especially considering the circumstances under which it was produced. How the history came to be written is just as interesting and troublesome as the book itself. Rarely, if ever, had the production of a literary text and the writing of history been assigned directly to the OGPU, a fact that has complicated any interpretation of the Belomor volume. Moreover, *The History of Construction* was posited on two kinds of collaboration: of the writers with the OGPU and of writers with other writers.

While it was publicly reported that the publishing house The History of Factories and Plants organized the writers trip to Belomor and the subsequent compilation of the volume, the OGPU firmly controlled the whole process, evident in the presence of Semyon Firin as tour guide on the Writers Brigade and coeditor of the Belomor volume. In fact, nothing could have been written about Belomor had the OGPU not sanctioned such activities and provided necessary documents, as noted in the bibliography of *The History of Construction*. Currently inaccessible OGPU documents, the "Agent's Notes" and the "Testimonials of Soviet Writers," substantiate the fact that the OGPU monitored every moment of the writers' journey along the Belomor Canal. Even post-Brigade meetings between the book's authors and the former engineers of the Belomor project, many of whom were working on the OGPU-supervised Moscow–Volga Canal project, could not have occurred without the direct intervention of OGPU personnel.

Contrary to the rhetoric in the newspapers, it is questionable how many of the approximately 110,000 copies of the Belomor volume ever reached a mass readership; most copies eventually were either relegated to "special" (read inaccessible) archives and libraries or destroyed after the purges in 1937, during which the majority of OGPU personnel who managed and directed the construction of the Canal, not least among them Genrikh Yagoda, head of the OGPU, were imprisoned or exterminated. Copies in private libraries were hidden or ignored.

At the time *The History of Construction* was published, OGPU sponsorship of the endeavor was not viewed publicly in a negative light. Privately scores of people knew and understood precisely what OGPU sponsorship of the Belomor project meant in real terms—senseless arrests, hard-labor camps, unjust penal practices—but were unable or unwilling to expose or even to discuss them. This unspoken knowledge about Belomor cast a pall over reader reception of the Belomor volume long before the documented practices and excesses of the OGPU and its successor agencies were more fully revealed. After the initial fanfare and enthusiasm that surrounded the Belomor project had subsided, this volume became one of the most censored books in Stalinist literature, a fact that for many years made it an untouchable and undesirable text. The proscription was double-edged, for the government essentially censored the text and made it unavailable, while those readers who might have had access to it neither chose nor wanted to discuss it openly or acknowledge it.

The taboo surrounding the text went beyond the simple fact that most of the project personnel perished in the purges. The official Belomor narrative was also "untouchable" because of all the concomitant moral and ethical concerns that reading and interpreting the narrative inevitably raised. The public approbation that the Belomor volume sought for a construction project that relied on forced labor, that forced prisoners to work in dire hardship and under severe conditions, that completely ignored the unjust and often life-taking imprisonment of guiltless political prisoners defied the moral and ethical code of most readers and participants. Yet this censure has emerged most forcefully with hindsight; only now do we understand and appreciate all the difficult moments in the construction of the Belomor Canal that failed to make it into print in the Belomor volume. Because most contemporary readers assume that *The History of Construction* can offer no fresh insights or elements of truth about the era in which it was published, it has been an almost invisible text for the past sixty years.

Most recently, archival holdings and personal memoirs that document the Belomor project have contributed to a weakening of this taboo. Moreover, the restorative power of time allows for a more objective treatment of the narrative, which goes beyond exclusive attention to the obvious transgressions against basic concepts of justice, humanity, and honor, values that were all too frequently absent from Stalinist projects.

To dismiss a close reading of the Belomor volume itself because of the taboo that has surrounded it is also to dismiss the important issues the book raises through its content and the method with which it was written. Unbeknownst to many readers, *The History of Construction* promotes key concepts that contribute to a deeper understanding of Stalinist culture and to subsequent ideological programs promulgated by the state. The ensuing discussion explores three critical areas that have been largely ignored in previous discussions of *The History of Construction* because the moral and ethical issues took precedence.

This text, more than any other work produced during prewar Stalinism, vividly and persuasively exemplifies what happens when the boundary between literature and history is breeched by writers within a system that seemed officially to allow no opinion other than its own. In addition, *The History of Construction* explores and implements for the first time central ideas about and approaches to the collective production of literature. Finally, the program of reforging, perekovka, receives its first and fullest treatment in the Belomor volume. Consequently, the *History* unites these three seemingly disparate issues under one rubric and suggests the rationale behind them and their potential for further implementation and exploitation in the Stalinist system.

Let History Be Judged

Whether the Belomor Canal project was worthy of history, as Sergei Budantsev claims, turns out to be the fundamental point on which any discussion of the Belomor volume rests. Indeed, the first two words of the volume's title, *The History,* indicate the pivotal point on which any interpretation of this volume turns, for the title immediately prescribes reader expectation and narrative presentation. Such a title promises much, for it claims to present the *history,* the official retelling of the Belomor project. Moreover, while the Russian word *istoriia* can mean either history in its traditional sense or a story or an anecdote, as it is used in conjunction with the Belomor project it absolutely connotes the meaning of *history*—the retelling of the facts of an actual event.

As such, the Belomor volume poses a paradox that stems from its consideration as the "official" historical account of the Belomor project. Both the terms *history* and *record* suggest a certain degree of veracity and faithfulness to actual events. How is it then that the official report on the construction of the Belomor Canal seems to strive to document truthfully the construction of Belomor, yet, no less faithfully, does not present what we would call the whole truth about the project? The reasons underpinning this paradox are varied and reside not only on the practical level but on the theoretical level as well.

Consider the issue of Soviet writers assuming the role of historians. Most obviously, when the writing of history is coopted by literary figures, the first impulse is to conclude that the integrity of the telling is jeopardized. Can artists, versed in the art of creating a fictional world, be entrusted to depict, with any accuracy, an actual event? In this case, is not the accuracy of the Belomor volume compromised not only by the organizers (the OGPU) but also by the people chosen to tell the tale? Arguably, literary figures are as committed to the truth as are historians; only their mode of presentation differs. As any student of Russian literature knows, Russian literary figures consistently viewed many of their fictional works as attempts to capture the reality of an era. *The History of Construction* continues that tradition. Therefore, it is impossible to dismiss *The History of Construction* as an historical text on the grounds that Soviet writers wrote it. Such a dismissal would discount this important tradition in Russian and Soviet literature and overlook an intriguing approach to the writing of history that the Belomor Canal project engendered.

As Andrew Wachtel argues in his recent study *An Obsession with History: Russian Writers Confront the Past,* the belief among Russian writers that they were better suited to write history than were historians was not new. Wachtel artfully traces the development of this practice from Novgorodian times to Solzhenitsyn. His study makes clear that "Russian writers traditionally write multiple monologic narratives on the same historical material" (11), thereby producing what he terms an "intergeneric dialogue" between and within a writer's fictional and non-fictional works. While Wachtel contends that "it is not surprising that the period of Stalinism marked an interregnum of sorts in the Russian tradition of intergeneric dialogue" (ibid., 197), he also asserts that "even in the darkest period of the Stalinist night, however, there were writers who continued to believe that it was their right and duty to interpret the nation's past. They published nothing on Russian history, however, preferring to wait for more propitious times, preserving the tradition in silence" (ibid., 197). As regards this discussion, contrary to Wachtel's argument, while many Soviet writers might not have openly continued an "intergeneric dialogue" within their own body of writing during Stalinism, some continued to write history and to document actual events in literature, for example, Valentine Kataev's novel about the construction of the city Magnitogorsk, *Time, Forward!*

For many contemporary readers, the presentation of the Belomor volume as history is complicated by the fact that the Party officially validated it by charging the OGPU with the task of organizing the Writers Brigade. We naturally question whether either the Party or the OGPU could have published an accurate account of Belomor, given the activities of both organizations. Yet at the time, no organization but the Party could have mandated the Belomor volume, especially in an era in which literary groups were being consolidated and controlled. In addition, our expectations about the boundaries between literature and history are frustrated by a work that seems to promise and deliver both.[3]

Two issues emerge from this discussion and are realized in the production of the Belomor volume. First, how the book was written provokes a consideration of the intrinsic properties of literature and how they reach fruition. Second, the writing of the Belomor volume displays one of the earliest Soviet efforts to exercise full political control over literature.

Rather than leaving the development of the book strictly to the artistic sensibilities of its authors, the Party authorized the OGPU to supervise its production, just as they supervised the construction of the Canal. This does not mean that the writers relinquished their creativity and artistry; it simply means that a more powerful agent of control made its presence known throughout the creative process. Indeed, the OGPU was charged with writing the history of its own project. Surely the "history" produced by an OGPU-controlled project on the most publicly applauded forced labor project in the First Five-Year Plan could be nothing but compromised, not even remotely factual.

These criticisms, however, are not fully substantiated. Does *The History of Construction* reshape the narrative of the actual event? Yes, by focusing only on common criminals and neglecting to discuss any political prisoners, by ignoring the inhuman conditions on the construction site, and by enthusiastically praising the work of the OGPU in bringing the project to fruition. Consonant with the age in which it was produced, the book accentuates only the positive; and we should not expect otherwise. Does this mean that it avoids the truth and fails to achieve a modicum of accuracy? No, because *The History of Construction* presents one kind of truth about Belomor that is as valid as any other discussion of the event. Its accuracy hinges on the firsthand accounts provided to the writers by some of the engineers, workers, and OGPU personnel on the Canal. For the kind of truth it sought to convey, the volume was accurate.

That the Belomor episode was immediately historicized and that the writing of the official history of Belomor was charged to Soviet writers raises questions about the book's validity, but it also hints that different processes were at work that defy our conventional understanding about how history is made and recorded. Within Belomor's context, it is not odd that writers were called into service by the state as makeshift historians. As is commonly known, the Party and Stalin demanded quick results in a short period of time so as to both justify its/his practices and demonstrate its/his ability to control and produce. Recall Stalin's pronouncement that enjoined Soviet writers to be "engineers of the human soul." While it was not unique to Stalinism that literature and literary practice were enlisted in advancing the cause of the state (precedents for this practice can be found throughout the history of Russian literature, most notably in the early chronicles that frequently privileged one political position or prince over another), never before had literature been employed to create the history of a forced-labor project.

And this, perhaps, is one of the most intriguing elements in the entire

Belomor episode. Never before had a forced-labor construction project received as much public attention and acclaim. In fact, not until the First Five-Year Plan was forced labor even considered a justifiable component of large construction projects. Although subsequent projects, the Moscow Metro and the Moscow–Volga Canal among them, were built by forced labor, publicly acknowledged, and perceived as viable topics for literary works, no single project approached the level of fanfare and public scrutiny as Belomor. The main reason for this distinction stemmed from the promotion of the program of perekovka and the use of the Belomor project as ground zero for the implementation of it, but that discussion does not fully explain the interest in and practice of history writing by Soviet writers. The early work of the critic Hayden White suggests another explanation for the overlapping of historical and literary discourse.[4]

In writing about the gray area in which historical and literary narratives intersect, White asserts that the writing of history is essentially a literary act, subject to the same method of emplotment and organization of events as a literary work. As he notes, the difference between literary and historical narrative is that, "unlike the novelist, the historian confronts a veritable chaos of events already constituted, out of which he must choose the elements of the story he would tell. He makes his story by including some events and excluding others, by stressing some and subordinating others" (*Metahistory*, 6). In the process, the historian emplots the narrative in a particular way that suggests to the reader how the account is to be read.

White's approach speaks to the very nature of *The History of Construction* when he discusses what he calls "the fictions of factual representation" in which "the discourse of the historian and that of the imaginative writer overlap, resemble, or correspond with each other" (*Tropics of Discourse*, 121). This does not mean that every imaginative writer is an historian, nor is every historian a master of imaginative writing. Instead, White suggests that the boundary between these two "tropics" of discourse is not firm. In fact, the two discourses frequently yield to or invade each other to differing degrees, depending on the topic and the writer. White does not argue that the historian creates a fiction in the most rigid sense. Rather, the historian frequently engages in the same method as does the imaginative writer, but with different results. Important to this discussion is the logical reverse movement of that process. The imaginative writer, while bringing an impressive arsenal of literary devices to the text, invades the domain of history when he/she attempts to record an actual event in a documentary genre. As Richard Wortman argues, the imaginative writer is aided in this endeavor by a fundamental difference between history and literature. Namely, he says—and here he takes issue with White's argument—literature inherently possesses greater narrative flexibility than history. As a result, those narrative strategies impermissible in the writing of history operate with impunity in literary texts (Wortman, 277).

Given White's proposition, who better to capture masterfully and vividly the energy and success of this monumental construction project than Soviet writers? What in White's schema is the domain of the historian is assigned to the imaginative writer in the Belomor project, the role of historian and imaginative writer are reversed. This reversal is especially significant in the Soviet-Russian context, given the deep appreciation of and reverence for literary figures and the written word.[5]

Added to this is the preponderance of rhetoric uttered both in the Soviet press of the time and by writers from the Belomor Brigade about the specifically "historical" nature of the project. Pronouncements such as Budantsev's "The Belomorstroi is worthy of history" reinforced this rhetoric, as did this excerpt from *Leningradskaia Pravda* cited as an epigraph to chapter 1: "The White Sea–Baltic Canal will go down in history as more than a school of the newest technology in hydroconstruction. It will go down in history also as a gigantic school of reeducation, of the remaking of people driven by capitalism from the path of labor" (29 June 1933, 1). Not only was the event conceived of as an appropriate topic for the writing of history; it was also practically historicized as it was occurring. This concept of "instant historicization" suggests that an event of such magnitude did not need to endure the test of time so as to gain its status as worthy of a prominent place in history. Arguably, all events as soon as they happen are history. But precisely the marking of the Belomor project as a *notable* event demonstrates White's notion of "emplotment"—the event itself does not necessarily determine its own importance. Rather, the person organizing the narrative of events determines which event predominates.

The fluidity, even permeability of the boundary between history and literature that White describes does not, however, completely explain why Soviet writers, not professional historians, were given the responsibility for creating the official history of Belomor. The most persuasive explanation for this strategy, as well as its genesis, are located in the writings and pronouncements of Maksim Gorky. Gorky's ideas operated not only on the theoretical level but the practical as well. The evidence to be presented here suggests that the writing of history by Soviet writers, especially at this point, was a well-conceived, planned idea that Gorky advanced. The development of the History of Factories and Plants series in itself implies the narrating of actual events, that is, the writing of history. Few wrote or spoke more extensively about the need to write the history of the new Soviet state than Maksim Gorky.

Throughout Gorky's writings of the early 1930s, especially those devoted to the function of literature in the new Soviet society and the development of the History of Factories and Plants series, the notion of collecting and writing history prevails. Granted, Gorky proposes a proscribed domain for the field of history: the construction and development of the working class and their workplaces—the factories, plants, mines, and construction sites of socialist construction and Stalinist five-year plans. Gorky argues that the telling of history should, for the most part, be undertaken by workers, who are to become literary figures themselves through their writing. Yet Gorky also challenges literary figures to assume this task. This proposition is not unexpected, given that both the quality and quantity of literary production by nonprofessional writers, i.e., workers, were uneven at best. To ensure the successful and proper promotion of socialist construction, professional writers had to assume the writing of history. Professional historians could not do it because they lacked the arsenal of literary devices and techniques common to imaginative literature. (In this regard Gorky's ideas prefigure White's later theoretical work.) Nor could they provide the depth and breadth of genre and narrative treatment that the history of the new Soviet Union deserved. If a new country and new approach to life and labor actually had been created, then how the history of this new phenomenon was recorded needed to be fresh and innovative as well.

In a number of articles Gorky discusses the need to create a history of industrialization in the Soviet Union, as well as the need for writers to be thoroughly and intimately involved in this task. In the article "About Hills and Hummocks" Gorky demands that the "literary figures of the USSR must expand their field of vision in order to broaden and deepen their activities. The epoch, the new history created by the proletariat of the Union, demands this of them; children who will soon be young men demand this so that they can pose a series of staggering questions to their fathers; and, finally, art demands this of them" ("About Hills," 177). He enjoins Soviet writers to participate in the building of the USSR by recording how it is being built and by whom. This serves as the function of the History of Factories and Plants series, for on the most basic level the series promotes this "history" through *literary* works.

To achieve the goals of the the History series, Gorky asserts that prerevolutionary history must be rewritten so as to reflect the development of the working class up to its victory during the 1917 revolution. As he notes, "The History of Factories and Plants is the history of the working class," and "that means the History of Factories and Plants until October 1917 is the history of the growth and development of the class, of the revolutionary self-consciousness of the proletariat under the conditions of the capitalist state" ("About the Work on the History of Factories and Plants," 270–71). While this article is addressed to worker-writers under the tutelage of RAPP (the Russian Association of Proletarian Writers), the method and ideas Gorky promulgates apply also to every literary writer, proletarian and nonproletarian, in the Soviet context. We sense, however, that Gorky directs his comments most pointedly to nonproletarian literary figures. He exploits the traditional Bolshevik rhetoric while unmistakably encouraging the notion that history must be created for the newly privileged working class.

As regards postrevolutionary history, Gorky's plan continues to promote the working class through the efforts of everyone, even those who were considered enemies of the revolution (ibid., 275). He repeats the demand made of prerevolutionary history that "the process of working on the History of Factories and Plants must in and of itself serve the matter of the development of the class, the revolutionary self-consciousness of the proletariat, the matter of the deepening of Marxist-Leninist ideology" (ibid.). Although the goals of pre- and postrevolutionary history in the series mirrored each other, the means through which these goals were to be achieved differed.

Logically, prerevolutionary history needed to be reinterpreted so as to reflect the reality of the workers' revolution, a project not without its problems. Yet this proposal supported the basic idea that a supposedly new society, such as that in the Soviet Union, needed a new history, even if that meant rewriting the past. (The essay "About the Work" explores in detail the notion of creating a new history and revising already recorded history. The limited nature of the present study precludes a fuller treatment of the ideas in "About the Work." Suffice it to say that they merit closer examination against the broad backdrop of all the work in the History of Factories and Plants series.) Gorky proposed to put into effect the very practice that Hayden White described forty years later—that the writing of history is an essentially literary task in which the writer "emplots" the narrative based on the events or facts he chooses to privilege. White broadens this definition when he applies this position to all history writing. Nonetheless, the privileging of certain events or facts is often motivated by the belief that they are the key to the most truthful reading or telling of the event, a contention that White and Gorky would probably support.

More important to the discussion of the Belomor Canal project, Gorky's method for writing the new history of the new Soviet Union details the approach followed in writing the Belomor Canal volume. As noted previously, writers needed to know and experience the development of the Soviet Union. To that end, they needed to visit the places in which industrialization and nation building were proceeding. *The History of Construction* embodies this enterprise, for the authors of the volume did as Gorky bid—they explored the "reality" of the Belomor project and reported what they saw. No matter that what they saw was a carefully manipulated reality. In effect, the act of creating the history took precedence over the veracity of the account. In essence, "the discourse of industrialization triumphed over the facts of industrialization—which is what we expect in a logocentric society."[6]

Once at a site, writers would collect the raw materials necessary for the construction of the narrative. As Gorky notes, "Any work begins with the mining and collection of raw materials" (ibid., 276). Note that Gorky himself uses metaphors of labor and construction to describe the process of writing. As a result he links the "industry" of writing with the broader industrial metaphor that shaped the time and casts literary activity in the practical sphere of production. For the writing of prerevolutionary narratives, the stories of older workers must be collected and analyzed. As he notes, "An historical account of events demands consistency and connectedness" (ibid.). For postrevolutionary narratives, "literary figures must know if not everything, then as much as possible about astronomy and metalworking, about biology and tailoring, about engineering and shepherding, etc." ("About Hills," 173).

Instead of outdated aphorisms, writers need to know the reality of the workers and their efforts toward industrialization. In Gorky's view, "literary folk care little about their audience and the readability of the work for the working class audience. Rather, they concern themselves with art for art's sake!" (ibid.). The times demand otherwise of writers, for in Gorky's opinion, "nowhere in the past, even in the epochs of the greatest bursts of energy, as, for example, in the epoch of the Renaissance, has a quantity of talent grown with such rapidity and in such abundance, as it has grown in our country since October. The basic striving of our talent is the audacious striving to change all the basic conditions of life, to build a new world" (ibid., 171).

The ultimate goal of the History of Factories and Plants series necessitates that writers "must study our reality in all its forms, [they] need to know firsthand all our plants and factories, all enterprises, all work on the construction of the state. [They] must know in detail all sides of everything that was inherited from the past, all that was created in the last fourteen years, and all that is being created in the present" ("History of Factories and Plants," 143). In his speech to the First Congress of Writers, Vsevolod Ivanov echoes Gorky's sentiments when he argues that "every one of us creates around himself an archive of documents of the epoch, but we still have no public archive of documents of our time. The Union of Writers must create such an archive.... We must collect diaries, personal correspondence, we must write the biographies of our neighbors, we must write the history of the Soviet family, we must take special note of the changes observed by us and taking place in the Russian, Ukrainian, Turkmen, and other languages of our Union" (*Pervyi s"ezd,* 231). Like Gorky, Ivanov argues for the creation of a history of the time that documents the "reality" of life in the Soviet Union. How fitting that Ivanov was one of the more enthusiastic participants in both the Belomor Brigade and the Belomor volume.

Yet the continuing interest of Soviet literary figures in writing history is not enough to account for the compulsion among many to enthusiastically and publicly document events like the Belomor project. One potential key to understanding this practice again lies in Gorky's writings. The overarching idea that guided Gorky's pronouncements about the History of Factory and Plants series stressed that the function of literature was not to entertain but to inform and educate. Hence the need for literary figures to involve themselves deeply in documenting the growth of Soviet power in its various physical manifestations. Literature was brought into the service of cultural education or, at times, reeducation.

In discussing specifically the Belomor Canal project, Gorky contended that while the construction of the Canal undoubtedly had great economic importance, its chief importance to him was its "social-cultural significance" ("About Hills," 169). The Belomor project, with its attendant "cultural-education cells," produced results not only in the construction of the Canal but in reforming the social and criminal enemies of the Soviet state as well. Literary figures must understand this. "On the example of the pedagogical experience of the White Sea–Baltic Canal . . . and other colonies of that type, we, literary figures, must understand what fantastic results our system of education with the truth provides and how great the power of this single truly revolutionary truth is" (ibid., 175). Thus, histories of construction projects and other undertakings of socialist construction serve not only to document those projects but also to inform and educate readers about their positive results. In the case of Belomor, Gorky's comments suggest that he applauded the use of forced labor to construct the Canal, given that the ultimate tandem goals of the project—to build the waterway and reform social miscreants—were supposedly achieved.

Of course, there are two possible caveats to the program just outlined. First, as Wachtel also suggests, written discourse under Stalinism steadily became monologic. Increasingly the state tolerated no opinion that differed from its own. This monologism applied not only to literary and poetic discourse but also to historical, juridical, publicistic discourse; the pressures of totalitarian rule forced, or tried to force, all modes of written discourse into one—the voice of the state. (Recent events in Russia suggest the futility and failure of such a strategy.) Individual voices often were sacrificed to one for the ultimate goal of creating the first communist society.

Remember that the early 1930s were a time of rapid and great industrialization during which the state mobilized all resources, from forced labor to natural resources, to achieve quick results. The atmosphere of the time reverberated with the enthusiasm and energy many people actually experienced in the process of making the Soviet Union an industrial power built by collective labor and communist ideology. Events such as the building of the Belomor Canal were instantly historicized, not so much because they were worthy of the value that being recognized as part of history could impart to them, but because there was no other Soviet history. This new country needed a new history totally unlike anything that had preceded it and distinct from parallel histories that were developing in other places. Chronicling the history of factories and construction projects and, as a consequence, the working class, provided a method through which the rapidity of the industrialization, replete with its excesses, could be legitimized. How could such projects be harmful if they were actually history in the making, history made by workers in the first Marxist state?

In addition to this first caveat, the subsumption of many voices to one might be thought to jeopardize the accuracy of the telling of the history; however, this caveat understates the importance and ingenuity of collective authorship. Granted, it might be thought that collective authorship drowns out an individual author's voice. But it also offers those same individuals collective protection. Collective authorship, while conforming to one of the dominant metaphors of the time, offered the promise of collective responsibility. Narrative and factual accuracy were not as important as conveying the energy and enthusiasm of the era. The goal of histories such as the Belomor volume was to create an immediate collective experience while quelling any other attempts to record history.

This privileging of the history of industrialization and workers, while most appropriate in the Soviet context of the time, proved fleeting. As other scholars have suggested, in the early 1930s attention focused on collective projects and collective labor, the collective construction of the new Soviet state; however, the emphasis on collectivity in agriculture, literature, and industry fell out of vogue as the thirties progressed. Emphasis on individual heroes replaced the emphasis on collective deeds and successes.[7]

For the time in which it was exploited, the impulse toward collective labor permeated most aspects of Soviet society and reflected the strongest concerns of the day. Writers, both through the creation of the Union of Writers in 1932 and through projects such as Belomor, also accepted the practice of collective labor, an endeavor that produced uneven results. As the following section discusses, collective labor, as it applied to literature and when underpinned by specific political goals, was possible but not necessarily sustainable in the long term.

Constructing the Belomor Volume

While it might be tempting to attribute the *History* to hack writers who operated behind the scenes and who were never credited with the authorship of this book, in fact the opposite is true: The thirty-six writers listed as the authors of the Belomor volume did indeed write it. (See Appendix II.) Archival holdings contain the manuscripts for the Belomor volume, replete with drafts marked as such, edited versions, and handwritten copies of each chapter of *The History of Construction*. There are also index cards whereby individual writers noted the topics on which they would focus in the Belomor volume, as well as their progress in their work. In addition, the archives also boast draft manuscripts of those submissions *not* accepted by the volume editors.[8] Contemporary newspapers further substantiate the truth of authorship, for many contributors to the Belomor volume also published excerpts from their respective chapters in leading publications, including *Literaturnaia gazeta*, *Pravda*, and *Leningradskaia Pravda*.[9] Thus, several of the authors of the Belomor volume very publicly advertised and described their participation in producing it.

As if published excerpts of *The History of Construction* were not enough, many of its authors also proposed writing additional works, from poems to novels, inspired by the Belomor experience; in this regard they joined those colleagues who did not participate in the *History* project but still pursued the

Belomor topic. Lev Nikulin planned to conclude his book *The Seven Seas* with an epilogue that featured materials he had collected while in the Belomor Brigade. L. Kassil' (who did not participate in writing the Belomor volume) promised a host of sketches (*ocherki*) that would be published in the central newspapers, as well as children's stories about the Belomor Canal. Evgeny Gabrilovich intended to write a book of short stories about the people at the Belomor construction site (*Literaturnaia gazeta*, 29 August 1933, 4). However, none of these projects came to fruition, in spite of the good intentions of the authors.

These aborted attempts do not mean that other literary works about the Belomor Canal were not written. On the contrary, a few writers both involved in and excluded from the Belomor Brigade composed poems, plays, and prose works dedicated to the Belomor project. But the subsequent burst of literary activity, for which some Brigade writers publicly proclaimed Belomor as the inspiration, ultimately failed to materialize. As it turned out, it was most appropriate to write about Belomor almost immediately after its completion, through the initial publication of the *History*, right up to and including the first Congress of Writers in 1934. The currency of Belomor as a literary topic waned within a year of its completion. (Note, however, that Prishvin's novel about the Belomor project, *The Tsar's Road*, was the only work that was published significantly later—see chapter 4.) Consequently, other construction projects as well as other literary and political agendas replaced Belomor as the prime topic.

Before attention to the Belomor project diminished, its attendant volume functioned as a unique example of what many critics and writers had thought impossible: a collectively written literary work. That the whole premise of collective authorship confounded the traditional understanding of how literature was created did not deter those, chief among them Gorky, who viewed collective authorship as the natural and obvious outgrowth of the whole movement toward collective labor. If collective labor supposedly worked in all other spheres of Soviet life, why could it not succeed as well in literary endeavors? Conventional thinking held that even that most private and individual activity—the creation of a work of art—could be reshaped into a collective activity.

This conception of the production of art was put into practice in *The History of Construction* project and, on the most basic level, it succeeded; that is, the physical act of collective labor was achieved. The opening pages of the Belomor volume established the notion of collective authorship and collective responsibility as the bedrock of the project. As a companion piece to the list of collaborators, the narrative's authors provide this preface: "All the authors answer for the text of this book. They helped each other, complemented each other, corrected each other. Therefore it was extremely difficult to assign individual authorship. We note here the authors of the basic sections that were included in one chapter or another, once more reminding [the reader] that the actual author of this book is the full staff that worked on the history of the Stalin White Sea–Baltic Canal" (*HC,* 7). Each chapter lists the numerous authors who contributed to it, and archival documents bear out the true multi-author nature of each chapter.

In fact, the archival manuscripts and notes for the book supply a great deal of information about the stylistic and thematic choices many contributors made; archival entries verify the authorship of sections and chapters and buttress the argument that the Belomor volume attempted to applaud the work of the OGPU and record the construction of the Canal itself. One additional detail deserves further examination. A close reading of the "Authors' Notes for Chapters of the Book," one of the files in the archival holding on the Belomor volume, illuminates aspects of collective authorship that were heretofore undocumented.

The "Authors' Notes" was a series of pages on which reader comments were recorded. Judging from the file, it seems that as selected writers read draft manuscripts for chapters, they noted their comments on a sheet, which was then submitted to the editors. It is unclear how the "Authors' Notes" were collected. The only principle of organization seemed to be to assemble the documents in chapter order, and even then notes do not exist for every chapter, nor does it seem that every Brigade participant submitted notes. The general format of the notes lists the chapter number at the top of the page, followed either by a paragraph or two of commentary or by specific references to pages. If the writer references a particular page, then he/she usually recommends specific revisions. The content ranges widely from stylistic rephrasings to historical addenda to assessments of the content and form of the given chapter.

The following discussion catalogues some of these "Notes" and contextualizes them within the framework of collective authorship as a prelude to the discussion of how individual chapters were compiled. For example, in response to chapter 4, "The Prisoners," Boris Lapin notes: "The chapter is successful. A few more section headings ought to still be included. This will help the reader make sense of the people [being discussed]. In my opinion, it is absolutely necessary that the section on Anan'ev [one of the Belomor engineers] begins with a phrase that would talk about the people of the construction site in general and about the fact that we will make sense of the story of one of them and, based on that example, we will understand a whole stratum of people. Otherwise Anan'ev sticks out."[10] Because Lapin functioned as one of the montage editors for the Belomor volume, he was concerned with the connections within the narrative as well as with reader comprehension.

In commenting on chapter 5, "The Chekists," Lev Nikulin delineates precise editorial changes both in structure and content. (A close analysis of his notes reveals that they are mismarked in the archival record. According to the notation on the document they are supposed to apply to chapter 4; however, the comments relate to the content and people profiled in chapter 5. There is no explanation for this discrepancy.) At the top of the page, Nikulin remarks that "the pages shown refer to the edited version [of the chapter]."[11] Nikulin's concise comments point to exact changes:

—Verify the connection between pages 18 and 19.

—The technical description of the Povenets Steps should be made more readable.

—On pages 20 and 21, Budassi's conversation with Uspensky. Enliven Budassi's dialogue.

—Develop the transition so that there is no stage direction: On that note Engineer Budassi walked out.[12]

The specificity of Nikulin's comments underscores his close reading of the text and his attention to detail. Moreover, this example strengthens the argument that, in addition to those writers who specifically managed the montage of the entire work, other project members also actively participated in the rewriting of the narrative. Nikulin's comment "Enliven Budassi's dialogue" exemplifies White's notion of emplotment—real events and conversations are modified so as to enhance their significance or dramatic effect.

Both Sergei Budantsev and Gleb Gauzner comment on Chapter 6, "People Change Their Professions." The brevity of Gauzner's comments ("A wonderful chapter") serves as a counterpoint to Budantsev's detailed, lengthier analysis. Budantsev generally criticizes the chapter's structure. According to him, the piece is not tied together successfully. He calls for strong revision and editing, concluding his comments with the statement "And so everyone needs authorial cunning (Gabrilovich and Khatsrevin need little) and there needs to be a general spirit of the chapter. In my opinion, without this the chapter is not ready for publication."[13] The archival materials do not enlighten us as to whether Budantsev's comments were heeded and implemented, although the published version reads smoothly. The materials illustrate, however, that not everyone agreed about the compilation of the volume. Yet it seems the authors felt comfortable enough with the process to be able to criticize those parts with which they did not agree. Presumably, there was still room for debate and the exchange of opinions, practices that increasingly disappeared from the literary process as the 1930s progressed. Perhaps this is why collective authorship, with the give and take of criticism and advice, passed out of vogue.

In his brief comments about chapter 11, Victor Shklovsky states, "The Chapter is approved. It seems to me that the end, about the *natsmen* [non-Slavic nationalities] is, to a certain extent, not clearly motivated."[14] There is no way to confirm whether the author of that section heeded Shklovsky's comments. In the final printed version, the text discusses canalworkers from the non-Slavic republics and their participation in the project, but it is not clear how substantially this section had been altered in response to those comments.

"Authors' Notes" for other chapters run the gamut from praise ("The chapter is good") to strong criticism ("We ought to shorten Alymov. It goes on for too long. After Gabrilovich it is boring and dry. . . . In general the transition is unclear.")[15] Comments also range from personal critiques of one author by another to general comments about inaccuracies in historical or technical data. Most telling remain the comments directed at style and structure. These comments in particular suggest that the reciprocity of collective authorship functioned somewhat successfully. This evidence independently supports the statements of the writers in the collective as to the true nature of the editing of *The History of Construction*. Indeed, such evidence deflates the myth that the Belomor volume was penned by hack writers forced to write it without any attention to artistic integrity. The writers who participated cared about how they wrote, even if they later had misgivings about what they wrote, and the archival and textual evidence both indicate that *The History of Construction* truly is a collectively written work.

Indeed, both archival evidence and the detailed reminiscences of Victor Shklovksy reveal how the writers collective "constructed" the Belomor *History*. In examining this evidence, a counterpoint to the publicly stated method of collective authorship emerges. As it happens, *The History of Construction* paradoxically united both the impulse toward the new (socialist realism) and strong elements of the old (avant-garde theory). This work simultaneously epitomized the program of socialist construction and collective labor, while relying on a highly modernist technique—montage—to achieve its end. As such, *The History of Construction* embodied the contradiction between avant-garde theory and socialist realist practice: It revealed that the imposition of ideology and dogma on writers, attempted since the Bolshevik uprising, had not and could not fully expunge artistic tendencies and instincts that were still very much ingrained in many of the writers who produced the volume. The following discussion reveals those points where avant-garde technique supported Soviet ideology and, conversely, where Soviet ideology was no match for literary instinct and tradition.

Constructing the Montage

While not always a success, the process of montage—not simply editing, but real montage in its richest cinematographic meaning—often prevailed in the composition of *The History of Construction*. Not only did those applying it—Lapin, Gauzner, Inber and Shklovsky—impose montage on the text, it also was embraced as the method through which a truly collective literary enterprise could be achieved. Granted, Shklovsky's comments suggest that while it was easy to embrace the rhetoric of collective authorship, it was not as easy to forsake individual authorial control for the greater literary good. Yet this tension points to one of the key ideas motivating this discussion. *The History of Construction* became, perhaps de facto, the decisive moment at which the modernist aesthetic (montage) combined with, repelled, and sometimes overcame the impending socialist realist mandate. Collective authorship, while squaring nicely with the imminent demands of socialist realism, simultaneously embodied some of the most important elements of the modernist aesthetic. If "the form favored by the 'progressive' artists of our time is, accordingly, the open one which not only permits a free and constant interchange between art and life—both in themselves fragmented—but also enables the *artist-engineer* [italics, CR] to add, subtract, dismantle and reassemble, almost at will, the parts which make up the artificial whole," then, as Ulrich Weisstein argues, "this is precisely what we mean when we speak of montage as a characteristically modern technique" (Weisstein, 131).

The History of Construction was most appropriate to the Belomor Canal project, which emphasized construction, labor, and engineering. Those writers who oversaw the montage, as well as the other writers who participated in the give-and-take process of writing the volume, worked as the "artist-engineers" to which Weisstein ascribes a modernist position. They "add[ed], subtract[ed], dismantl[ed], and reassembl[ed]" the parts of the whole so as to achieve the apparent effect of unity. To extend the construction metaphor, the authors of *The History of Construction* built the volume by joining "bricks" of text in an effort to produce a single, connected narrative. If, as Matthew Teitelbaum and Margarita Tupitsyn contend, the practitioners of photomontage became the message makers and bearers in the Soviet context, so, too, did the practitioners of literary montage.[16]

This is a logical linkage, given what Weisstein posits as the only type of cinematographic montage appropriated successfully into the literary sphere. As he notes, "The second, and more distinctly esthetic sense in which montage occurs (and which finds its most exact literary equivalent in Flaubert's handling of the *comice agricole* scene of *Madame Bovary*) attaches to the creative, specifically rhythmic, application of a technique developed (in partial emulation of D. W. Griffith) by Russian directors like Kuleshov and Pudovkin, and perfected by Sergei Eisenstein. In this instance what is meant is 'a style of film editing in which contrasting shots or sequences are juxtaposed for the purpose of suggesting a total idea or impression'" (ibid., 127). This same definition applies to *The History of Construction*.

However, that montage could be used to further a platform that was distinctly *not* avant-garde is also not remarkable, given the nature and appeal of montage in its various forms. In writing about an exhibit of Soviet photomontage, Matthew Teitelbaum suggests that it "elucidates moments in the USSR . . . at the point when an established modernist avant-garde was challenged by the need to reach a mass audience" (Teitelbaum, 8). (As regards photomontage, Teitelbaum has in mind a much longer time period, ranging from the early twenties to the advent of World War II.) In addition, in writing about photomontagist Gustave Klutsis, Margarita Tupitsyn "trace[s] the history of political photomontage in the Soviet Union that was inspired by the paradigmatic change from the artist as formalist to the artist as an active message maker" (Tupitsyn, 87). As these critics suggest, the art of photomontage was linked closely, either consciously or unconsciously, to the idea that in the modern age the role of the artist, whether writer, photographer, filmmaker, or painter, had changed.

While this is not a novel idea, given what we know about the function and practice of art as espoused by nineteenth-century realism, the more recent practice foregrounds the distinctly political, ideologically based function that prevailed in Soviet art and literature in the 1930s. Theoretically, the artist was duty bound to create not a personal message but the message thought to be most appropriate by the state. Here the practice of realism clearly diverges from the role of artist as message maker in prewar Stalinism, since the majority of individual voices seemed, increasingly, to become officially subjugated to and subsumed under one voice, the voice of the state.

This situation implies that a very modernist undertaking holds the promise of being exploitable in a nonmodernist framework. Montage, be it film, photo, or literary, as practiced in the Soviet context and especially as applied to *The History of Construction* was important not so much to achieve artistic goals as to convey the message. Literary montage made the Belomor *History* the physical embodiment of the notion of collective labor.

The technique of montage was most widely theorized and practiced in Soviet film and photography. This rich montage tradition encompasses most notably the work of Pudovkin, Vertov, and Eisenstein in Soviet cinematography and the work of Rodchenko and Klutsis in photomontage. (In fact, in a forthcoming dissertation, Erika Wolf, University of Michigan, will explore Rodchenko's photomontage work at Belomor as depicted in the pages of the magazine *SSSR na stroike* [The USSR on the Building Site].) This use of montage, a use that does *not* imply simply cutting and editing, in turn was applied to a literary text. This is not to suggest that there was no tradition of literary montage prior to the writing of *The History of Construction*. In fact, one of the chief practioners of montage in the Belomor project was Boris Lapin, himself a proponent of literary montage as evident in his early works, among them the tale "Krokus Prim."

Underpinning the connection between the application of montage to a non-avant-garde project is a logic that stems from the fact that Russian modernism was posited on the notion of remaking life. Many Russian modernists embraced the fervor and vitality of the revolution and saw in it an opportunity to create something new and to infuse life and art with these artistic attitudes. Montage, then, is associated with the making of the new; the consistency between the enthusiasm of the period that initially spawned montage and of that which produced Belomor links these two seemingly disparate entities. In his seminal work *The Total Art of Stalinism,* Boris Groys argues exactly this point and extrapolates it even further. According to Groys, the practitioners of Stalinist art and culture were more avant-garde than their modernist predecessors. What avant-gardists advocated only in theory, the Bolsheviks and their successors put into practice. If modernism urged the development of a "new" life, postrevolutionary Soviet culture actually created it.[17] The distinction between the avant-gardists and their Bolshevik successors derives from the perception of modernism when it was associated with individualism, formalism, and inaccessibility. In this regard, modernist technique represents the opposite of that which was demanded in socialist realist art.

Furthermore, it is montage and not collage that is the operative method, the chief principle of organization, of *The History of Construction*. The fundamental goal of collage is to have disparate parts create the illusion of unity without each constituent part losing its individuality or otherness. The viewer/reader perceives each element of the collage while comprehending the total idea of the work. In contrast, montage strives not to disrupt the narrative per se but to join seemingly disparate narrative segments to produce a unified whole. The segments lose their individual qualities for the sake of creating a single message or idea. The *History* embodied this principle, since writers as diverse as Alexei Tolstoy, Ilf and Petrov, and Alexander Avdeenko collaborated to produce a work that advanced the single cause of reforging Soviet society through intense physical and collective labor. If montage in film could be used to provide a positive spin on an event or idea to propagandize it for mass consumption, then a literary rendering of montage could achieve the same goal.

In regard to the montage practiced in writing *The History of Construction*, one of the most influential participants in this enterprise was Victor Shklovsky. Shklovsky not only worked on the actual writing of the volume but also was responsible for much of the montage, as well as for publicly promoting both the volume and the literary process that produced it. Added to Shklovsky's filmwork and intimate knowledge of the principles of montage was his active support of and participation in the campaign for "the literature of fact" as a viable literary alternative to traditional prose fiction.

In an article about the *faktoviki* (proponents of the notion that the presentation of objective facts through literary forms such as biography, notes, and sketches should be the highest form of literary activity), Natasha Kolchevska wrote about their attempts to advance the "literature of fact" in the pages of the journal *Novyi Lef* [The New Left] (1927–28). She argued that the impulse behind this program was a desire to probe "the possibilities for responsive, contemporary prose forms which would adequately convey the spirit and wealth of material arising out of the new social and economic order in Soviet Russia" (Kolchevska, 452). Shklovsky, along with Osip Brik and Sergei Tretiakov, actively discussed these possibilities in the pages of *Novyi Lef*. As Kolchevska notes, Shklovsky's approach to the literature of fact meant that "he envisioned ... the development of 'hybrid' prose forms which combined journalism's respect for material with narrative or compositional techniques which could most expressively 'organize' that material" (ibid., 453). Shklovsky's implementation of these ideas is most forcefully evident in his experimental works of the late twenties—*Sentimental Journey, Hamburg Account,* and *Zoo*. In "constructing" these works, Shklovsky shared a belief (with other faktoviki) "in the material and scientific bases of literature which required of the writer an intimate understanding of material from a 'producer's' point of view. In Shklovsky's case, the material was often the literary form itself, which he approached rather as an *engineer* [italics CR] would, taking it apart, distinguishing the discrete pieces . . . and nakedly recombining them in his own experimental works" (ibid., 460). Perhaps unwittingly, Kolchevska succinctly described the process of employment that Shklovsky was practicing long before White's theoretical formulation of it.

Moreover, it is no accident that Kolchevska ascribes to Shklovsky the epithet "engineer," a description even more apt in the context of the Belomor volume. Kolchevska's assessment of Shklovsky's work in factography dovetails nicely with the montage procedure followed in assembling *The History of Construction*. Even more important, as Kolchevska notes, "While the faktoviki's output was small and their attacks on fictional prose simplistic and ultimately self-defeating, their demand that literature actively participate in the transformation of society is not to be taken lightly even today" (ibid., 461). Here we find an accurate, concise description of one of the most important motives equally applicable to the *History*. The Writers Brigade to Belomor and the subsequent volume were intended to demonstrate literature's "active participation" in the transformation of Russian society into Soviet society.

In a speech about Belomor that Shklovsky delivered in January 1934, he delineates both the theory and methodology of writing the Belomor volume. In discussing how the book was compiled, he notes, "There were three types of montage. Lapin and Gauzner edited the photographs and edicts, Vera Inber [edited] for the continuity of transitions, for continuity of action, and I edited for internal thematic unity."[18] Shklovsky further explains, "I worked on the montage, on the art of uniting the parts. I worked a lot in film, a great deal in fact, and for the most part, on interweaving fragments. . . . We argued a lot about the montage. One needs to learn collective labor from encyclopedists. . . . There were long arguments about language, about figures, about people, about the external appearance of a person, about the sunsets and about the rocks necessary or unnecessary to the construction project—the collective of Belomorstroi raised these issues."[19] He concludes that "this [the Belomor volume] is a very interesting piece, for it truly changed the internal mutual relations of authorial powers,"[20] and adds, "There were thirty-six of us. Disputes arose, manuscripts were returned to their authors . . . [ultimately though] there was not a single instance when opinions diverged."[21] Shklovsky's commentary suggests that while differences of opinion were the natural outgrowth of individual writers working together, compromises could be reached, especially when they were achieved by collectively sharing both constructive criticism and editorial responsibility. Alas, Shklovsky's opinion is one of the few documented opinions of the writing process. It is unclear how most of his colleagues viewed this process.

This lack of documentation does not mean, however, that the notion of collective authorship was not conceptualized by other writers. Repeatedly during speeches at the First Congress of Writers in 1934, various literary figures returned to the idea of collective authorship as a new approach to literary production. In her speech Lidiia Seifullina notes that only true comradeship and collective responsibility would enable Soviet writers to reach new levels of literary production (*Pervyi s"ezd,* 237). Kuz'ma Gorbunov, another participant in the Belomor Brigade and volume, noted in his speech, "The experience of work on the book about the Belomor Canal brilliantly confirms that it is possible to write collectively, and in other circumstances; when it is a matter of the assimilation of a large amount of material and the mastery of life, it is completely imperative. A writer's originality does not suffer from [collective authorship]. On the contrary, one's originality develops more clearly when collaboration is involved. Not for nothing did the writers, the authors of the book about the Belomor Canal, not want to split up, and with great enthusiasm they greeted the proposal to create a work dedicated to the people of the Second Five-Year Plan" (ibid., 602). Speeches like Gorbunov's, repeated throughout the First Congress of Writers, continued to applaud, at least in public, the feasibility and appropriateness of collective authorship for the new Soviet literature.

In further discussing how the Belomor volume was produced, Shklovsky notes, "This book demonstrated that the methodology of cinematographers [when used] in literature turned out to be well grounded. This was clear to every writer.... We wanted to make this book a general work of the collective, but there arose such an uproar, that we signed every chapter."[22] Significantly, this last statement indicates that in spite of the spirit and rhetoric of collective authorship the project supposedly engendered, the aspiration to individual authorship and fame had not diminished. He continues, "Then we started to read excerpts to each other and to reject [some]. It turned out that writers are most of all similar to each other in their shortcomings. When we started to reject pieces, something akin to individuality was rejected. Beginning writers make the mistake of striving to be similar to others. And this is true not only among beginning writers."[23] The tension between individual authorship and collective responsibility persisted in spite of the desire (or demand) to produce a collectively written work. Yet the aspiration to collective authorship, at least overtly, won out in the project.

Official pronouncements of the Belomor volume writers' collective efforts attested to this victory of sorts. As they noted in an article in *Pravda*, "We decided to write about everything in a new way. We worked on the book collectively. We jointly devised a plan for the book. Each line was written by every one of us and discussed by all the others. We added material to each other's stories. In the course of the last ten days we, all together, edited the book that will be a wholly collective work" (*Pravda*, 7 December 1933, 1).

In addition, the move to collective authorship sought to galvanize the methodology of collective labor and socialist collaboration. In keeping with the shift from writer as artist to writer as conveyer of "the message," at least officially, *The History of Construction* writers collective reinforced this idea. In a jointly authored article dated 23 December 1933, they also state, "We in no way think that the time of individual artistic activity has passed. But we are convinced that in place of individual competition there should be collective mutual assistance. And we know that this is a new experience of socialist collaboration of Soviet writers; this is the first example of close and urgent cooperation [based] not on the principle of a stylistic school or an organized literary grouping, but on real, collective creative work" (*Literaturnaia gazeta*, 23 December 1933, 4).

This public pronouncement of the Belomor volume's authors predates the charter of the Union of Soviet Writers of the USSR, presented at the First Congress of Writers in 1934. The charter stipulates that writers must actively participate in socialist construction and in the documentation of concrete Soviet reality (*Pervyi s"ezd*, 712). The charter demands, among other things,

> the active participation in socialist construction of Soviet writers with their artistic creativity, the defense of working-class interests and the strengthening of the Soviet Union on the path toward justly depicting the history of the proletariat's class struggle, the class struggle and the construction of socialism in our country, and the path of educating the broad laboring masses in the socialist spirit, along with the creative competition of writers, their mutual assistance to each other with the goal of engendering the more successful growth of artistic power and the ever-deepening and many-sided development of forms, styles, and genres of artistic creation on the basis of socialist realism, depending on the individual talent and creative interests of writers (ibid., 712–13).

On the most basic level, the writers who produced the Belomor volume instituted and promulgated the principles that a year later would be officially incorporated into the charter of the Union of Writers. Thus the significance of the Belomor project in terms of the codification and adoption of the socialist realist program is unmistakable.

As is widely known, socialist realism in literature, however we choose to describe it—method, dogma, program, mandate—developed post facto. That is, the defining texts used to prescribe its parameters appeared prior to its official adoption and the actual coining of the term.[24] Clearly, the method and content of the Belomor volume further buttressed the basic premise of socialist realism, for not only did the book espouse collective authorship, but it also promoted the basic concepts underpinning the socialist realist doctrine—*partiinost'* (Party-mindedness), *narodnost'* (popular/national quality), *ideinost'* (ideological content). This means that a work of socialist realism must portray the Party, or the spirit of the Party, as it displays itself in the population at large. In turn, all thought and action must be infused with Communist ideology. In terms of Belomor, the Party, through the efforts of the OGPU, promoted and executed the writing project. The canalworkers highlighted in the volume—criminals, kulaks, and wreckers—were melded into the *narod* (the people) through Party intervention and Communist ideology. And the ideinost'—that socialist construction and Communist ideology imbued its workers with a sense of devotion to the cause and a renewed feeling of worth because of their newly gained skills—permeates the entire text.

In turn, the promotion of reformed criminals who were now well equipped to continue to participate in socialist construction afforded *The History of Construction* writers and, consequently, their readers, a plethora of positive heroes. Here again, the Belomor volume prefigured the official adoption of the positive hero as a literary type. Those inmates singled out in the narrative as the best examples of the reforging process served as prototypes for a workers' model of the positive hero. More important, the authors of the *History* depicted the Chekists as the true embodiment of the positive hero as mentor. The socialist realist schema justifies this choice, for the Chekists, even more than the canalworkers, were imbued with a sense of Party activism and ideology. They were the ultimate positive heroes, for they accepted the challenge that the Belomor project presented, thereby overcoming physical and ideological obstacles to achieve their goal. As a result of their endeavors, they gained a greater awareness of the power and correctness of the Party, socialist construction, and comrade Stalin.

The final socialist realist flourish obtains in the canonical happy ending that concludes the Belomor account—the Canal was completed and opened, former enemies of the state were reformed, and the Chekists succeeded in implementing the plan, thanks to Communist ideology. A photograph of a female canalworker with a jackhammer that prefaces chapter 8 is captioned with a quotation from Marx: "In changing nature a person changes himself" (HC, 318), thereby overtly linking ideology to action.

Hence, the flexibility of socialist realism, at least in its earliest manifestation. The unstable climate in Soviet literature of the early 1930s often produced narratives that did not cleanly fall into the socialist realist category because they were not completely devoid of modernist elements. Valentin Kataev's novel *Time, Forward!* exemplifies this possibility: the omission of the first chapter of the novel with the remark that it will be included later in the novel, thereby disrupting the logical narrative flow. While the 1920s are a period that critics generally consider a time of great literary experimentation and diversity, to a lesser extent the same can be argued for the early 1930s. In that regard, the Belomor volume remains a text with mixed pedigree that fell under neither the socialist realist nor the modernist rubric.

This blurring raises the question of whether the finished product of the montage process really was a seamless whole. On the level of narrative structure and style, the text supports the argument that the narrative reads rather choppily (Carleton, 996–1000). Segments frequently seem out of place or totally unconnected to preceding ones. Or in a complete chapter, the disparate parts remain disjointed and lack unity. That is, the authors of certain chapters wander across a particular thematic terrain and hardly link the various segments under one stylistic rubric. This apparent narrative inconsistency demands closer attention in order to explain the frequently rough transitions and narrative disconnections in the text.

Within this context montage could very well be the most appropriate strategy through which texts created by many authors can be united. The nature of collective authorship (and any collaborative undertaking) is such that there inevitably are different styles, voices, and disjunctures that somehow must be brought together. If the goal of a collective endeavor is a collective resolution of the difficulties encountered therein, then montage can help surmount, though not alleviate entirely, these difficulties.

A close analysis of the text reveals much about the interdependency of montage and collective authorship. For all the information the archival manuscripts of the Belomor volume provide, they are not exhaustive. These materials must be used with discretion, for the authorship of every section of every chapter is not precisely attributed, while the information some materials provide is more complete than others. Likewise, the information that is available must be matched closely with the published version of the text so as to compare variants of the same text and to document the connections between them. The following analysis in no way pretends to be exhaustive, but where appropriate the archival drafts and notes are included judiciously in order to understand how the text is constructed.

These materials will be considered in this analysis: drafts of chapters of *The History of Construction*, drafts of individual manuscripts submitted by the authors and included in the volume, notes of the authors on chapters they did not write, and author cards on which certain writers noted different types of information—work completed, themes undertaken, progress to date, and the like. Even though this study will be the closest examination of that process to date, bringing these various kinds of information to bear on the text will not answer all the questions about the construction of the Belomor volume itself.

The Practical Application of Montage and Collective Authorship

An analysis of both the drafts and final versions of selected chapters illustrates the peculiarities in the narrative and provides those unfamiliar with the text itself a better understanding of form and content. A word of caution, however. Those who would seek to match the following examples and analyses with the English translation of *The History of Construction* will find themselves confounded. Unfortunately the English translation fails to preserve the order and presentation of the material in the Russian original. Likewise large segments of text were omitted and the general principle of organization behind the translation remains a mystery. (See chapter 4 for a fuller discussion of the English translation.)

While the following analysis does not discuss every chapter in great detail, the hope is to convey enough of the flavor of the Belomor narrative so that the reader can better understand the volume, especially in the contexts in which it was presented. The interplay between draft manuscripts and published versions accentuates the unique processes that produced the book.

Moroever, this analysis will address questions pertinent to a fuller understanding of the Belomor volume and collective authorship: Did the collectively authored volume succeed? How well did collective authorship work? What could collective authorship accomplish that single authorship could not? While not a new concept per se (the Bible was, after all, a collectively written work), collective authorship within the Soviet context prompts a reappraisal of this approach.

Chapter 5, "The Chekists," coauthored by Alymov, Berzin, Ivanov, Kataev, Korabel'nikov, Nikulin, Rykachev, and Shklovsky, affords a rich starting point. Because of the title, the reader assumes that the chapter will describe the Chekists and their role in the construction of the Canal. Some sections, such as those devoted to two of the most prominent Chekists—Yakov Rapoport, assistant director of the project, and Lazar Kogan, project director—support this assumption. (See Appendix IV for a list of the camp directorate.) Interspersed among these passages are sections seemingly unrelated to the Chekists, such as "A Conversation at the Washbasin," "He Became Different," or "At the Threshold of the Povenets Steps," all of which focus on the attitudes, labor, and reforging of Canal inmates. In fact, of the thirteen individual segments in the chapter, half devote their attention to the prisoners and not to the Chekists. Precisely this topical distribution underscores the principle of montage, for although each segment does not necessarily follow from its predecessor, the overriding message endures: Thanks to the efforts and the abilities of the Chekists, the Canal was completed and the process of reforging was achieved.

A closer examination of the text reveals how this interweaving of theme and authorship operates. While the archival documents do not clarify who authored each particular section of chapter 5, it is possible to determine the authorship of at least a few sections.

Chapter 5 begins with a fourteen-and-a-half page section devoted to Rapoport. The opening line establishes the tone of the ensuing description, "The style of Chekist labor completely excludes any uncertainty about one's own powers" (*HC,* 154). Rapoport embodies the prototypical Chekist—intelligent, self-assured, and iron-willed. The discussion stresses Rapoport's sharp mind—he awakens ready to greet the day: "The most valuable [thing] for him is the inner firmness and clarity of the mind" (ibid., 155). In addition, as a child he loved brainteasers and would doggedly pursue the solution to problems for days if necessary (ibid.). The author of this section (it is unclear from archival documents who this is) stresses Rapoport's mental acumen because that is the quality that the construction of the Belomor Canal necessitates. When Rapoport arrives at the construction site nothing exists. Therefore, to him falls the task of building everything from the ground up, including the prison camp. As Rapoport claims, "First of all we need to give the camp inmates a place to live. A person cannot work when he has no place to sleep and nowhere to cook his rations"(ibid., 158). According to the Belomor narrative, the OGPU personnel prioritized equally both the construction of the Canal and worker welfare, a myth perpetuated by *The History of Construction* and not substantiated in reality. (Recall that prisoners sent to Belomor in the first convoy were ordered to build their own barracks out of little more than snow and bogs.)

Added to Rapoport's Chekist biography, which is presented as the prototype for this kind of narrative hero, is the fact that even at the university fellow students dubbed him a "mathematician" and predicted great things for him (ibid., 159). Early in his career, he realized that the future did not lie with the tsar but with Bolshevik power. This fundamental element foretold Rapoport's dedication to the cause, a dedication that prompted him to proclaim modestly, "I simply fulfill the directives of the OGPU" (ibid., 160). The discussion continues to reveal the underlying structure of his personality, which enables him to succeed at Belomor. Always thinking, always calculating, Rapoport achieves the impossible, for out of nothing he creates something and in so doing remains true to his Bolshevik convictions and the spirit of collectivism. Even when unpleasant situations arise, Rapoport is always ready to accept the challenge and solve the problem. As such he becomes one kind of model for the positive hero—the example whom others can try to emulate.

The ultimate test of his strength of will comes when Rapoport recognizes an old acquaintance among the prisoner-engineers brought to the Canal. Rapoport initially wants to approach the man, grab him under the chin, and demand, "Who gave us away?" (ibid., 169). It seems this person informed on Rapoport and his revolutionary comrades in 1917. But true to his Chekist character, Rapoport restrains himself and tells the man's section head, "I request that you carefully follow the one who is now presenting. If in actuality he is sincere, then report to me about him in a month" (169). Like an elephant, Rapoport never forgets, yet he is willing to give the "saboteur" the benefit of the doubt and the opportunity to redeem himself. This concluding flourish underscores the wisdom, self-control, and sharp memory with which Rapoport is blessed. In turn, although this is never directly stated, the narrative intimates that the Canal project benefits from his fine qualities and exemplary behavior. Never does the writer utter a negative word or phrase about Rapoport, and the tone throughout the piece unwaveringly conveys confidence in and respect for such an excellent example of an OGPU officer.

Chapter 5 continues with two sections, "A Threesome on the Site," which discusses other Chekists on the project, and "The First Meeting," devoted to the first meeting of the directors of the administrative-technical workers. Central to these narratives is the justification for the use of slave labor to build the Canal. The writer of these sections reports (again we do not know who penned them) that the use of this labor was justified. As Kogan, head of the construction project, argues, "Where is the machine that could, according to demand, produce the required specializations? There is no such machine. We have a reserve of labor. You say that there are no masons here? That's correct. But there are also no honest Soviet citizens here either; we must create both masons and honest Soviet citizens. One is worth the other"(ibid., 177). Kogan's remarks underscore the need for specialists who do not have bourgeois roots and have been produced by the Soviet system. The scarcity of such specialists prompted the mass arrests of "bourgeois" engineers to design the Canal. Actually, construction of the Canal remained a task that could have been accomplished only by enlisting the labor of prison camp inmates, which triggered the move to guarantee a large labor supply. While Kogan's contention that "there are also no honest Soviet citizens here either" rings false when matched against what we know of Belomor, the impetus for that remark—reforging—is transparent.

Subsequent sections, "A Conversation at the Washbasin," "Listen to Headquarters," and the "The Camp Director's Day," generally continue this narrative line, but there is a distinct change of tone and style beginning with "A Conversation." This section recounts an exchange between two prisoner-engineers in which they question the OGPU's plan to complete the Canal in five hundred days. One speaker contends that they need three thousand days. (This discussion echoes the concerns about Magnitogorsk voiced in Kataev's *Time, Forward!* in which the rapidity with which the project must be completed is questioned.) The other man questions the source of the workforce needed. Perhaps it will be imported from America? Both interlocutors lament the poor food rations, for they are certain they will not be having peas and ham. "Instead the tempo of work is increased" (ibid., 178). The odd thing about this exchange is that it at first appears to be a narrative non sequitur. The texts that precede and follow this conversation focus on the wise foresight and planning of the OGPU, not on the prisoners or on dissenting opinions.

Yet connections between the sections exist nonetheless. "A Conversation" is linked to its framing texts by the slimmest of threads. Note that the closing line of the section preceding "A Conversation" states, "A year later, when they showed the engineers the transcript of this meeting [with the Canal administration] they were ashamed" (ibid.). At this meeting, the engineers voice their doubts over their ability to construct the Canal in such a short period of time. The section that immediately follows "A Conversation" begins, "But whatever the weather we observe a strange occurrence: an unusual number of long dark threads stretching in all directions along the ground" (ibid.), a description that refers to the lines of workers fanning out along the Canal route in an effort to complete the construction project. The existence of these "long dark threads" proves that the engineers referred to in the preceding section were mistaken. Again the planning and organizational prowess of the OGPU prevails, for in spite of the reservations that the engineers voice, the Canal project commences, marking a victory over dissenting voices.

Physically, stylistically, and thematically, the framing sections isolate "A Conversation," hence underscoring the engineers' mistaken preconceptions about the project more sharply. The framing sections convey neither the conversational tone nor the familiarity found in "A Conversation." Instead they emphasize, in the strongest possible terms, that the OGPU will succeed. "The headquarters of the construction project wishes to be listened to" (ibid., 180). According to the narrative, headquarters achieves this goal by mounting radios throughout the construction site that constantly broadcast information about the success of the Canal project and the response to it in Moscow, among the Chekists, and from the Party (ibid.). The implication is that blaring radios, in sharp contrast to personal conversations, drown out other, less important discussions and convey more important and credible information. Despite changes in tone and style, the overall message of the chapter continues to prevail.

In fact, the message never gets lost, no matter what the tone or topic of each section. The section "The Chief of Construction's Day" continues the theme and mood, for it describes not only the harried, activity-filled life of construction chief Kogan but also relates his personal history. This biography turns out, yet again, to be the quintessential Chekist life story. Kogan, like many of his OGPU peers, was jailed as an anarchist against the tsarist government. However, upon his release from prison, he joined ranks with Felix Dzerzhinsky (first head of the Soviet secret police) and pursued the Bolshevik cause, receiving his Party card in 1918. An ever vigilant OGPU man, Kogan worked his way through the ranks, moving from the leadership of a provincial Party school to the head of the secret police within the Ninth Army to the assistant directorship of the troops of the OGPU. Having served three years in the division of border security, he assumed the leadership of organizing the GULag, a position that led him directly to his joint appointment as head of the Belomor project (ibid., 183). Kogan, like Rapoport before him, emerges as the prototypical mentor.

The author of this section wedges this biographical vignette between descriptions of Kogan's duties and his hectic life on the Canal. This structure buttresses the argument that he represents the best that the OGPU has to offer, and it continues the thematic treatment of the Chekists.

While the narrative preserves its thematic connectedness in the ensuing two sections, "KVO (Kulturno-vospitatel'nyi otdel)" [The Cultural-Education Section] and "The Rally," its attention shifts somewhat to the camp inmates. Both of these sections, authored by Sergei Alymov, discuss the implementation of the OGPU plans in the prisoners' lives. It is no accident that Alymov authored precisely these two parts; as an inmate at Belomor and the editor of the camp newspaper, *Perekovka*, he was intimately acquainted with the activities of the KVO and assisted it in using the paper as the mouthpiece through which the message of reeducation was proffered to camp inmates.

The section entitled "KVO" focuses on the educational function of the OGPU as it pertains to the construction project. The KVO is the organizational structure that, next to hard labor itself, promoted the reforging and reeducation of camp inmates. These KVOs, usually run by an "educator," taught illiterate prisoners to read and write while indoctrinating them with the Marxist-Leninist ideology and the program of perekovka. In addition, the KVOs frequently served as the foci of entertainment and cultural programs for the Belomor camp inmates. But their main purpose was to indoctrinate and agitate.

The section "KVO" details the meeting among heads of various KVOs. Their task is to "mobilize" themselves and the workers. A night of "storming" at the construction site is on the agenda. *Shturm*, or storming, involved working at a furious pace, frequently the whole night or days on end, in order to accomplish a particularly difficult task in the construction project. In essence, the storming places the responsibility for the completion of the task on the collective whole. There are community responsibility and socialist competition, two recurrent themes in the rhetoric of the time. This description of storming accurately reflects some of the strategies used to encourage, or force, people to work more efficiently.

In a prelude to the storming, the canalworkers were encouraged, even goaded, to perform at their highest levels of productivity and their quickest work pace. As the main speaker in the section "KVO" notes, "We must without ceremony, with all harshness beat away all defects, drown out the tortoise tempo. Our main task is to mobilize the community and force them to accept the responsibility for the completion of the Canal on time" (ibid., 186). To the objection that there are not enough KVO workers to attend to all the sections personally, the main speaker replies that "we will mobilize the brigades for a competition" (ibid.), a common method of inducing and bolstering productivity on the Canal site.

However, the idea that overrides all other concerns and generates all this activity is that "we must swiftly reconstruct all our work," a challenge that, in this case, applies to the KVO but subsequently applies to all areas of labor on the Canal. The reader encounters this idea repeatedly. Added to this notion, of course, is the important fact that the head of the construction project, Kogan, directs the KVO to engage in these organizational and agitational activities (ibid., 185). In effect, the OGPU is responsible not only for the construction of the Canal but for the reeducation of the workers on it as well.

Alymov also contributed the next section, "The Rally," which narrates the agitational gathering that was organized to prepare the canalworkers for the "storming night." Throughout this section, the narrative returns to the theme of greater production and reforged workers. The official presiding over the rally presents "the calling card of the shock-worker" to those present—a fragment of diabase dotted with crystals of golden pyrite.[25] On the fragment a piece of paper is pasted that reads "No natural obstacles will break our doggedness in the battle for the Canal" (ibid., 188). This demonstration is accompanied by music, banners, and placards all aimed at raising the enthusiasm and energy of those who will be participating in the storming night. Alymov caps off the section with the phrase "Thousands of hands, that are blocking rivers, stopping waterfalls, removing cliffs, vote for the birth of the Canal, and together with it, for the birth of mankind" (ibid., 188). Here he returns to the umbrella idea of reforging through hard labor. In addition, earlier in the section, one of the rally participants suggests that "we send it [the chunk of diabase] to the head of the construction project—let it be our collective signature" (ibid.). Although Alymov shifts the focus of discussion from the OGPU personnel to the camp inmates/laborers, he nonetheless does not lose the thread that connects each section of the chapter—the OGPU presence on the Belomor project.

Yet how is it possible to determine that Alymov authored these sections? In the final published copies of the Belomor volume, section authors, while noted alphabetically in the table of contents, are never alluded to in the body of the text. Nor can the reader assume automatically that the alphabetical listing in the table of contents parallels the order of appearance of sections in any given chapter. We must instead turn to the draft manuscripts for each chapter as well as to individual author manuscripts to authenticate the authorship of particular sections in various chapters. As regards chapter 5, the draft manuscript of the whole chapter provides no concrete evidence of authorship. In this case, the authors' individual draft manuscripts contain the original versions of Alymov's contributions to this chapter and others.

Interestingly, the draft manuscripts for Alymov's contributions just discussed differ slightly from their final versions. While the section "The Rally" begins identically, the final version omits entirely the draft line "Tarah-tarah-tarah-tarah-rah. At the rah there was a deafening blow." Perhaps the most important sentence in the entire section—the conclusion—also differs from the final version which reads: "Thousands of hands, that are blocking rivers, stopping waterfalls, removing cliffs, vote for the birth of the Canal and together with it, for the birth of mankind." On the other hand, the draft sentence reads: "One hundred thirty thousand hands . . . vote for the birth of the Canal and the birth of mankind."[26] The enthusiasm that the narrative tries to capture and generate is unmistakable in this passage; a sense of the atmosphere remains with the reader, even though the monumentality expressed by "one hundred thirty thousand hands" has been deleted.

While no concrete explanation emerges for the differences, however slight, between the two texts, we can conjecture why the texts differ. Perhaps the accuracy of the number of hands belied an intimacy with the rally that the editors of the volume did not want to reveal. Remember that Alymov, as newspaper editor and prisoner, was probably present not only at the rally but at the storming meeting of the KVO. Thus, he had access to information and witnessed events to which no other writer in the Brigade was privy and that allowed him a degree of accuracy that no other contributor to the Canal volume could match (perhaps with the exception of Victor Shklovsky).

Contrary to this point of view would be the supposition that the exact number of canalworkers might have been considered a state secret, as it were, or a negative detail that would alert readers to the size of the work force on the Canal. This fact might have been unpalatable to the camp administration or to the main editorial committee—Gorky, Averbakh, and, most important, Firin, who did not want to dampen the overall positive tone of the volume. The camp administration never released any accurate figures regarding the number of workers. To do so would have afforded critics an opportunity to compute exactly how many prisoners perished on the Canal, as well as to note the total number of laborers required to complete a project that was supposed to be carried out with the greatest efficiency.

Perhaps the most contradictory element of the "Rally" section in the published version of the text rests on its opening word—*comrades*. Such a salutation is unexpected in this context because prisoners, throughout the existence of the camp system in the Soviet Union, were deprived of the "privilege" of being called comrade. For common criminals and political prisoners alike, the title *comrade* had to be earned; it was not granted gratuitously. That the rally's moderator refers to the assembled mass as "comrades" confounds expectation and suggests that Alymov was there to hear and report it accurately.

Comparing the draft and final copy of the "KVO" section also yields strange results. While the section begins identically in both versions, it ends differently in each. Whereas the draft version concludes "The stove is dying out. The wind howls in the holes above the ceiling. The workers of the cultural-education section with fervor are working out a detailed plan for the storm night," the final version does not conclude with these sentences.[27] Instead they appear two paragraphs before the concluding paragraph. In addition, the final version changes the word in Russian describing the stove that is dying out from *potukhaet* to *gasnet*, a subtle lexical change from the more colloquial to the more literary.

More important, though, the actual concluding sentences of the "KVO" section provide a much smoother, more effective thematic transition between this section and "The Rally." The final version reads "On the construction site the campfires are burning. Cauldrons steam under the pine awnings. People are shaking the trees loose. People are cursing, while pulling the branches furiously" (ibid., 186). This conclusion affords the perfect transition to the next section, for it continues the line of narrative that focuses on the camp inmates. In effect, the section's ultimate paragraph answers the question posed in the subsequent opening lines of the next section—"Comrades, what are you doing?" (ibid.). Again, the detail with which Alymov's narrator describes the scene testifies to the author's first-hand observation of the event. We base this conclusion on the factors that set apart "KVO" and "The Rally" from the rest of the chapter: The narration presents events in great detail and focuses on activities that occurred well in advance of the Writers Brigade to Belomor. Only Alymov could have written about events such as agitational rallies and storm-work sessions that occurred *during* the construction of the Canal and not afterward.

This first-person narration continues into the section entitled "The Night of the Storm." Although the tone of this section is quite similar to that of the sections authored by Alymov, archival materials attribute this section to Nikolai Dmitriev.[28] Yet Dmitriev is not listed as a contributor to the published version of chapter 5. Nevertheless, the published description of the sign that hangs on the doors of the Canal administration building, "Tonight is the Storm Night. The camp community is giving an account of its work" (ibid., 188), echoes verbatim the lines included in Dmitriev's author's manuscript for that section.

The same narrative style continues in this section, as does the theme. Dmitriev returns to the work of the KVO, repeats the exhortations to work at a brisk pace, and emphasizes the importance of the construction of the Canal and its reforging powers. One orator is quoted as saying, "The Canal is our general task. Only together, having mobilized science and creative experience with common effort, can we be victorious over the Karelian cliffs" (ibid., 189). The narrator voices the opinion that the main concern was to complete the project as quickly as possible, a statement that, when considered together with the quotation just cited, reinforces the ideology that drove the Canal project: fast-paced, collective labor will achieve physical feats unachievable in other systems. The section concludes with the sentence, "The buses, going to Povenets and the Watershed, the trains running to the north, were taking the brigades of the Administration's first shock-workers to the construction site" (ibid.). Limited success had already been attained because these first shock-workers had appeared. In fact, the "storm night" becomes an appropriate metaphor not only for the Belomor project but also for the era that produced it: the excitement and enthusiasm of a big effort, the communal push to accomplish the task, the fast-paced tempo of the work. All these elements would become hallmarks of many socialist realist production novels as well as of the public discourse through which other construction projects were described.

Nonetheless, the strange turn in authorial attribution in this section puzzles the reader. If Dmitriev's name does not appear in the final list for the chapter, does that mean that he did not write this section? Did Dmitriev actually write the section, while Alymov took credit for it? The more believable scenario is that the archival documents somehow were mislabeled and Alymov is the actual author of this section. Yet how does this explain the attribution of the section to Dmitriev in the author's manuscripts, which were catalogued and filed alphabetically with each writer's contributions? Did Alymov's special status as inmate/contributor affect the attribution of some of his work? Alymov's own archival materials do not indicate whether or not he authored this section. Or was Dmitriev a victim of political oppression? His name appears in the author's list of all three editions. Nevertheless, the discrepancy still stands out, especially considering that every other comparison of authorial attribution between the final and draft versions of the Belomor volume reaffirms the original authorship cited in the drafts.

All things considered, Alymov's contribution to this chapter is significant for a number of reasons. He manages to include descriptions of a certain kind of prisoner existence that he himself witnessed, he provides examples of how the OGPU implemented their plans, and he, alone among all the other contributors to the chapter, writes about the camp inmates. These three sections create a centerpiece in the chapter around which those sections pertaining either to OGPU personnel or to reforged engineers are grouped. Although it might seem that these three sections disrupt the continuity and narrative flow of the chapter, in fact they contribute to it for, as noted, they do not lose the main thematic lines that unite the chapter. Rather they contribute to the overall portrait of the Chekists on the one hand and demonstrate the effectiveness of the montage on the other hand.

With the exception of one section, entitled "At the Threshold of the Povenets Steps," the remaining three out of four sections of chapter 5 focus not on Chekists but on selected canalworkers who were reforged through their labor on the Canal. The section that follows Alymov's and Dmitriev's contributions, "He Became Different," focuses on the reforging of the engineer Budassi who is transformed from a supposed saboteur into an active participant in the Canal project. As the writer notes, engineer Budassi was a "fantastic worker" (ibid., 193). He worked so effectively that he was freed ahead of schedule from the labor camp. The conclusion of the section on Budassi affirms that "the experience of working on Belomor was not for nothing for [Budassi]. He was freed from the shortcomings of the social stratum in which he lived and worked for a significant part of his life. On the contrary, his worthiness developed under the conditions of socialist labor, which changed his character and many of his personal traits" (ibid.).

The entire passage resonates with the familiar rhetoric of the era. Phrases such as "shortcomings of the social stratum," "the conditions of socialist labor," even references to the change in character and personal traits, connect the narrative not only to the theme of reforging but to the world outside the camp as well. As with other reforgings discussed in the Belomor volume, Budassi's serves as a prototype that can be duplicated perpetually. Of course, his reforging succeeded thanks to the disciplined management of the OGPU, an opinion subtly intimated by the phrases "the experience of working on Belomor" and "conditions of socialist labor." The code word Belomor, when linked with socialist labor, could imply nothing else.

Perhaps the only section in chapter 5 that seems out of place follows the account of Budassi's reforging. This section, "The Threshold of the Povenets Steps" mentioned earlier, digresses to discuss the arduous task of mastering the confluence of the Povenets River and Lake Onega. In part, the difficulty stemmed from the sharp drop of the Povenets River as it worked its way toward Lake Onega—seventy meters within twelve kilometers. This elevation required a system of locks that acted as "steps" through which ships would pass and rise up to the level of the first lakes, against the current of the Povenets River.

Not only does this section relate the physical difficulties of this portion of the Canal, but it also contextualizes the Povenets area in history. Even today, not far from the banks of the Canal, visitors can see remnants of smelting ovens built during the reign of Peter the Great. The narrator is quick to point out that Peter the Great dragged great frigates up the Povenets River on the backs of what amounted to slave laborers. "Big ships or steamers could be dragged by means of portage only under petrine conditions—at the expense of cheap labor. How do we now raise steamships up the [Povenets] elevation?" (ibid., 195). Of course, the irony in the narrator's comments derives from the reference to cheap labor. Conventional wisdom on the subject held that Peter the Great had exploited the labor force available to him to attempt an impossible feat, the transport of naval vessels over difficult terrain. Yet the narrator inadvertently reveals that the very practice for which the Soviet regime condemned its tsarist predecessors (even though Soviet versions of history tended to consider Peter the Great a "progressive" monarch) was its chief means of construction. It was not for nothing that the slogan of the Belomor project was "Cheaper, faster, less raw materials, no foreign capital."

While the archival documents do not suggest either the author or purpose of this digression on Povenets, there might be a logical explanation for its placement precisely at this point. Among other thematic threads, the description of the actual construction of the Canal and its attendant physical challenges runs throughout the Belomor narrative. It is most fitting in this chapter, which sets the parameters for how the work will be carried out and discusses the initial construction feat. Up to this point the narrative has not delved into the actual construction of the Canal because the groundwork and rationale for subsequent themes and events were being laid out. Only after the OGPU has arrived at the Belomor site and set up the camp administration can construction commence. And the most logical starting point was, of course, the historic spot of Povenets. While no direct narrative elements link this section and those that precede and follow it, thematically the section furthers the continuum that describes the actual construction of the Belomor Canal; it emphasizes the difficulty of the task and the achievements of the OGPU.

Chapter 5 closes with three sections all devoted to discussions of the reforging of former state enemies. The section "A Battle with the Kungurs" immediately follows the Povenets digression. In this section the reader learns of the steady recovery of the *kulak* Novichok (no first name given) from the dregs of his existence.[29] In spite of the difficulties on the Canal, Novichok, like many other kulaks, reportedly learns the benefits of socialist construction and collective labor. His brigade ultimately overfulfills its plan by 160 percent, much to the delight of all those involved. Novichok himself even dreams that his ox has been reforged: "They have de-kulakized [him]" (ibid., 208). Novichok's dream equates man and beast, thereby leading to two possible conclusions. Either the dream signifies both the leveling of class and rank and the dehumanization that the system of reforging produces (this would seem to be a sort of subversion of the official rhetoric on reforging, which never casts doubt on its positive outcomes), or the dream elevates the ox to the level of comrade, with a touch of humor, so as to reinforce the idea that everyone and everything can be brought into the collective effort.

Yet the success of Novichok's (and by association the ox's) reforging is not the most striking aspect of this section. Unlike all the other sections in chapter 5, this part is told in the vernacular of the person being reforged. The section opens with the statement in quotation marks: "It is shameful and painful to remember the past. I was a kulak. I had a large farmstead. They de-kulakized me and in me boiled a deafening, wild spite against the [Soviet] regime. One idea was deeply imprinted: I'll get revenge!" (ibid., 196). The ensuing text describes how Novichok seeks revenge but instead finds reformation at the hands of the very Soviet regime that he detests (ibid., 196–208). The section remains almost exclusively in quotation marks as Novichok tells his story. The narrator invades the text only to introduce the continuation of the personal narrative or to close the section; however, this narratorial intervention reminds us that Novichok's story has been "reforged" as well on a variety of levels—by the narrator, the author, and the editors of the volume. Strangely perhaps, the final sentence of the section concludes with three dots, thus suggesting either a continuation or an unfinished thought. The actual function of the three dots is to unite this section with the one that follows it, for the section "Canalarmyists" begins with three dots. The connection between them, of course, emphasizes Novichok's status as reforged canalarmyist, a title of honor in this context.

The brief section "Canalarmyists" describes how the name *canalarmyist* originated and simultaneously promotes the ideas of worker enthusiasm on the Canal and the efficiency of the OGPU. The action of the section occurs during the visit of Anastas Mikoyan to the Belomor site on 23 March 1932. Mikoyan (1895–1978) was a member of the Communist Party, and from 1926 to 1946, Minister of Trade (internal and external), Supply, and the Food Industry. Kogan escorts him on an excursion along the construction site, and when the day draws to a close, Mikoyan requests two copies of a report on the status of the work, one copy of which is for Stalin personally. Mikoyan marvels at Kogan's efficiency, especially when he learns that the report reflects that day's activities. While Kogan weighs whether or not to request permission from Mikoyan to get a shipment of supplies for the project, he "suddenly, unexpectedly even to himself, says: 'Comrade Mikoyan, how shall we call them [the Canal prisoner/workers]? To say "comrade" is still not appropriate. "Prisoners"—that is offensive. "Camp inmates"—that is colorless. I thought up a word—"canalarmyists." What do you think?'" To Kogan's suggestion, especially after having seen the Canal for himself, Mikoyan agrees: "That is absolutely true. They are your canalarmyists" (ibid., 209). His quick-thinking and diplomatic repartee with Mikoyan further embellish his portrayal as a model OGPU officer whose character and deeds are fit to emulate. Not only is Kogan efficient; he is resourceful as well!

In reporting Mikoyan's visit to the OGPU, Kogan notes:

> Two thousand people, identically well-dressed, are digging a gigantic pit. Thousands of hands, flying up, throwing dirt into wheelbarrows. Hundreds of wheelbarrows, in an uninterrupted flow, moving along the scaffolding and walkways from pit to pit. It is a clear sunny day. People are healthy, cheerful, happy. We stood on this spot for several minutes. And it seemed that not a single person stopped for a minute. We passed the pit and examined the chopping of the cribwork. All these carpenters spread out all over had learned their trade on the Canal (ibid.).

Kogan's positive assessment of worker attitudes, while only partially reflected in reality (his notation that they were "well-dressed" is particularly questionable), makes for good copy in his report to the OGPU. We also can surmise that the author of this section had access either to Kogan's letter or to Kogan himself as a source for the narrative.

Finally, in answer to the ongoing query—does this section connect with its surrounding sections?—we can answer in the affirmative. In fact, the penultimate section in chapter 7, "Canalarmyists," functions as a conclusion, for it unites the thematic lines of reforging (the carpenters learned their trade on the Canal), OGPU effectiveness (a report that reflects the day's labor), and the ideology the OGPU promulgates (the hard work creates canalarmyists, a new kind of Soviet citizen).

The chapter's actual concluding section, devoted to the biography of the engineer Anan'ev, closes the continuing discussion of perekovka. Oddly, however, this section differs slightly from the rest of the chapter, for it directly focuses on Anan'ev's biography and his reform, and not on the efforts of the OGPU. Arguably, the fact of the reforging effectively concludes the chapter, for it demonstrates, though the references are oblique, the power of the OGPU program, even on those persons—educated, intelligent engineers—who were among the categories considered most difficult to reforge.

More important, the section on engineer Anan'ev affords the perfect transition into chapter 6, entitled "People Change Their Professions," because Anan'ev's attitude toward his work and dedication to the project change for the better, according to the prevailing wisdom of the time. The fundamental point of his story rests on the fact that he did change. What better way to lead into a discussion of the drastic changes that many canalarmyists made in their professions after they arrived on the Canal? Although nothing in the last paragraph of chapter 5 signals this connection, the totality of the discussion promotes such an interpretation.

This detailed analysis of chapter 7 provides insights into one way in which the montage method was applied. Although it is impossible to document the authorship of each section, certain patterns emerge, as do connections between sections and chapters. While initially some of these connections might seem strained, they nevertheless exist. That each part does not fit hand-in-glove with what precedes or follows it is not the main issue. Rather, each section informs and develops the general theme. In addition, the chapter collects under one rubric a variety of narrative styles that generally work together. This is not to claim that chapter 5 or any of the others in the collection is a masterwork of literary creation. Instead, the method of writing the chapter underscores both the use of montage and the drive to produce a new literary genre that operated differently from anything that had preceded it.

Oddly enough, though, the disjointed quality of the narrative does not detract from the overall message *The History of Construction* is designed to impart. These lapses in narrative flow further substantiate the modernist elements and structure of the text. Greg Carleton has recently argued that narrative choppiness might not have been the central concern for the authors of the Belomor volume; instead, ideological concerns replaced issues of genre and style (Carleton, 992–1009). While Carleton's argument has some merit, I believe all elements were of prime concern for the authors of the Belomor volume, that ideology, genre, and style were inseparable in *The History of Construction*. Considering the context that produced the Belomor volume and the ensuing drive to promote socialist realism, ideology and narrative presentation cannot not be excluded from each other.

As a totality, chapter 5 displays the most clear-cut features of montage and collective authorship; individual elements of other chapters also illustrate these elements. While the following analysis considers these chapters in the order in which they appear in the final version of *The History of Construction*, this approach should not suggest that these are the only segments where we can trace how the work was constructed. Instead, the chapters to be analyzed function as the best examples of how discrete elements of the compositional process were employed by the authors of the Belomor volume.

Consider, for example, chapter 4, entitled "Prisoners," a rather ironic twist, given that in chapter 5 Kogan himself thinks calling the Belomor workers "prisoners" is insulting (*HC*, 209). Presumably the authors of chapter 4 (Gorbunov, Ivanov, Inber, Khatsrevin, and Shklovsky) and the volume's editors did not share his view. Or was Kogan, given his rank and responsibility in the Canal project, one of the few people accorded such lexical freedom? In any case, chapter 4 consists of seven sections: three reveal how the prisoners reached Belomor ("Echelons on the Move," "To the North," "The Distant Staging Ground"), two describe Medvezhegorsk and the scope of the project that the Canal headquarters in Medvezhegorsk will control ("Medvezh'ia gora" and "About the Project"), and two discuss ideological-propagandistic issues ("Working on Trust" and "About Truth"). The themes of collective labor, reforging, and stalinist ideology unite each section, with tenuous transitions similar to those found in chapter 5.

As the archival materials on chapter 4 indicate, however, the authors and montage editors wove segments of text written by different authors into one total narrative. The manuscript for chapter 4, subtitled the "first montage," illustrates how this textual weaving was employed. On the manuscript, next to the section title "Echelons on the Move," Zakhar Khatsrevin's name was written. Although not all subsequent sections were titled in the manuscript, each subsequent section bears the last name of the author of that section. For example, following Khatsrevin's contribution we find Vera Inber's name next to the section that was ultimately titled "Medvezh'ia gora." The third section, although not identified as "To the North," bears Vsevolod Ivanov's name in the draft. The fourth section, attributed to Khatsrevin, was titled "The Tashkent Staging Ground" in the manuscript but was changed to "The Distant Staging Ground" in the final version. Section 5, "Working on Trust," belongs to Ivanov, with the last two sections, "About the Project" and "About Truth," attributed to Ivanov and Inber respectively. In fact, in the first draft of the chapter, the only section specifically given a title was Khatsrevin's opening contribution. Only in a later draft do we find the title "Tashkent Staging Ground" added to the manuscript. Initially at least, the text reads as one unbroken narrative that was not necessarily separated by thematic or authorial dictates. This changed in the final version.

Together with the draft manuscripts of chapter 4, the archives also hold the final edited manuscript of the chapter. In this version, similar to those mentioned above, notes were included in the text in order to signal the placement of photographs. The most puzzling element that the draft manuscripts for this chapter introduce is the changing lists of contributors. As noted above, the final published version of *The History of Construction* lists five authors for chapter 4, including Gorbunov and Shklovsky, yet nowhere in the manuscripts can we find a specific reference to Gorbunov's contribution.

In addition, based on handwriting matches between original texts and notes that Shklovsky authored and the marginal notes contained in the draft manuscripts, it seems that Shklovsky was responsible for editing the pieces into a manageable whole but not for writing original copy. His comments include cross-outs of pieces of text as well as sentences added to provide transitions between sections. The manuscripts bear out Shklovsky's own claims regarding the scope and nature of his work on the volume. Finally, the list of authors provided in the last edited version of the manuscript for chapter 4 does not include Gorbunov's name but does include Lapin's and Gauzner's. According to Shklovsky, Lapin and Gauzner were two of the four members of the montage team (the fourth member being Inber), so it must have seemed logical, at least in a draft version, to attribute the writing of the chapter to those who edited it as well. Yet Gauzner and Lapin do not appear in the final published list of contributors to chapter 4.

Aside from these discrepancies between manuscript and published version, the textual deletions that mark the final version differ significantly from the draft. Appendix V illustrates the comparison. Note that in the final published version, the section entitled "Working on Trust" (marked in the text with brackets) opens with the sentence "Never leaving the tables, Medvezhegorsk worked with insomnia, with unceasing gatherings, with tireless telephone calls" (ibid., 145). The second paragraph begins "For example," followed by two single-sentence paragraphs: "To trust" and "And they trust. And they travel on." The next paragraph begins, "In the Belbaltlag they started to confer." The narrative continues with a one-sentence paragraph, "Let's confer; how are we going to work together?" and then moves into the next paragraph which opens with the line "They reminisce about this briefly. . . . " The narrative flow reveals a sense of economy and directness. From the section's opening lines, the ideas of the greatness of the project and all that it entails, as well as the umbrella theme for the section—trust—echo from the lines.

As the sample in Appendix V demonstrates, significant editing occurred. Written ever so faintly in the margin is the author's name—Ivanov. More significantly, though, whole paragraphs of text from the draft have been eliminated, although the draft bears no markings to that effect. The draft page begins with a sentence that continues from the preceding manuscript page; in the final version a completely different sentence and section precede this part of the text. Moreover, the draft bears no section heading, while the final version has "Working on Trust." The draft and final versions mirror each other with the paragraph "Medvezhegorsk was working . . . " but instead of concluding the final paragraph with two sentences that begin "For example," those phrases are offset into their own paragraph with the draft notation "Who" added into the final version.

The two versions then briefly parallel each other until we read to the draft paragraph "Barracks need to be put up quickly," which has been deleted in the final version along with the following paragraph, "In the Belbalt camp." Only after this two-paragraph deletion do the two texts again mirror each other for the next two paragraphs. Finally, the paragraph that in the final version begins "They reminisce" opens in the draft version with the line "Those reminiscing speak about this briefly." The process of deleting words, phrases, or whole paragraphs continues throughout the section, although not all deletions are marked in the draft. Only a close comparison of the final version with the draft reveals these changes. And because there are few, if any notations in the draft version, with the exception of random words, it is unclear just who performed the editing. The only clue is that those scant notations found in this section seem to be in Shklovsky's handwriting, although no firm evidence exists to confirm that he was responsible for all the changes.

These alterations suggest that whoever handled this editing paid close attention to the narrative flow as well as to the ideas a particular author wanted to convey. Indeed, it is entirely possible that the edition's chief editors—Gorky, Leopold Averbakh, and Firin—might have exercised a control over the editing process that is not documented anywhere.

Further evidence of montage is found in the draft manuscripts for chapter 6, "People Change Their Professions," and chapter 11, "Spring Tests the Canal." In some instances the drafts of these chapters contain copies of documents as well as copied versions of poems, mandates, and decrees taken from the camp newspaper, *Perekovka*.

To a lesser degree than in the manuscripts for chapter 4, the manuscripts for chapter 6 also specifically cite some of the contributors to the chapter. What is peculiar about this chapter, however, is the clear difference between the manuscript version, the outside documentary materials it contains, and the finished version in *The History of Construction*.

The official list of contributors to chapter 6 includes Alymov, Berzin, Gabrilovich, Dmitriev, Lebedenko, Khatsrevin, and Shklovsky. In the draft manuscripts, however, the only section attributed to a specific author is "The Story of a Rifleman of the Internal Guard," which is titled "By the Sluice with a Rifle" in the draft.[30] Authorship of this section belongs to Lebedenko, and the versions themselves match each other closely.

The segment focuses on the life and experiences of one of the guards who belong to the internal security force of the Belomor camp. A prisoner himself, this unnamed guard is called upon for duty in part because of his experiences as a volunteer in the Red Army—he knows how to handle a rifle. (Here we find another ironic subtext because according to official propaganda about the Belomor project and other sections of the Belomor volume itself, guards were not really required because the Belomor inmates were so content and devoted to their labor. Even the single reference to this prisoner/guard would suggest otherwise to discerning readers.) Thus he is pressed into service. In the draft and final version, Lebedenko allows the rifleman to "tell his own story" in his own vernacular with minimal intervention on the part of the narrator. The chief difference, though, between draft and final versions lies in the disposition of the narrative in the text.

Whereas in the draft Lebedenko has submitted one ongoing sketch about the rifleman, in the final version this sketch is divided into three separate segments. The first segment, the title of which is noted above, occupies the second section of the chapter. Only in the fifteenth chapter section does the general narrative resume the story of the rifleman. This section, titled "The Rifleman of Internal Security Continues His Story," does precisely that—the rifleman resumes the narration and continues to describe his experiences on the Canal. Finally, in chapter section 19, "The Rifleman of Internal Security Completes His Story," the penultimate section of the chapter, the rifleman concludes his personal tale.

Aside from allowing the reader a glimpse of the rifleman's life and change of profession, the division of the sketch into three parts permits a physical connection that unites the chapter as well as provides a thematic connection between text and chapter title. The rifleman's unfinished story prods the reader to proceed through the chapter so as to learn how the tale concludes. Theoretically, in moving through the chapter without skipping ahead, the reader would also have to read those segments that narrate the change in profession among other Belomor inmates as well.

The theme of changing professions recurs throughout the chapter but takes a negative turn in the segments "Lederkin's Refusal" and "Lederkin Maims a Horse in the Name of God," which do not appear consecutively. The kulak Lederkin refuses to work and vents his anger over his predicament at a horse that he subsequently maims—it can no longer work owing to its back (beaten raw), its lame legs, and its poor sight. Nothing makes Lederkin work, and as a result he is sent to solitary confinement (ibid., 259). While the draft manuscript does not ascribe these sections to a particular author, other archival documents reveal that Evgeny Gabrilovich wrote them.

The "author's manuscript" for the Lederkin story provides initial evidence of Gabrilovich's writing. It and the final version of "Lederkin's Refusal" differ in the introductory paragraphs and concluding sentences. The draft immediately relates biographical details of Lederkin's life: "Foma Lederkin, fifty years old, a native of the hamlet of Stafanadar, was de-kulakized in the fall of 1930,"[31] information that appears in the final version only in paragraph 2. Instead, the published version reads, "Not everyone worked in good conscience. Among the inmates there were evil loiterers, refusniks who shirked from work for months. There were fictional invalids, those who created illnesses, those who would do anything to avoid going to the foundation pits. There were naysayers—people who agitated against labor. There were saboteurs" (ibid., 251). The insertion of this politicized rhetoric, replete with key words *evil loiterers* and *saboteurs*, provides the necessary ideological introduction to the Lederkin story. It was insufficient simply to relate the biography; rather the ideological framework within which the biography is meant to be understood had to be supplied, although it is unclear by whom. Only after this point do the draft and final versions coincide—"Foma Lederkin was fifty years old . . . " (ibid.). The other slight difference between draft and final versions appears in the change of the active verb in "they *de-*

kulakized him," a conversational form, to the literary short-form past participle construction, "He was *de-kulakized*," a grammatical structure that leaves the agent of the action unspecified.

Even more revealing, though, is the evidence for Gabrilovich's authorship found in his personal archive. Materials there include versions of the Lederkin story that Gabrilovich published separately in *Pravda* in 1934. In addition, a French version of Lederkin's story appeared in France on 26 January 1934.[32] The publication of the Lederkin story as a separate item was not the exception, but the rule. Many excerpts and segments of *The History of Construction* were published individually shortly before and after the volume appeared. They functioned as advertisements for and enticements to read the entire book.

Aside from the story about Lederkin which stretched over two sections, Gabrilovich also contributed the last section of the chapter, again about a kulak who finds himself bewildered in the camp. While the draft titles the section "Kulaks," it appears in the final version as "A Man and His Ox." This section serves as a counterpoint to the Lederkin story, for the peasant Balabukh becomes a first-rate metalworker who ultimately refuses to forfeit his new profession in favor of tending his ox, which, like Balabukh, has also been de-kulakized. Whereas Lederkin resisted reforging and did not embrace his new profession, Balabukh did. Gabrilovich's sketch neatly concludes the chapter because it presents the ultimate change of profession, from farmer to metalworker in a positive, reaffirming light. Moreover, it underscores the true measure of perekovka, which involved not only a change in profession but, more important, a change in psychology. According to Soviet thinking, independent, individualistic kulaks were not necessary; collectivized skilled workers were.

In addition to questions of authorship, the draft manuscripts for chapter 6 also illuminate some interesting features concerning how it was assembled and how it differed from the final version. For example, among the "Materials for Chapter 6" we find two interesting items. First, the archival holdings include the complete texts of two official orders, one, Order Number 1, dated 8 March 1932, and the other, Order Number 4, dated 22 March 1932. Only Order Number 1 was reprinted in full in the final version of the Belomor volume. This order, authored by Kogan, mandated that the scientific journal *Inventions and Rationalization Measures* be made available throughout the construction site. He also directed readers of the journal to make special note of the authors, inventions, and methods discussed so as to be able to apply that knowledge to the Belomor project. Kogan's rationale behind this move was to "complete the Canal quickly and to use unerring measures for incentives and bonuses for the canalworkers" (ibid., 244).

The inclusion of this order precisely at this point in the chapter makes sense. Appearing as it does between the sections entitled "People Study without Leaving the Construction Site" and "One's Own Industry," Order Number 1 discloses how the Canal administration attempts to assist people in changing their professions. (As an aside, the section "People Study" is noted in one draft of the chapter as a "cliché." Who considered the section clichéd remains unclear, especially since it was not deleted from the final version.)[33] The only drawback to this system, unintentionally emphasized in Order Number 1, is that bonuses and incentives were needed to induce workers to perform more effectively. Clearly collective labor unto itself and its reforging powers were not enough to motivate workers to be more productive. Instead, like many other workers, the canalworkers needed some incentive beyond their own labor to continue working. While contemporaneous official interpretations would argue that incentives and bonuses were the just reward for socialist construction, the astute reader could not help but interpret that these "bonuses" and not Soviet ideology ultimately inspired the labor.

More important, the unintentional emphasis on this flaw in the system could point to a minor subversion of the narrative. As we now know, some of the authors viewed the project ambivalently. As a result, they subtly attempted to depict a truer picture of the project, which a discerning reader would be able to apprehend.[34]

Nonetheless, the inclusion of Order Number 1 enhances the "documentary" quality of the Belomor volume because it affords some grounding in reality for the rest of the narrative of chapter 6. The authors did not base their work simply on their own observations and opinions but on actual documents as well. In turn, the documents provided the narrative with a legitimacy that seemed to guarantee its nonfictional quality, an important factor in the drive to present *The History of Construction* as precisely that—history.

Aside from the documents included in the archival materials, the first montage of chapter 6 contains notations about the placement of photographs throughout the text. Of greater interest is the opening of chapter 6 presented in this first montage. Contrary to the final version, this particular draft of the chapter opens with a sizeable quotation from Mikhail Prishvin that describes the geography and geology of the area in which the Canal is being built. The draft narrative follows the direct quotation from Prishvin with commentary. Both of these items are conspicuously absent from the final version, which reads as a much drier account, presumably assumed to be a more fitting tone for a "history." Conversely, it is also possible that Prishvin's expressiveness and technical mastery would be so obviously superior to the prose surrounding it that it could not be included.

The need for a less poetic and more prosaic approach to the material demanded that the Prishvin citation and subsequent introductory paragraph be omitted. On a more political level, it would have been problematic to insert his prose in the narrative for a few key reasons. Most obvious, Prishvin, who had wanted to participate in the Writers Brigade, was denied that opportunity. Thus, the Prishvin citation would seem to be an insult to the author; his prose could be included in the project, but he could not. On the other hand, this citation could have been a way of "sneaking" him into the text despite undocumented, official objections to his participation.

Related to this idea is the fact that Prishvin, more than any participant in the Writers Brigade or member of the Belomor administration, knew a great deal about Karelia intimately. But this knowledge was not as critical as his love of and respect for the area, which motivated and nourished his artistic endeavors. Given his writings on the region and his keen appreciation for the natural world, there would be no way to reconcile his approach with the destruction that the Canal project was about to inflict on the land and its human and animal inhabitants. He opposed the ideology that argued for the reforging of nature, for he believed it unnecessary and damaging, an opinion that would exclude him from being considered a writer for the new Soviet age, in spite of the respect he had garnered for his work. If anything, Prishvin's work harked back to pre-Soviet Russia and therefore did not belong. To include Prishvin in a work like *The History of Construction* was to validate an anachronism that had no place in a work of the new Soviet literature.[35]

Cited below are the introductory paragraphs from both versions so that the reader can appreciate the critical divergence between the two. Note that the photograph that introduces the chapter bears the caption "We'll teach nature and receive freedom," a quotation attributed to the Povenets agitational brigade (ibid., 230). In the published version this caption sets the tone for the chapter, especially because, in changing their professions, the workers on the Belomor Canal project were changing nature as well.

The first montage version begins:

> Moss and more moss, hummocks, little lakes, puddles. The water whistles in your boots, like old pumps; you are powerless to drag

them out of the boggy swamp. You stop, exhausted. The husky, also overworked, falls down on the spot, breathing heavily, sticking out its tongue . . . over the moss and through the forest. You go and go and then you fall down in the dampness and sleep. The poor dog, approaches, yawns, thinks—he's dead, but you will rest up and once more stride off. From the mossy areas to the forest, from the forest to the mossy areas, from the peaks to the valleys, from the valley to the peaks. (Prishvin)

Thus M. Prishvin describes "The Land of Brave Birds," now the construction site of the Canal. This is the taiga. Tundra. In Lapp *tantura* means cliff. But the tundra is a swamp. Tundra—this is swampland, not rock faces. These swamps must be measured, the amount of water in them must be determined, the swamps and lakes must be precisely marked on the construction site, on exact maps, their water cycles must be investigated. This is the site, the red line of the site, carried out on the map.[36]

Now contrast that introduction with the actual opening of the published version of chapter 6:

The swamps and lakes had to be carefully measured, and marked on exact maps, their water cycles had to be investigated. Along the taiga, along the tundra, along the swamps walk the people of the construction project. They arrived from Moscow with the project plans but without exact data about the geological surveys. They were forced to formulate the project in a summer, dragging out of the geologists data that they still had not filed in their map cases. They reconsidered the question of the height of the ascent. Because of a change in some of the data, the entire path [of the Canal] changed (*HC*, 231).

Without question the second, published variant exudes a more scientific, serious tone, devoid of the rich lexicon and vivid descriptions that mark Prishvin's passage. Even the second paragraph of the *draft* version, presumably penned by the same author, reads more poetically. In that paragraph the writer relies on some of the same devices that so enrich Prishvin's prose—repetition, short sentences, precise lexicon—all equally at home in prose and in poetry, elements missing from the final published version.

For the purposes of the Belomor volume, especially in the context of the industrialization and mechanization of Soviet society, luxuriant prose like Prishvin's was extraneous. His prose poeticized nature and emanated from a writer who pursued the task as an individual, not as part of a collective. Soviet ideology required prose to be well written yet at the same time clear, concise, scientific if the situation demanded it, but most of all accessible to all readers and bland if need be. The insight that this comparison of draft and final versions brings to the discussion of *The History of Construction* proves significant. Not only does it reveal the mechanism that guided the compilation of the Belomor volume, but it also lends credence to the contention that new times demanded new literary forms, even if that meant losing some of the poeticization, or the artistry, of prose. It was as if the wildness of nature was being tamed along with the wildness of prose.[37]

This concept is not to suggest that poetry was absent in the Belomor volume. The authors of the book managed to include a variety of inmate poetry ranging from the more sophisticated verse of the futurist poet Igor Terent'ev, a Belomor inmate, to the less successful attempts of other camp inmates who were not poets by profession. Chapter 11, coauthored by Agapov, Alymov, Berzin, Dikovsky, Dmitriev, Ivanov, Inber, Nikulin, Shklovsky, and Erlikh, is one of the richest chapters in terms of the interweaving of verse into the narrative. Three draft manuscripts exist for chapter 11, "Spring Tests the Canal." The first document contains separate manuscripts that were later combined into the chapter. The second and third manuscripts represent the original and second version of the entire chapter. Each document includes examples of the poetry that appears in the final version.

As we have seen in comparing other draft manuscripts with the published version, it is possible to trace authorship for some, although not all, of the sections within chapter 11. For example, Vera Inber penned the opening section "Spring in the Country," the fourth section "A Conversation about Cleanliness," and the seventh, "The Agitbrigade." While Inber is the main author of this last section, it seems that Berzin assisted in its writing. Berzin, by the way, also contributed section 8, "Sosnovets." Section 5, "The Story of Pavlova, Written on the Construction Site," belongs to Dikovsky, while the penultimate section, "A Letter from Home," owes its composition to Shklovsky.

Interestingly, Shklovsky's section describes a Belomor camp barracks in which an economist reads a letter from home (ibid., 487–88). In all probability, Shklovsky recounts this scene in such detail because he was there. Among his archival materials devoted to Belomor we find not only his official permit to visit the construction site and move freely within the camp; we also encounter a detailed description of the various barracks at Belomor.[38] In comparing his depiction with the published text, we find elements that subtly, though unmistakably, link the two texts—the log cabin structure of the barracks and the warmth generated by a cast-iron stove.[39] As we know, besides Sergei Alymov, Shklovsky was the only participant in the book who experienced life at Belomor while it was being built, and not afterward, unlike the majority of the participants in the Writers Brigade.

None of the poetry in either the drafts or the final version of Chapter 11 reaches the level of artistic competence found in a brief citation from Terent'ev's poem. This means that Terent'ev managed to preserve some semblance of technical merit and artistry even though the poems he wrote at Belomor were propaganda pieces designed to applaud the Canal project.[40] Within the Belomor volume the authors of chapter 11 cite one brief verse from Terent'ev:

The bourgeois abroad
Have pained fingers.
The red canalists
Are stuck in their throat.

Let them not believe abroad—
The fools are mistaken,
Here every brother has
This—a fine physique. (ibid., 473)

In this verse Terent'ev juxtaposes Western propaganda with the reality of Belomor. The success of the canalworkers "sticks in the throat" of the foreign bourgeois, especially because, as Terent'ev implies, through their labor the canalworkers are becoming physically strong and powerful. In addition, direct references to Terent'ev elsewhere in the text include: "The agitbrigade is led by Igor Terent'ev, a talented director and himself a poet" (ibid., 476). In a later reference, Vera Inber notes that Terent'ev is one of the "Belomor poets" (ibid.).

Aside from the brief citation of Terent'ev's poem, a collection of manuscripts filed separately from those for chapter 11 indicate that Inber copied down a number of the ditties that Terent'ev's agitational Brigade used in its performances.[41] Many of these songs were subsequently incorporated into the final version. Among them are "We will sing this ditty to you" (ibid., 475) and "In socialist competition we signed an agreement" (ibid., 476).

The significant point to note about these inclusions is that many of these poems were taken from the newspaper *Perekovka*, not the poets themselves. The original manuscript for chapter 11 includes two fragments of poems that are taped to the manuscript, with an arrow pointing to where they are to be inserted. It is obvious from the paper and typeset that these excerpts were cut out of the camp newspaper and then positioned in the appropriate place. Such is the case with the verse fragment "Where I'll be singing tomorrow," which appears on page 476 in *The History of Construction* and is attached to the left side of page 26 of the original manuscript.[42] In addition, an Alymov poem cited later in chapter 11, on page 487 and plainly attributed to him, is quoted in full in the manuscript, although without the name of the author. In the manuscript the only allusion to the source of the poem is the notation that it was taken from the 22 May 1933 issue of *Perekovka*.[43]

Draft manuscripts for chapter 11 include other excerpts from *Perekovka*, an unremarkable fact considering that the list of sources at the end of *The History of Construction* openly lists the newspaper as a source of information and documentation for the Writers Brigade. By including excerpts that were originally published in *Perekovka,* the authors of Chapter 11 further underpin the documentary quality of the work. In a sense they extend the authorship of the Belomor volume beyond the writers collective and further legitimize the telling of the tale. Eyewitnesses to the construction project lend their compositions and personal experiences to the narrative, thereby enhancing its credibility.

Theoretical Constructs

The application of montage to *The History of Construction* is appropriate because the ultimate intent of the work was "to suggest a total impression or idea." The goal of the book was to present a total view not only of the successful Belomor construction project but also of the implementation of perekovka and its attendant phenomenon of collective labor. In all these areas, the method of montage insured this unity of impression or theme. Why? Because collective authorship initially seemed impossible. How could thirty-six individual writers, with thirty-six individual perspectives, blend such diversity of background, literary approach, and, in many cases, ideology into a meaningful whole that, as a collective work, reflected all that was considered good and successful in the Belomor project? Montage facilitated the achievement of this goal.

This effort also suggests that elements of avant-garde practice were still being played out in Soviet culture, a supposition that lends credence to Boris Groys's argument that many ideas of imaginative artists were extrapolated to their limits under socialist realism, thereby making many practitioners of socialist realism more avant-garde than professed avant-gardists.[44] Yet this does not mean that this daringly creative element automatically engendered totalitarian art. As Igor Golomshtock eloquently argues, totalitarian art was not necessarily posited on the tenets of the avant-garde. By the same token, Golomshtock notes that "it is equally illegitimate, however, entirely to deny the role of the avant-garde in the formation of the totalitarian artistic ideology, to consider any such assertion 'as absurd as to blame the Western democracies for their dictatorships.' . . . Just as the words of Rousseau (in Heine's phrase) turned into the bloody machine of Robespierre, so—and only so—did certain aspects of the artistic ideology of the avant-garde become incorporated into the foundation of the megamachine of totalitarian culture" (Golomshtock [b], 28).

Golomshtock's precise observations return this discussion to its original contention. The contradiction inherent in *The History of Construction* indicates a fundamental truth about literature and literary history of the early 1930s: namely, the usurpation of literary activity by socialist realism was neither complete nor all-encompassing. That vestiges of modernist thought and practice persisted implies that not only were the tenets of modernism firmly embedded in the consciousness of many Soviet writers but also that the mere imposition of a new ideology, no matter how forceful, was not enough to completely replace one literary consciousness with another. No less important is the contention that some elements of modernism turned out to be most appropriate to, and consequently were included in, the socialist realist paradigm; the devices were similar, but the content of the message was quite different. The contention that both modernism and socialist realism reacted to and interacted with each other not only informs our knowledge of the complexities of Soviet literary history of the early 1930s but also confirms that the nature of Soviet literature and Soviet literary life was complex and contradictory.

Katerina Clark reached a similar conclusion in developing a typology for socialist realist production novels in which elements of myth were exploited to produce a socialist realist reality. In calling on Tynianov and Jakobson's theory of literary evolution, Clark notes that "the particular literary possibilities canonized in socialist realism were those that had power to interact with the new ideologies that had become dominant. What was kept was kept because it served a function in the new conditions; yet, as part of the new tradition, these surviving elements of the old tradition would have an effect on literature's further evolution. Thus, as socialist realism was taking form in the 1920s, it adopted elements from disparate literary schools, including even symbolism, but it did so only insofar as these elements could illuminate the unique needs of the twenties" (Clark [b], 253).

Clark's conclusion also pertains to the early 1930s, in which literary devices had to serve a function in the new context. As we have seen, the strategies that guided the authors of *The History of Construction* in writing and editing the volume were applied in just the right measure to support the ideology. Ironically, reviews of and articles about *The History of Construction* support the assertions discussed here, while alluding to the very quality of the narrative that was derived from modernism—its uneven flow.

(Re)Constructing Critical Response

For the most part, and not surprisingly, reviewers tended to assess *The History of Construction* favorably. I. Eventov considered the Belomor volume one of the leading examples of the attempt by Soviet writers to capture the flavor and document the period "of socialist restructuring of the economy and people's psychology" (Eventov, 153). While Eventov believed that Soviet writers still had not completely succeeded in the task of documenting socialist construction, at least books like the Belomor volume took a step in the right direction. A. Bolotnikov echoes Eventov's dismay at the paucity of well-written works devoted to socialist construction. Nonetheless, he praises the Belomor volume, saying that "before us is not simply a literary work, neither is it a tediously scrupulous scientific treatise. No, both science and literature are presented in the book in a synthesis that is possible only by observing the demands of socialist realism, the artistic base of Soviet writers" (Bolotnikov, 2).

Similarly, A. Erlikh notes the unique nature of this literary work: "Before us is the first attempt at collective creativity. *The Stalin White Sea–Baltic Canal* is a complete narrative. It is not various and sundry excerpts mechanically connected by the generality or similarity of theme. It is not a series of portraits, existing independently and only joined on the most general level. . . . This is a sketch novel about the miracle in Karelia" (Erlikh, 9). And S. Fin concludes, "This book is worthy of the most concentrated attention of our readers, of our critics, of all of Soviet society" (Fin, 4).

While these sentiments recurred in each review of the Belomor volume, reviewers also detailed how the volume was written and included the most significant facts about the construction of the Canal itself. This is not to suggest that reviewers did not cast a critical gaze at the book. While they noted its flaws and inadequacies, their criticisms never overshadowed the generally positive assessments of the volume.

Criticisms of *The History of Construction* focused on two main points:

problems with the narrative and problems with the presentation of socialist construction "in its revolutionary development." In his review of the Belomor volume, Iogann Al'tman noted that the book's "collective style did not find its expression in the heights of artistic, collective mastery. We must note the following most important inadequacies: a certain chaotic quality in the distribution of the material, an insurmountable scrappiness, the insufficiently high artistic level of a number of chapters, their 'newspaper articlelike' quality" (Al'tman, 261). Al'tman contends that the Belomor Canal topic is so rich that the book did not do it justice; it would also be possible to compose numerous other literary works from the material. Yet precisely the newspaper articlelike quality imbues the Belomor volume with much of its documentariness and contributes to its classification as a history. And the "scrappiness" stems not so much from insufficient artistic ability as from the montage process.

A review by Lage (first name not given) reinforces these sentiments and adds a criticism of Mikhail Zoshchenko's contribution to *The History of Construction*. The reviewer contends that Zoshchenko's stylized prose is, in the case of the Belomor volume, excessive. In addition, Lage criticizes the publicistic and reportage qualities of a number of sections in the book (Lage, 61) on the grounds that they also are too stylized. Yet such reservations do not diminish his overall positive assessment of the volume. E. Troshchenko laments the fact that the Belomor volume does not adequately convey the technical aspects of the canal construction project (Troshchenko, 250). He also critiques the same unevenness in narrative presentation and adds that as a product of collective authorship the *History* did not succeed in creating a "new, special collective genre" (ibid., 254). Finally, Bolotnikov speaks to the deficiencies in the volume's handling of the economic and historical significance of the Canal. He insists that a necessary addition would be a chapter that compares the inability of the capitalist system to achieve such a feat and the victory of the Soviet system in creating the Belomor Canal (Bolotnikov, 2).

These criticisms notwithstanding, every reviewer of the Belomor volume promoted one idea that superseded even comments about collective authorship and literary innovation: the importance and success of the program of perekovka, especially with the prudent and wise direction of the OGPU. Perekovka emerged as the overriding idea not only of the Belomor volume itself but of the reviews as well. The program permeated all areas of life and literature connected with the waterway construction. Reforging demanded that practically everything change so as to complement and support the new Soviet society that socialist construction strove to build.

In Reconstructing Literature, We Reconstruct Life

The desire to create a new literature with new genres, to remake supposed state enemies into Soviet citizens, to build a new society and to construct new industrial complexes to achieve that goal (even if it meant tampering with nature) all interesected in the program of perekovka.

At Belomor this reeducation was achieved through the *kulturnye-vospitatel'nye otdeli* or "cultural-education cells," which not only taught inmates to read but also indoctrinated them into Marxist-Leninist ideology. Texts that inmates read and any writing assignments focused on the history of the revolution and the teachings of Marx, Lenin, and Stalin, albeit in watered-down versions. Honor rolls were mounted on walls, and whole newspapers were posted to laud achievement. The culmination of the reforging activities for inmates was the camp newspaper, *Perekovka* (see figure 16 in chapter 2); they were invited to submit original poems and stories that detailed either their personal reforgings or praised the Belomor project and all its attendant events and programs. The newspaper also served as the official mouthpiece for camp policy and for the dissemination of ideology either from the pen of OGPU administrators or the newspaper's editor, Sergei Alymov. The inmates' literary efforts, which will be discussed in greater detail in the next chapter, further attest to the overriding emphasis on perekovka.

Hence, perekovka emerged as the public justification for using forced labor on construction projects. Note, however, that the policy served this purpose most assiduously concurrent with the Belomor project and shortly thereafter. By the mid 1930s, public approbation for perekovka, as well as documentation of its success appeared less frequently, until it ceased to be mentioned. Granted, those works that narrate other large construction projects hint at and frequently speak directly about perekovka, but the Belomor project proved to be the apex of reforging.

This short-lived prominence is not surprising for two basic reasons. First, the authorities exploited perekovka only during that initial period in which rapid and intense labor was required of the populace to industrialize. The government needed to convince the population of the need to reform, to become model citizens who were dedicated to the cause of socialist construction and willing to work and sacrifice to achieve those goals. Once the seeds of collective labor and ideology were planted, there was no impetus to continue to justify reforging. The use of forced labor on construction and mining sites became institutionalized and increasingly less public. Thus, the continued publicity surrounding perekovka would only direct attention to a practice that the authorities advertised as a success with the culmination of the First Five-Year Plan. Second, as noted earlier in this chapter, during the Second Five-Year Plan (around 1934), official pronouncements as well as literary works began to focus with increasing intensity on individual feats of achievement—*stakhanovism,* aviation exploits, and the like—instead of on communal, collective achievements such as those that the large construction projects engendered. In short, perekovka as a publicly acclaimed program was no longer useful.

For the purposes of the Belomor project, however, perekovka served as the perfect propaganda tool. In fact, the volume panegyrizes the program of perekovka at every opportunity. Practically every chapter of the book includes references to and descriptions of various instances of reforging. The most obvious example is, of course, Zoshchenko's chapter, "The Story of One Reforging." As we have seen, Zoshchenko dedicated the narrative to the description of the reforging of the thief and swindler Rottenburg who becomes a well-trained, committed Soviet worker thanks to his experience at Belomor. Reportedly intense labor fostered this change in Rottenburg's character (*HC,* 492–524).

Yet Rottenburg's reforging is only one of many. The methodology of perekovka is summed up best in chapter 4, "The Prisoners," which concludes with a brief exegesis on truth and maintains that "we will create the Canal only with strict discipline, only with strict rules, and these strict rules must emanate not from somewhere outside, but from within oneself" (ibid., 151). Critical, of course, to the success of this rigid discipline, is the work of the Chekists, for, as the author of this passage goes on to note, "The Chekists speak in long ash-gray overcoats, in leather jackets, having pulled their caps over their foreheads. . . . They know what truth is; they know what socialism is; they—the true sons of the Party, the most important Bolsheviks—have been defending it for fourteen years" (ibid., 152). *The History of Construction* tries to convince the reader that no one, save the Chekists, is up to the task.

The results of the efforts of the OGPU are reported in chapter 6, "People Change Their Professions." Fundamental to a true reforging is the ability of the person being reforged to gain a new profession and new expertise so as to become useful to socialist society. Former thieves, prostitutes, and swindlers are remade into welders, construction workers, laborers, all as a result of their work on the Belomor Canal. For example, engineers and average canalworkers find themselves capable of devising new and efficient ways of building the Canal without traditional materials. According to the Belomor volume, "High technology is simple and easy; the amazing thing about

Belomorstroi is not that it's big, but that it's easy" (ibid., 241). The simplicity of the Belomor Canal is in large part due to the efforts of the canalworkers and engineers who, because of the scarcity of materials and heavy equipment, were forced, in the most literal sense, to devise construction methods and structures based on the materials at hand.

Reforging was not limited to thieves and prostitutes, for, as the story of Balabukh reveals, even state enemies as vile as private farmers (kulaks) were capable of being reforged. According to the narrative, Balabukh mounted an armed protest against the de-kulakization of his farm. For this he was sent to Belomor. Once there he became a respectable metalworker, in fact a shock-worker. However, one day Balabukh discovered his ox in the herd of cattle attached to Belomor. Upon his request to the authorities to return him to cattle farming so that he could be with his own livestock, the authorities replied, "All its life the ox worked for the peasant and the peasant worked for the ox. They moved about on a squeaky wheel—why do you need that, when you are a master metalworker?" To this Balabukh replied, "OK. I'll visit the ox on my days off" (ibid., 278). The author of this segment of text concludes with, "Thus ended the wooden age on Belomor and commenced the metal age" (ibid.). (Note the irony of this conclusion when we consider that all of the major dam and lock structures on the Belomor Canal were constructed not of metal but of wood, peat, cement, and dirt. By the same token, it is also paradoxical that the narrator must reach back to almost prehistoric times in order to find an analogy with which to describe a modern socialist state.)

This pattern recurs in the Belomor narrative and is consistent with the development of positive heroes in literature. A positive hero often overcomes some sort of adversity—be it class origin, physical limitations, or personal circumstances—in order to become a productive member of Soviet society. Largely, this development stems from a psychological and ideological change in the person. In keeping with this literary model, the book argues that anyone, no matter his or her status, background, or previous occupation, can be reforged successfully.

These reinventions extended even to some of the Chekists involved in the Canal project, among them Semyon Firin. According to *The History of Construction,* Firin underwent the same profound transformation from nonbeliever to avid supporter of the Bolshevik cause, an enthusiasm that enabled him to become the head of the Belomor prison camp. According to the Belomor narrative, after Firin served in the tsarist army, he was demobilized and intended to go to America, "the concrete paved land of all failures" (ibid., 364). However, he never reached the United States and cast about without money and was constantly in trouble until he was saved by the October 1917 uprising. From that point on he worked his way through the ranks and was devoted to the cause of the Party (ibid., 366–67).

Thus perekovka embraced not only outright criminals but those individuals who succeeded by promoting the Bolshevik cause. The underlying connection here between reforging and people like Firin, of course, emphasizes that the Party attracted to itself and continued to motivate and develop people who would be faithful to its ideology. This is not to suggest that every laborer on the Belomor Canal required reforging. Arguably, kulaks like Balabukha, as well as political prisoners including such great intellects as Dostoevsky's grandson Andrei (see figs. 18 and 19, pp. 186–87), the ethnographer Antsiferov, and the philosopher Losev, required no reforging, for they already were productive, thinking members of society.

Yet perekovka did not involve simple professional retraining. It implied a change of ideological perspective, a change in the *psychology* of the person. This was the fundamental goal of and idea behind reforging. The inmates mentioned earlier lacked the prescribed class consciousness and ideological inclination required of new Soviet citizens. In addition, their consciousness had been formed under bourgeois conditions, thereby tainting them even more. Perekovka was intended to be a multilayered process that sought to remake individuals from the inside out. Because there were greater and more visible successes with common criminals, the presupposed reforging of political prisoners never appeared on the pages of *The History of Construction*. Added to this is the fact that the authors of the Belomor volume were never shown political prisoners, nor were politicals ever held up as fine examples of reforged inmates. This is probably because they were not successfully reforged and probably could never be.

To assist in the implementation of perekovka the camp administration assaulted inmate senses with a barrage of pro-Soviet, pro-reforging propaganda. The Belbaltlag administration established a theater that mounted some of the classics of Russian drama—*Woe from Wit*, *The Thunderstorm*, and other plays. The choice of the dramatic repertoire is striking in its lack of contemporary, Soviet theatrical material. This reliance on the classics emphasized that there was not much to choose from among more modern pieces and that these plays would be familiar to the viewers and somehow elevate their sensibilities, for reforging involved literacy in both the literal and cultural senses.

Of course, artists from the major Soviet theaters did not visit the Belomor camp to perform. On the contrary, the entire theatrical company consisted of camp inmates. The biography of Ivan Nikolaevich Rusinov (see fig. 17) typifies the fate of these artists. Although he became an Honored Artist of the Soviet Theater later in his life, Rusinov frequently was a lead actor in the Belomor theater. Based on his recollections, it seems his only crime against Soviet power was that his father was a priest. Although Nikolai Rusinov was arrested, detained for a short time, and then released, his son Ivan served a full term at Belomor, from which he was released into exile in the provinces. Ivan Nikolaevich continued his acting career in provincial theaters. Eventually he was permitted to return to Moscow, where he appeared in the leading theaters of the capital.[45]

In remembering the theater at Belomor, Ivan Nikolaevich related that if the company needed a young tenor for a light opera performance, a young tenor almost immediately appeared at the theater; he was arrested for the specific purpose of performing in a Belomor theater production. (Although this practice seems to run counter to the underlying philosophy of reforg-

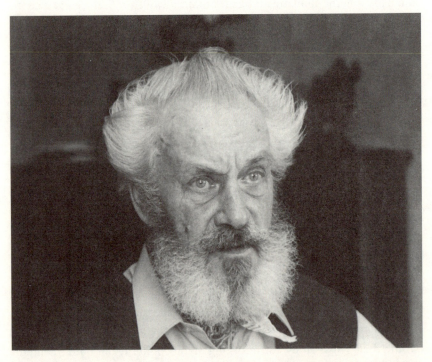

17. Ivan Nikolaevich Rusinov, Honored Artist of the USSR and actor in the Belomor camp theater. Photographed in his apartment in Moscow, July 1993. Used by permission of Igor V. Sopronenko.

ing, it nonetheless reinforced the idea that whatever was necessary for the success of Belomor was supplied. Actually, any case could have been made against the young tenor so as to reconcile his appearance at Belomor with the need to reforge him.) The Belomor theater was intended to provide not only entertainment for canalworkers but also to provide a forum in which propaganda plays and shows could be staged so as to reinforce the idea of reforging even during an inmate's recreational time.[46]

Similarly, musicians were assembled in order to provide accompaniment for the work on the Canal. Ensembles dotted the construction sites, often playing incessantly for fifteen hours so as to inspire in the canalarmyists a fervor for work that did not wane. As with the theater, if a trumpet player was needed, then he suddenly appeared at the site. Music, especially marches, were thought to be able to provide inmates with a renewed spirit of labor. It is difficult to imagine, however, that the musicians, having played for so long, shared this exhilaration for their labor at the end of their shifts.[47]

Agitational brigades, or *agitbrigady*, were organized to involve inmates as fully as possible in the production of propaganda that could be disseminated throughout the camp. The theme of perekovka reverberated throughout their performances. Each brigade was assigned a particular sector of the camp. The brigade members would then travel around that sector and perform for other inmates. Their repertoire included the recitation of inmate poetry, as well as the singing of pro-Belomor, pro-reforging songs. Skits were staged that visually reinforced the oral portions of the program. No matter what the genre or the setting of the work being presented, the purpose was the same: to instill in prisoners Soviet ideology and a commitment to their personal reforgings.

By extension, perekovka changed not only people, it changed the environment in which they worked. Conversely, in changing one's surroundings one also effected change in oneself. *The History of Construction* quotes Marx: "By changing nature, man changes himself" (ibid., 318) and also notes that "here passed the Canal—a new nature was created" (ibid., 280). The impulse of perekovka was strong enough to reforge not only people but to restructure their natural surroundings as well. It was as if the Soviets had no notion that they could harm nature but sought, based on an ideology similar to that of premodern people, to control it. As noted in chapter 1, the canalworkers stopped waterfalls, dammed rivers, moved railroads, made islands disappear—all in the ultimate quest to reform themselves. In so doing, they recreated nature as well with questionable results. Nonetheless, the importance of these actions stemmed not from the damage wrought on the natural surroundings, but from the new physical world created as a result of the overall plan of perekovka.

Because the implied intention of perekovka demanded that any element of the old system be reforged, the arts, and in this case, literature, fell under the purview of the program. To that end, writers needed to be reforged in order to produce new literary forms and a new literature that befitted the new Soviet society. On a more basic level, the new ideology demanded that writers accept and integrate that ideology into their literary works. To do so required that writers recast their approach to and perception of literature and of the role of the author.

The intent of this program emerged both in the actual writing of *The History of Construction* and its critical reception. In his speech at the First Congress of Writers, Gorbunov heralds the practice of collective authorship as a "new" way to produce literature: "Skeptics are also not considering that as a result of collaboration, new genres [and] books that are not subordinated to the usual scholastic definition, are being produced. The experience of 'The History of Factories and Plants' [and] 'The History of the Civil War', aside from their special significance, represents enormously successful genre innovations that attract the very best writers.... It must be noted that no one intends to proclaim collective collaboration the only method of work for beginning [writers]. We must invent such methods of work so that, having searched for a path and pushed ahead the organized and planned cultivation of writers' cadres, the living idea emerges in the collective" (*Pervyi s"ezd,* 602). More traditional discussions of the literature of the 1930s frequently neglect to mention or ignore the idea that innovation was still a pressing issue for writers, a fact to which Gorbunov's speech attests and that squares nicely with the implementation of perekovka.

In theory the incorporation of perekovka in literature seemed plausible, and in the case of *The History of Construction* it modestly succeeded; in reality it was impossible to sustain simply because many writers could not and would not subjugate their creativity and innovation to it. The program demanded that its practitioners accept a single discourse, in this case the discourse of Soviet ideology. Put differently, perekovka demanded silence from writers who would not comply and monologism, in its true Bakhtinian sense, from those who would. The annals of socialist realism would be empty were it not for those writers who were willing to subjugate, replace, or adjust their individual artistic impulses in favor of the officially accepted artistic program. Of course, such a replacement cost a writer like Budantsev nothing in terms of creativity or innovation if, in fact, the Bolshevik ideology meshed with his personal philosophy and artistic approach. This seems to be the case with other writers, but it is not the only scenario, for many Soviet writers could not accommodate themselves to the mandated ideology just because it was demanded of them.

In practice, each review of the Belomor volume alluded to or openly discussed perekovka. If the Belomor volume failed to propagate the program widely, reviews potentially reached a larger audience, thereby expanding the impact of the idea. In A. Starchkov's review "A Second Birth" he discusses not only the newness of the literary form of the *History of Construction,* but he also notes that "the enormous educational significance of the Belomorstroi book, a book that millions of readers will begin to read tomorrow, is in the fact that it takes people with great inner conflict, while entering into their battle with a society building socialism . . . and shows the process of their 'second birth'" (Starchkov, 3).

In his review of the *History,* Troshchenko argues that the fundamental truth of the volume rests on the fact that "the book about Belomorstroi shows numerous instances, when people changed and were reformed *against their own will.* . . . On Belomor a person underwent such deep changes that it is possible to speak about a change in his very nature, which, being neither good nor evil, was nevertheless a monstrous incarnation of his previous history" (244). Ultimately, contends Troshchenko, "the Belomor book reveals the dialectic of this transformation, it shows the connection of the moral remaking of a person with practice, with practical participation in revolutionary matters" (247).

In his review, Al'tman echoes these sentiments and even more forcefully argues for the success of perekovka on the Belomor project. He states that "the greatness of the construction of the BBK is expressed in the fact that it decided not only the greatest economic and political problems, but also the greatest scientific-psychological and philosophical problem of the remaking of people, of those who, according to bourgeois science, are the least capable of being educated, the least susceptible to the intervention of others" (Al'tman, 255).

In keeping with his argument that precisely the socialist system in the Soviet Union manages to reform social enemies through labor, Al'tman contends that "it is no accident, but deeply symptomatic that precisely the keenest weapon of the dictatorship of the proletariat, the 'guarding sword' of the proletariat—the GPU is not only the weapon of repression, but, as has been shown based on the experience of many years, the organ of *the education and reeducation of people*" (255–56). In his judgment, the OGPU's pedagogical and organizational functions distinguish the Soviet world from the capitalist one. The Belomor volume convincingly demonstrates this and confirms that "only in the Soviet state, where a single socialist plan is possible, where such gigantic structures as the Belomor Canal are possible, does a planned organization characterize not only our economy, it characterizes our relationship to life as well, to the existence of the millions of laboring people in our country. And, finally, how the revolutionary relationship to nature, to the world, to all reality changes the psychology of people themselves is graphically confirmed once more" (ibid., 256).

Perekovka thus operates not only because it embodies the spirit of socialist construction, but also because the ideology that unites all activity under socialist construction and revolutionary development firmly underpins the concept. In their comments, the reviewers of the Belomor volume directly link perekovka to Marxism. The program becomes the next step on the path of revolutionary development, for it creates anew workers who are freshly steeped in Soviet and, by extension, Marxist ideology. Hence the ideology justifies and legitimizes the process of creating "new" people through labor. In practice Belomor may not have fully succeeded in reforging people, but the ideology and rhetoric of perekovka seemed persuasive enough in theory to have been able to convince at least some people of its merits.

Ultimately, the Belomor volume united three ideas central to the establishment of Soviet ideology in the early 1930s under the rubric of socialist construction. In fact, socialist construction proved to be the testing ground for the ideology in a most practical way. Each element of *The History of Construction* discussed—the (re)writing of Soviet history, the collective/Brigade construction of the Belomor volume, the commitment to the implementation and dissemination of perekovka—deflected the focus back onto the ideology. Without it there presumably would have been no motivation to embark on such projects. The converse also rings true since the rewriting of history and the implementation of collective authorship and reforging justified the ideology, thereby justifying the project, no matter what the means used to achieve its goals.

This circularity should not surprise us, for as Katerina Clark persuasively argued in her work on the Soviet novel, mythmaking, as practiced in socialist realism, evolved as the chief means through which Soviet reality was created. As she concludes, "The function of socialist realism was to provide political allegories. It became a repository of official myths which affirmed the status quo" (Clark [b], 269). This analysis captures the essence of *The History of Construction,* for it was one of the first works not only to create the myth of perekovka but also to establish the status quo of which Clark writes. As such, *The History of Construction,* like those texts commonly considered to have prefigured socialist realism, defines not only the status quo but also the paradigm for large construction projects. In effect, it mythologizes, institutionalizes, and legitimizes the use of forced labor and the authority of the OGPU as a method necessitated by the desire to create a new Soviet society. Of course, the ultimate question that this text raises is the most compelling: Can the use of force to promote ideology actually succeed? If recent events are any indication, then the answer to this question is a resounding *No!*

4
Converging Narratives and the Emerging Truth

> I think that what committed us to the work, despite all our differences of interests and approaches, was that it was a "dossier," that is to say, a case, an affair, an event that provided the intersection of discourses that differed in origin, form, organization, and function. . . . All of them speak, or appear to be speaking, of one and the same thing; . . . But in their totality and their variety they form neither a composite work nor an exemplary text, but rather a strange contest, a confrontation, a power relation, a battle among discourses and through discourses.
>
> Michel Foucault, *I, Pierre Riviere, having slaughtered my mother, my sister, and my brother* . . .

The power relationship between texts that Foucault describes applies equally well to the constellation of literary works that accompanied the construction of the Canal. Each text, through the discursive possibilities inherent in it, struggles to exert its influence in the interpretive structure that derives from the Belomor event. For our purposes, the Foucault model offers the chance to glean from Belomor conclusions that have never been drawn before simply because the event and its literary manifestations were never documented before. The following examination of these texts will not detract from the truth. Rather, it will bring us closer to the reality of the Belomor episode and provide a truth about it that previously had been avoided.

This approach demands, then, that we analyze the other narratives that converged on Belomor with two goals in mind: Not only must we assess these discourses to determine their own relationship to Belomor; we must also look at the interplay between discourses so as to distill away the critical issues. Hence, the following discussion will systematically trace each narrative's path to Belomor in the hope that their convergence will offer conclusions for further consideration.

Converging Narratives

While other works were produced to glorify Soviet construction projects, *The History of the Construction of the Stalin White Sea–Baltic Canal* ultimately stands alone for a number of reasons. It was the foremost example of a truly collectively written work, uniting ideology and method under one event and thereby applauding and justifying both in a most public way. Other collective works were produced, among them the *People of the Stalingrad Tractor Factory*. However, *The History of Construction* was the only collectively written work that joined Soviet writers, forced labor, and Soviet ideology into an organic whole that would never be repeated in Soviet literature.

This unique feature does not preclude the existence of other texts that address the Belomor project, albeit in different and sometimes contrasting ways. Nikolai Pogodin's play *The Aristocrats*, Mikhail Prishvin's novel *The Tsar's Road,* and poems of varying complexity all intersect at the Belomor Canal project. The metaphor of an intersection fits this context because each of these narrative interpretations approaches the topic from a distinct perspective generated by the individual author's stance, the features of the discourse, and the power relation it maintains among texts.

If *The History of Construction* represents the most sympathetic literary response to the Canal project, then the other narratives that converge on Belomor display varying degrees of sympathy, or the lack of it, with the goals of the Soviet regime. Like *The History of Construction,* Pogodin's play *The Aristocrats* sympathizes with the regime's programs. In contrast, Prishvin's *The Tsar's Road* was designed with its own agenda, which does not actively promote the goals of regime. Inmate poems, stories, and songs, at least those that have been discovered, tended to be more sympathetic, although many songs would defy such a classification. The poetry of Konstantine Simonov, Igor Terent'ev, and Nikolai Kluyev illustrates the diversity of the poetic response to Belomor.

The Comedy of Reforging: Pogodin's *The Aristocrats*

For the Soviet playwright Nikolai Pogodin, no two topics were more inspiring or appealing than Vladimir Lenin and Soviet socialist construction. For his trilogy of plays devoted to Lenin—*Lenin: Man with a Weapon, The Kremlin Chimes,* and *The Third Pathétique*—Pogodin was awarded a Lenin Prize in 1958. He received no such prize for his 1934 play *The Aristocrats,* a comedy inspired by the construction of the Belomor Canal. Yet as the only dramatic work devoted to retelling the Belomor story, this play occupies an important place in the literary history of Belomor. *The Aristocrats,* like other literary works about the episode, focuses on one pivotal theme that provides unity not only within this one work but also among the various Belomor histories—perekovka. As such, the relationship enables us to examine yet another work that supports the idea that hard work and socialist construction successfully reforge former miscreants into productive Soviet citizens. Among all the fictional variations on the Belomor topic, Pogodin's play is the most faithfully Soviet in that it unquestioningly supports the programs of socialist construction and social reforging.

Of the diverse discourses that center on Belomor, *The Aristocrats* illustrates how Pogodin manipulated dramatic discourse, steeped in theatricality and dependent on performance, to create and visually sustain the notion of reforging. Although it initially might seem an odd selection, the playwright deliberately chose the comic mode through which to achieve his goal.

Certainly a powerful approach, the use of comedy to lessen the terror of that which is actually terrifying distances the reality of the historical event from the "reality" achieved on the stage. In discussing the effect of distancing on the viewer/reader's perception of comic elements in folk humor, Mikhail Bakhtin contends that "the medieval and Renaissance grotesque, filled with the spirit of carnival, liberates the world from all that is dark and terrifying.... All that was frightening in ordinary life is turned into amusing or ludicrous monstrosities" (Bakhtin, 47). These strategies provide the distance that defuses the viewer's fear. As Amy Williamsen argues, "distance allows the [viewer] to perceive the humorous reduction of that which is 'dark and terrifying'" (Williamsen, 117). Hence even a fear-inducing event such as the construction of the Belomor Canal can be made comic, an effect that contemporary critics might find difficult to bear, but that Pogodin's audiences found delightful.

Pogodin viewed the Belomor project as a most appropriate topic for a dramatist. In his speech to the First Congress of Writers in 1934, he noted that the Belomor project provided him with three elements that appealed especially to a playwright: the colorful blend of various social strata in one place, the conflicting goals among all the participants at Belomor, from OGPU men to common criminals, and the victory of the most powerful force (the OGPU and perekovka, CR) over its opposing forces (*Pervyi s"ezd*, 385–86). In order for the Soviet regime to successfully promote a project like the Canal, it required methods and cultural statements that camouflaged the horror or injustice of an event for the sake of credibility. The socialist realist stage became one platform through which public opinion could successfully be manipulated. In this particular case, it could persuade viewers to think that forced labor projects were not really detrimental, especially if they contributed to the increasing power and prestige of the new Soviet state.

From the beginning of his career, Nikolai Pogodin devoted himself to the

Soviet regime and the expansion and strengthening of the state. He believed that by depicting socialist construction and Soviet power in his plays he could capture the spirit of the time and the essence of what it meant to reforge people into model Soviet citizens. One commentator notes, "He [Pogodin] joyfully greet(ed) the intelligent reforging of people in *The Aristocrats*" (Markov, 8). As Pogodin commented, "But the main thing is to reveal, through the methods of the theater and in [visual] images, what the simple, brief word 'reforging' means in reality" (*Pervyi s"ezd*, 386).

The Belomor Canal project was not the first construction project that attracted Pogodin's attention. He frequented the construction sites of some of the most famous building projects in the Soviet Union. For example, his play *Tempo* (1930) was written in seven days after Pogodin had traveled to the construction site of the Stalingrad tractor factory on assignment for the newspaper *Pravda*. "While working on his first play, the writer strove to reflect his impressions of the construction of one of the first giants of the Five-Year Plan" (Pogodin, *Collected Works* 1:421). A sketch he wrote for *Pravda* in 1928 about the Lenin Zlatoustovsky metallurgy factory inspired his play *Epic of an Ax*. (While published in 1932, the play premiered only in 1951.) *My Friend*, which premiered in November 1932, resulted from a Pogodin trip to the construction site of the Gorky automobile plant. As his dramatic works illustrate, Pogodin acted politically correctly, in contemporary parlance, and was rewarded for it with success and publication.

Throughout his long career Pogodin did not focus exclusively on construction projects. His other plays ran the gamut of officially sanctioned Soviet topics. In *After the Ball* Pogodin dramatized the establishment of a collective farm. *The Lady Boatman* lauded Soviet efforts during the great Patriotic War (World War II). Other plays concentrated on particular segments of Soviet society—*When the Lances Break* featured the Soviet intelligentsia. *The Little Student* described the life of young Soviets. The Communist Party was the focus of *The Years Gone By*, while he paid tribute to the Red Army in *The Silver Fall*. Most important and most ideologically sound among all these plays was his trilogy, *Lenin: Man with a Weapon, The Kremlin Chimes,* and *The Third Pathétique*.

Even Pogodin's biography lends credence to his standing as a mainstream Soviet writer who complied with and supported the implementation of socialist realism and the need to positively convey the construction of Soviet society. Pogodin came from Tambov peasant stock. He was raised by his mother and educated at home because a lifelong eye ailment prevented him from attending school after the first grade. He started to work at fourteen and landed his first newspaper job at age twenty. According to an official biography he was instantly captivated by writing and had his first poem published in 1921 in *Trudovaia zhizn'* in the 1 May edition, no less (*Collected Works* 1:19). Pogodin eventually abandoned writing newspaper sketches and in the 1930s he began to devote himself to drama full-time. Over the next thirty years he was considered one of the leading Soviet dramatists and published more than thirty plays, some more well known than others.

In *The Aristocrats* we find evidence of the general theme of perekovka and elements that would have been perceived as comic by viewers of the day; however, both the evidence and our perception of it must be tempered by the fact that this play, like any other, was meant to be viewed, not read. Its peformance history is scant and not well documented. Reviews in various publications of the day are the only commentary on how the play was performed and received by audiences, but even that information sheds little light on the details of gesture and facial expression so important to the apprehension of the play's content and comic intent. This is not to suggest that reading the play fails to produce an interpretation. On the contrary, a reader gleans much from doing so, but as Matthew Stroud suggests, "As usual, the closer one can come to actual performance, the more performance will become a meaningful function of the literary text" (Stroud, 32). The words a character utters cannot be disengaged from the actions that character performs and vice versa. Any analysis of *The Aristocrats* must be posited on this.

Furthermore, understanding the action of the play reveals the success with which the Belomor event and the program of perekovka were purveyed to many Soviet writers who, in turn, sought to instill those ideas in readers and viewers. Perekovka, cited repeatedly in the play, also recurs in reviews of the play, thereby attesting not only to the success of the theme's presentation but to the strength of the idea as well. Even more important than the construction of the Canal was the idea of reforging that was institutionalized at Belomor.

If the comedic elements of a play are not convincing initially, then when it is read as a literary text the comedic elements may further weaken. At least with a performance, a weakly written comedic element can be strengthened through an actor's delivery—gesture, facial expression, intonation, enunciation. Expressions or linguistic peculiarities that were perceived as humorous or taboo in the 1930s have lost much of those qualities simply because they are no longer current. Arguably, the mark of a good comedy is its timelessness; no matter what the era or cultural context, the reader/

viewer always finds something humorous. This principle is not true for much political comedy because we lose the context in which it was written and therefore cannot interpret the signs—as is the case with *The Aristocrats*.

The Aristocrats is a comedy in four acts. As befits a work that strives to approximate reality in its socialist development, the cast of characters includes OGPU officers, thieves, imprisoned intellectuals, and various other personages who actually converged on the Belomor construction site. The list of characters include "'Chekists,' 'specialists,' bandits, thieves, prostitutes, unbelievers, kulaks, and others" in that order (*Collected Works* 3:97).[1] This arrangement reflects how the playwright expected the participants in the Belomor project to be perceived. He ranked the characters in descending order of importance to the Canal project.

The OGPU officers who supervised the construction and through whose determination and vision it was successfully completed rank first. Yet the Chekists could not have succeeded in their task had it not been for the "specialists" who contributed their expertise, willingly or otherwise, to the project. Significantly, these specialists—engineers in fact— were inmates in the Belomor camp and had no choice in whether or not to work; it was demanded of them. In the hierarchy of the fictional and actual Belomor world, the specialists ranked second. Finally included are the workers, a group comprised of common and political prisoners. This motley crew actually carried out the plans and designs of the preceding two groups. Without them no Canal would have been built. Thus, in the composition of the workforce of the waterway, Pogodin's cast of characters mirrors exactly those who joined in the actual construction project. Like the real event, the action of the play occurs on the Canal—in the offices of the administration, in the prisoners' barracks, and in the work rooms of the engineers. But no matter where a scene unfolds, it is part of a chain of events that describes and emphasizes the pervasive theme—perekovka.

While the viewer might surmise that only common criminals are subject to perekovka, the opposite is true. Parallel to the real situation at Belomor, in the play state enemies, among them kulaks and engineer-saboteurs, also merit reforging. While in reality it was questionable whether well-educated, erudite engineers or hardworking, productive farmers really needed to become model Soviet workers, in the play there is no question. As we have seen before, the likeliest candidates for change emerge as those people who were molded prior to the revolution, not during or after it. In the play this logical conclusion is borne out by the reforgings of engineers educated in tsarist academies and institutes and of criminals accustomed to a life of crime independent of any sociopolitical event.

To illustrate this point, Pogodin includes two engineers, Sadovsky and Botkin, who are imprisoned because it was perceived that they tried to sabotage other Soviet construction projects. To rid them of this saboteur mentality, they are sent to Belomor, where their skills will be put to the service of the Canal. Pogodin presents Sadovsky and Botkin as two sides of the same coin. The engineers are former colleagues, but Botkin is the first to embrace the construction project and begin his transformation. However, Sadovsky cannot comprehend the situaton in which he has been placed. He repeatedly mentions that he is a prisoner. The notion of perekovka is alien to him. To wit, this exchange with the supervising Chekist, Gromov:

Sadovsky: "I don't understand anything. They sent me here for ten years. I'm a prisoner. I'm a criminal."
Gromov: "Have the rumors reached you that a prisoner's sentence can be significantly shortened?"
Sadovsky: "I've heard that."
Gromov: "Or you can get a longer sentence."
Sadovsky: "How come?"
Gromov: "For new crimes, of course. . . . Let's get down to business."
Sadovsky: "Very well. As you command."
Gromov: "Tomorrow you will be the one giving commands. Let's get down to business" (ibid., 93).

As this episode illustrates, Sadovsky cannot fathom Gromov's words. Those who willingly participate in the construction project can receive shortened sentences. For those who continue to engage in sabotage, the sentence can be lengthened. Ultimately, though, the most important point, that Sadovsky can also become a commander if he obliges and participates enthusiastically in the construction project, is lost on him. Gromov implies that successfully reforged canalworkers can become the new leaders, a Soviet version of the Prodigal Son, only on a much larger scale. Conversely, while Botkin initially views his entire Belomor experience in a pained, sad light, he commits to the cause rather quickly. At first he reveals to Sadovsky that "I've been silent for a long time. What are these newspapers? Akh, *Perekovka*. (He reads.) 'Engineer Botkin has been authorized to design wooden sluices.' Yes, authorized to do that" (ibid., 112). When Sadovsky questions whether Botkin is designing structures for the Canal, Botkin confirms that he currently is, but adds, "They have some sunny, wonderful ideas about the cleansing of capitalist sludge from people. Here is that *Perekovka*. This is the fulfillment of their ideas. Think about it, Sadovsky, how will they reforge you and me? How stupid and boring!" (ibid.).

At first Botkin reacts with despair and spite, because he understands the falsity of perekovka. Engineers like Sadovsky and Botkin need no reforging, for they already are productive, educated members of society. That the OGPU believes them in need of it is a cruel joke. Yet in the reality of the play and of the actual construction project, this idea was ironic only to people like Botkin. Everyone else was convinced that any enemy of the state, even a productive one, still merited reforging. The crucial point here is that Botkin eventually succumbs to perekovka and participates actively in the construction project. As he later says to Sadovsky, "I simply wasn't doing anything, and I got tired of not doing anything. My mind is protesting. I was tired of believing in a future which I don't see. I can't live in isolation any longer" (ibid., 124). With this, Botkin plunges into his work and produces plans for the wooden locks that are implemented on the Canal, an act that replicates the actual situation on the Belomor construction site. Botkin even cajoles a brigade into fulfilling their quota. In effect, he becomes the boss, the very thing about which Gromov spoke to Sadovsky—he would become master of his own destiny and that of others if only he committed himself to the work of building the Canal.

More important, even Sadovsky alters his thinking and labors on the Canal. As he notes to his mother, "Here we are creating geography" (ibid., 156). He so fully and successfully immerses himself in the construction of the Canal that he receives an award for his labor and obtains an early release from the Belomor prison camp, the ultimate reward. As he tells Gromov, "I was a coward, confused, I deceived you and myself.... I was a real saboteur, I committed a crime" (ibid., 168). At one point Sadovsky even suggests to Botkin that they destroy the project for the wooden locks (ibid.). With these confessions Sadovsky emerges as the true candidate for reforging among the intellectuals. He has moved from state enemy to state hero through his work on the Canal. His self-doubt and unproductive thoughts recede. In their place emerge self-confidence and Soviet ideology. The same holds true for Botkin, but throughout the play Sadovsky is given a larger role. His dialogue more fully reveals his doubts not only about his ability to contribute to the Canal but about the whole enterprise, too. Through the persistent urging of the Chekist Gromov and his own ultimate commitment to his work, Sadovsky is reformed and emerges as the prototypical positive hero.

In this play Pogodin achieves the quintessential happy ending, a requisite feature of a work of socialist realism: Everyone reforms, realizes his or her ideological deviations, and becomes a devoted new member of Soviet society. The reforgings of Sonya and Kostya-Kapitan, the chief protagonists among the camp's criminal element, differ from Botkin's and Sadovsky's but with the same results.

Sonya's catalyst for change is a project supervisor who tries to persuade her to reform. Not one to give up, he repeatedly chats with Sonya until he convinces her that she has a future, if only she will work on the Canal. He encourages her to tell him her life story, an account filled with thievery, alcoholism, prostitution, and murder. As their conversations continue, he gains Sonya's confidence, although how he achieves this is unclear. In fact, she repeatedly resists his offer of reform. As she notes, "You can talk to me for a year if you want. . . . Good grief, like a broken record. I have never worked—and I don't want to now" (ibid., 112). After he spends four hours, tea, and cookies on Sonya, she exclaims, "You don't have to talk to me any more about your life. This is worse than being depressed" (ibid.). But a change has occurred, for she promises the supervisor, "I give you my solemn word that I will stop drinking vodka" (ibid., 113). This is all she promises, but it marks a significant point in her development; after this she even refuses to have a drink with Kostya-Kapitan when he offers, for she has given her "solemn word."

The level of Sonya's reforging rises to the point where she challenges Kostya to a competition to see whose brigade will overfulfill the work order by 150 percent. Although she doubts Kostya's newly exposed enthusiasm for his work, Sonya nonetheless presses on with the challenge. Ultimately she is awarded a medal for her labor. When asked to deliver a speech during the celebration of the particularly successful completion of a part of the Canal, Sonya is overcome with emotion. As she declares through her tears, "Gromov told me, as if he were talking to his sister, that the government is sending me an award. When he said that to me, as if to his sister . . . "(ibid., 169)—Sonya cannot continue. She has reaped the rewards of her labor and has been recognized with an award for her participation. More important, she has moved to a level of heightened consciousness, the mark of a truly reforged individual.

The ultimate reformation occurs in Kostya, the person most opposed to the Canal project and the most incorrigible. Precisely how this occurs remains a mystery to viewer and reader alike. In spite of the attempts of other characters, not least among them Sonya and Gromov, to persuade Kostya to work, he seems unmoved by their arguments. In fact, he continues to steal from anyone in the camp who affords him the opportunity. For example, he swipes a cap from one of his fellow thieves, steals port-cigars from Sadovsky's parcel from home, and even makes off with an Underwood typewriter from the office of the engineers' secretary, Margarita Ivanovna. This is the same Margarita Ivanovna whom Kostya won in a prisoners' card game and to whom he proposed, while telling her that he was a famous aviator. Being in the labor camp does nothing to deter him from his previous behavior. Even more enlightening, Pogodin's inclusion of Kostya's activities parallels actual events on the Canal site, where gambling, prostitution, and thievery flourished in spite of official efforts to the contrary. Indeed, life within the camp became a microcosm of life outside the camp.

In fact, from the time Kostya arrives in the camp until the penultimate scene of the play, he continually plots to escape. Early in the play, he discusses the possibility of escape with Sonya, who initially views escape as her only option (ibid., 91). Later, when the inmates are required to register, Kostya continues his opposition to work when he maintains, "I wonder how I will work here? . . . Sonya, have you really registered to build socialism?" (ibid., 93). Kostya further insists, "Sonya, stay close to me. We won't perish. Crooks must stick together" (ibid.). Finally, regarding their plans for escape, he quips, "First Class—to Manchuria and back" (ibid.). At the end of act 1, he poses one of the most crucial questions of the play: "I wonder, how are they going to reeducate me?" (ibid., 114).

The reeducation of Kostya superficially appears to succeed, for his conversations with some of his fellow inmates seem to alter his thinking. For example, he converses with Mitya, an inmate who "was a famous bandit" (ibid., 120) but now works on the Canal; for his labor he has received a reduced sentence. He even wears the pin of an *udarnik*—a shock-worker. Mitya repeatedly tries to convince Kostya to work, and one particular conversation strongly impresses Kostya. Mitya, in response to Kostya's question about his udarnik pin, says:

"This is the pin of a shock-worker."
Kostya: "And what does that mean for your life?"
Mitya: "I had a 10-year sentence, and now I have a 6-year sentence. See for yourself. (He shows Kostya his work record.) I'll build the Canal and leave."
Kostya: "And I'll spit on it and run away."
Mitya: "They'll catch you and bring you back, while I'll leave a free man."
Kostya: "Mitya, leave me alone. I'm tired of these conversations. I

ask you Mitya, leave me alone.... That bastard, he speaks very convincingly" (ibid., 122).

Slowly the ideas of freedom and reduced sentences, the common enticements actually provided to inmates on the Canal, penetrate Kostya's thinking. After the aforementioned conversation, he even turns to Sonya for solace, but she dramatically abandons her wheelbarrow and flees from him.

An appropriately dramatic moment later in the play provides yet another false turning point in Kostya's thinking. When Mitya confronts him anew for not working, he stabs himself, tearfully repeating the words "I won't work, I won't" (ibid., 127). Sonya delivers the ultimate blow when she labels Kostya a "fool" for resorting to such melodrama. In turn, he serves as the mouthpiece for the play's theme when he asks the medic, "Listen, medic, why did they think up this Canal?" (ibid., 128). After the stabbing episode, Kostya meets with Gromov, who berates him for wagering for Margarita Ivanovna in a card game. When Kostya responds, "OK, so shoot me," Gromov retorts, "You are bubbling with energy, will, intelligence, talent" (ibid., 131). After this vote of confidence, Gromov assigns him to a demolition unit that will be responsible for blowing up cliffs in order to build locks for the Canal. This is an ironic assignment for someone supposedly endowed with "energy, will, intelligence, talent," because working on an explosives brigade was the most dangerous, and often fatal, assignment. Workers frequently did not escape the detonations or were killed by careless handling of the explosives. If Gromov was outside the fictional confines of the play we might question his intent—was he trying to reforge or eliminate Kostya? Within the play, though, his motives are portrayed only as the most noble: Challenging work will reforge Kostya into a Soviet citizen.

This incident seems to suggest progress in Kostya's development. Nevertheless, as he confides to the inmate Alyosha, "I've already thought it out. I'll do a great job, earn their trust, then run away" (ibid., 139). True to his plan, Kostya leads the brigade to the completion of their work. For this he is written up in the camp paper and remarks, "They've been hypnotized by trust [in me]" (ibid., 144). As a result of his accomplishments, Sonya, in a dramatically fitting gesture, challenges him to a brigade competition to overfulfill the norm by 150 percent, a figure that he ups to 200 percent. Although Kostya's brigade loses the contest, they perform admirably. Not only do they successfully detonate and destroy cliffs and embankments, they also build a dam according to Sadovsky's plan. As Kostya notes to

Sadovsky, "Tomorrow we'll show them the high class of your dam," to which Sadovsky responds, "What a person will be released into society!" (ibid., 160). In the next scene Kostya even lulls Mitya into believing that he has reformed: "Mitya, this is very funny. I, an old thief, have become the head of a commune, I—a famous shock-worker, I—a builder of a world-class project. Mitya, how wonderfully you have reeducated me. Mitya, I'm thankful to you until my death. Mitya, hooray!" (ibid., 161). Apparently Kostya-Kapitan has evolved into the model shock-worker and reforged prisoner who ascribes his perekovka not to the OGPU but to his fellow inmate Mitya.

No sooner does Kostya utter these lovely phrases, than he flees the camp. It immediately becomes clear that he has escaped, and he is promptly rearrested. When Gromov questions him as to why he ran away, he responds, "I was fighting for my life in the Canal . . . with a guy who took me against my will, but I came back. He wanted to drown me in the Canal" (ibid., 166). In fact, this "guy" symbolically refers to Kostya himself, who tried to run away but was saved, albeit metaphorically, by the very Canal in which he almost drowned himself. The reader/viewer suspects that the hero has had a change of heart, having thrown himself into the Canal. Most appropriately, the Canal itself has saved him, and his personal perekovka is complete. Gromov underscores this transformation when, in answer to the Kommandant's query about the attempted escape, he replies, "Write this . . . 'freed from punishment, bayan [a Slavic string instrument] to be returned, glue given back'" (ibid.). Kostya receives no reprimand for his thievery, because the forthright, all-knowing Gromov understands that the inmate has changed. He knows, omnipotently, that Kostya, the bayan-playing thief who has romanticized his life of crime, understands what "real" work means and has found his "freedom" on the Canal.

Consistent with the profile of a socialist realist positive hero, Kostya also comprehends this. When he is called upon to give a speech on the occasion of the completion of work on Botkin's locks and Sadovsky's dam, he rambles on about the foresight of the Bolsheviks, Sonya's admirable labor, and his own high emotions at this moment. He caps off this speech with a panegyric to Gromov in which he proclaims, "I never expected that my fate would be intertwined with the life of the wonderful Chekist, comrade Gromov" (ibid., 170). Kostya's perekovka is complete, for not only has he worked on the Canal—he has also been honored for that work. He realizes that his reformation was possible through the thoughtful assistance of the Chekist Gromov. The ultimate proof of Kostya's reforging obtains in the shift from spontaneous action to consciousness. He no longer acts on whim or desire, instead thinking about his actions and their place in the larger picture. His is a reforging not just of skill but of intellect, too.

Pogodin romanticizes the events of Belomor to make them more palatable to viewers as well as to comply with the increasing demand of the socialist realist mandate to present a happy ending. Within his play the partial reality of the historical event, the romanticization of an historical episode, and the historicization of that episode converge. The story of Belomor is dramatized while it is historicized.

Because of the paucity of information about the actual performance of the play, we must rely on the actors' words to convey the comic-carnivalesque elements that Pogodin's use of language supports. Throughout the work we encounter expressions, dialogue, and misstatements that, at the time, either evoked laughter in the audience because the remarks were genuinely funny or prompted nervous laughter because a taboo subject had been lampooned verbally.

One of Kostya's cronies, Limon (or Lemon, who always displays a sour demeanor), makes a pun about another character tellingly named Beret. He tells him, "Beret, give the hat back to the hat" [Beret, otdai shliapu shliape] (ibid., 90). The pun revolves around the name *Beret* as well as the use of the Russian word for hat—*shliapa*—to refer not only to the thing itself but also to a person who is considered to be feeble. Similarly, when Sonya criticizes her fellow inmates, she says, "Here are the heroic ladies of the north. They are conducting the water. Where are you conducting the water to?" [Vot . . . geroicheskie damy severa. Oni more provodiat. Kuda vy more provodite?] (ibid., 106). A Russian audience would react to such a statement because of the link made with plumbing terminology: the word for pipes, *vodoprovody*, and plumber, *vodoprovodchik*. In addition, a listener might associate the verb *proVODit'* as a pun on the Russian word for water, *VODa*. Moreover, the *provodit'/provozhat'* verb pair, meaning to "see off" or to "escort," adds another comic element. In effect, Sonya questions where the women laborers are escorting the water to, not a usual activity to engage in with water.

Likewise, when the engineer Sadovsky asks Kostya, "Tell me, thief. Why did you start to work? How did that happen to you?" [Skazhite mne, vor, kak vy stali rabotat'? Kak eto s vami proizoshlo?], Kostya retorts, "What are you asking me for? Who am I, Dostoevsky?" [Chto vy u menia spra-shivaete? Razve ia Dostoevskii?] (ibid., 142). His remark to Sadovsky strikes a humorous note, for the comparison it draws between Kostya and the writer Dostoevsky is intensified with the comment "I'm not Dostoevsky, but I understand what's going on." [Ia ne Dostoevskii, no delo ponimaiu] (ibid., 143). Kostya is elevated to the level of Dostoevsky, which for the prisoner is positive—he has the same ability to know and comprehend as does the great writer. At the same time, Dostoevsky is lowered to the level of a prisoner (which he was at one point), a lessening of his stature and a rather insulting gesture. In Kostya's world, one does not need Dostoevsky's erudition in order to understand one's surroundings, while one can be as verbally adept as the great writer without being him. Finally, upon Kostya's victory in a card game for which a woman is the prize, another inmate responds, "They're playing for a live babe! These are my kind of people!" [Na zhivuiu babu igraiut! Vot eto liudi!] (ibid., 97). Fully appreciating the humor that these statements convey in Russian is somewhat difficult because of the cultural and social specifics that have lost some, although not all, of their relevance since the play was written.

In addition to the linguistic peculiarities of the language, characters in the play often misquote classic lines from Russian poetry. The poet Aleksander Pushkin proves to be the most frequent victim of these malaprops. For example, on Limon's lips Pushkin's poem "I erected to myself a monument not made by human hands, A common path to it will not be overgrown," [Ia pamiatnik sebe vozdvig nerukotvornyi, K nemu ne zarastet narodnaia tropa] becomes "I erected a monument to myself, pray you vermin, you won't be seeing Pushkin anymore." [Ia pamiatnik sebe vozdvig, molites' gady, bol'she Pushkina ne uvidite] (ibid., 126). In these lines Limon misquotes Pushkin in discussing escape with Kostya. Rather than "perish" among the "parasites" in the camp, Limon has procured a compass in order to expedite their escape—they won't see "Pushkin," i.e., Limon, any more.

Similarly, Gromov modifies the opening lines of Pushkin's poem "The Drowned Man" [Utoplennik] from "The children ran to the hut, Hurriedly calling their father" [Pribezhali v izbu deti, Vtoropiakh zovut ottsa] to "The drowned man arrived? Hurriedly calling his father?" [Utoplennik priplyl? Vtoropiakh zovut ottsa?] (ibid., 140). Gromov greets Sadovsky with these words when he arrives to report on an expedition the engineer Botkin completed with some of the inmate-thieves. The "drowned man," the engineer Sadovsky, greets "his father," the OGPU man Gromov, a comparison that suggests the fictional paternal relationship between the OGPU men and their inmates on Belomor. Limon utters the final literary paraphrase when he sings the opening lines of Pushkin's poem "The Black Shawl," subtitled "A Moldavian Song": "I gaze, like a viper, at the black shawl, and sadness tortures my sick soul." [Gliazhu, kak gadiuka, na chernuiu shal', I dushu bol'nuiu terzaet pechal'] (ibid., 164). The Pushkin original reads, "I gaze, as if insane, at the black shawl, And sadness torments my cold soul." [Gliazhu kak bezumnyi na chernuiu shal', I khladnuiu dushu terzaet pechal'.] Limon sings these lines in order to camouflage the fact that Kostya intends to escape within minutes. When questioned about the song, Limon simply replies he is singing out of joy (ibid.) and then bids Kostya farewell.

That Pogodin includes these literary misstatements implies two important points. First, Pogodin relies on classic Russian literature to inject comic elements into the play. The theater public of Pogodin's time was well versed in the Russian literary classics, to wit, the references to Dostoevsky and Pushkin. In fact, it is highly likely that many members of the audience could recite by heart the Pushkin poems to which Pogodin alludes. The resulting misstatements do not so much belittle Pushkin as they link the thieves' world with that of the theatergoers. Second, the misquotations bring into question other portrayals of the thieves, who appear less common and more educated than other sources would have readers believe. Given that most of the criminal inmates on Belomor were illiterate (there was a major campaign to eradicate illiteracy on the Canal), Limon's ability to manipulate Pushkinian verse rings a bit false. This is not the case, however, for Gromov, whom Pogodin systematically portrays as an educated, literate Chekist with sophisticated thoughts and tastes.

For a late-twentieth-century reader the most striking aspect of *The Aristocrats* is that Pogodin labels it a comedy. This categorization is perplexing if only because it is difficult to perceive the construction of the Belomor Canal cast in the comic mode. Yet this is what Pogodin has done, even though the play has some serious, dramatic moments. This issue—the comedy of terror—is pivotal in understanding how Pogodin's work fictionally treats an actual event, thereby striving to achieve veracity. In his speech to the First Congress of Writers, Pogodin repeatedly stressed the need to capture "reality" in Soviet literature; he viewed his dramaturgical pursuits as contributing to that depiction of reality (*Pervyi s"ezd*, 385). Moreover, the playwright sought both to document Soviet history accurately (a chronicle of socialist construction, if you will) and to legitimize the practice that was to be the mainstay of much of socialist construction, forced labor. He produced a stringently pro-Soviet play that applauds the achievements of Belomor while turning that engineering feat into a cultural act.

Initially Pogodin used the material he collected while in the Writers Brigade for a screenplay for the film *The Prisoners*. Having visited the Canal, he also felt compelled to write a play dedicated to this theme. To that end, the director of the Realistic Theater, Nikolai Okhlopkov, encouraged Pogodin to write a play about Belomor (*Sobranie* 3:482). The play debuted in

Okhlopkov's theater on 30 December 1934, and the director subtitled the performance *A Show-Carnival*. The play ran successfully there and was also staged at the Vakhtangov theater. The Vakhtangov premier in Leningrad was in early May 1935, with the Moscow premier following later that month. In addition, the play ran in theaters throughout the Soviet Union and was restaged by Okhlopkov in 1956 at the Mayakovsky Theater.

Audience and critics' reception of the play was quite favorable. In response to the Okhlopkov production, one playgoer noted, "*The Aristocrats* is a fantastic play, about which one can say that it is the best play of the 1934–35 season" (Boiarskii, n.p.). Another agreed "A wonderful play. Stirring, life-affirming, humane" (Zarkhi, n.p.). Still another exclaimed, "This play, which truthfully depicts Belomorstroi, must be shown in the provinces, and in particular, we invite you to Orenburg" (Stepanov, n.p.). Given the originality of the Okhlopkov production, it is questionable whether the viewers were responding more to the staging of the play than to the content.

Perhaps what so impressed viewers of the Okhlopkov production was the rather avant-garde staging as a carnival-play. To that end, the Moscow version unfolded on scaffolding. As reviewer S. Tsimbal noted, "In Okhlopkov's version, jolly stagehands spin around the stage, throwing confetti around themselves—it's cold, snow falls whirling and moving about" (7). Tsimbal also points out that Okhlopkov blended the ostentatiousness of Japanese theater with the folk comedy of Italian theater to produce a successful original effect (ibid.).

The desire to create a carnivallike atmosphere is not as far-fetched as it might initially seem. If, as Umberto Eco argues, "carnival can exist only as an authorized transgression" (Eco, 6), then Okhlopkov's approach is appropriate. The mishaps and missteps of the characters in *The Aristocrats* underscore not only their mistakes but the acceptable code of behavior as well. In permitting the carnival atmosphere, the Okhlopkov production emphasizes the opposite of how the characters behaved. Every time Kostya-Kapitan transgresses the moral or legal code of the Belomorstroi (and by extension the Soviet Union), the viewer sees more clearly the correct way to behave. Kostya's successive missteps form a totality of behavior, the opposite of which provides the prototype for the ideal Soviet worker, the *reforged* Soviet worker.

In order to shape viewer perception, Pogodin and subsequently Okhlopkov successfully instilled the idea of perekovka in the viewer through the use of the comic and carnival. As Eco points out, "Carnival, in order to be enjoyed, requires that rules and rituals be parodied, and that these rules and rituals already be recognized and respected. One must know to what degree certain behaviors are forbidden, and must feel the majesty of the forbidding norm, to appreciate their transgression" (ibid.). The atmosphere of the theater provides the viewer with the opportunity to laugh at the transgression, in this case Kostya's continuing thievery, deceit, and refusal to work. Simultaneously the spectator realizes the justice or truth of whatever Kostya sins against. "In this sense, comedy and carnival are not instances of real offenses; on the contrary, they represent paramount examples of law reinforcement. They remind us of the existence of the rule" (ibid.). Casting the Belomor episode in a comic, carnivalesque mode does not undermine but instead reinforces the notion of perekovka and the appropriateness of using forced labor for socialist construction.

That the Vakhtangov production of the play followed an opposite approach fails to diminish the power of either staging. In fact, for those who might have viewed the Okhlopkov production as too "experimental," the more traditional staging of the Vakhtangovtsy would serve to convey the same message, that only through hard labor and socialist construction will state enemies be reforged.

This does not mean that both stagings of Pogodin's play were completely successful. On the one hand, reviewers criticized Okhlopkov's lack of attention in working with the actors and the sometimes shallow portrayals this produced (Ermilov, 236). On the other hand, the desire of the Vakhtangovtsy to penetrate to the psychological inner workings of the characters was not always realized. As Tsimbal notes, "But here we find the well-known contradiction between Pogodin's dramatic method and the theatrical methods of the Vakhtangovtsy. Pogodin reveals his characters in leaps. The difficulties of remaking their personalities he reveals only in concrete actions and not through internal-psychological expressions. . . . Pogodin ignores psychological nuances. . . . The Vakhtangovsty, in overcoming this difficulty stemming from the peculiarities of Pogodin's dramatic method, took off on a different path. They tried to find a certain psychological 'continuity' of development for the play's images; they did a great deal in this regard, but in the end they could not avoid this situation" (Tsimbal, 8).

Arguably, in Pogodin's play the Vakhtangovtsy encountered one of the fundamental lapses in many socialist realist texts—little psychological continuity in character development. In many works of socialist realism, action, not subtleties of the evolution of one's psychological profile, merits attention. A socialist empire is not built on psychology but on strong wills and determined actions. Pogodin captures this essence in *The Aristocrats;* only those characters who reshape their lives into lives of action and labor succeed.

The most accomplished purveyors of this doctrine are the OGPU men, who consistently subjugate self-analysis to action. Throughout the play the chief OGPU protagonist, Gromov, neither lapses into self-examination nor expresses self-doubt. The purposefulness of his actions overcomes any of his weaknesses. This is not quite the case with all of the potentially re-forgible inmates. Many, be they political prisoner or common criminal, analyze their positions in the camp vis-à-vis the administration and its ideology. Yet this action also complies, to a certain extent, with the socialist realist mandate, for these characters are developing their consciousness. To do so requires an analysis of past actions with an eye toward future improvement. In the context of the developing program of socialist realism, Pogodin's play succeeded, for it captured onstage the spirit of the mandate. No small wonder that the Vakhtangov company, trained in the art of subtle psychological portrayals, did not succeed on this count; there was little psychology to convey.

The strongest criticism leveled against the production of *The Aristocrats* reverberates in a review article by Iurii Zubkov. Writing in early 1957, he discusses the restaging of the Okhlopkov production at the Mayakovsky theater. In keeping with the times, he mentions only once the program of perekovka and hardly dwells on the fact that the play unfolds in a forced labor camp. He argues that the play has not aged gracefully and has lost much of its currency, an accurate assessment given that its politics no longer resonate with contemporary audiences.

According to Zubkov, the actual process of perekovka occurs relatively quickly in the play, perhaps too quickly to be believable. As he notes, "After all, it has to be stated that the place where Pogodin clearly succeeded in showing the 'exoticism' and 'romance', the 'world of crime', is nowhere more evident than in the very process of the reforging of the psychology and consciousness of former criminals, a process that occurs surprisingly quickly: one, two conversations with the prison camp director, and the matter, as they say, is in the bag" (Zubkov, 3). Judging from Zubkov's comments and the tone of the entire review, by the time *The Aristocrats* was staged in late 1956, its appeal to the theater public had waned. This is not unexpected considering that the 1956 staging of Pogodin's play occurred during the period of de-Stalinization. Zubkov's review speaks to the issue of political comedy and its relativity within the time in which it originates. Any weakness in the play's original structure comes to the fore once its political context is removed.

The dichotomy between the contemporaneous reception and our understanding of Pogodin's *The Aristocrats* should diminish neither the important place the play occupies in the body of texts about the Belomor Canal, nor our reaction to the comic treatment of a truly uncomic event. Like other writers of the time, Pogodin used the Belomor project as a literary theme like any other, with little regard to the questions of morality and ethics.

Whether or not we agree with the politics of the play, there can be no doubt that Pogodin succeeds in dramatizing many of the details of daily life at Belomor. As viewers (or readers), we see life in the camp as it unfolds, replete with comic incidents, thievery, gambling, shock brigades, personal relationships—all the elements that actually comprised life at the Canal. In this regard Pogodin captures a reality like no other text about the place, for he reveals how, out of necessity, many inmates adapted creatively to the adversity. Given the thousands of men and women who worked on the Belomor Canal, there had to be interactions that moved beyond the overriding notion of forced labor. In fact, the playwright brings the camp to life through jokes, laughter, intrigue, romance, and melodrama—all elements of the real life of the camp.[2] This portrayal does not diminish the hard labor and suffering that drove the camp; rather, it expands our perception of Belomor beyond its traditional parameters, thereby bringing that perception closer to the truth. As Foucault argues in the passage that opens this chapter, examining all the discourse about an event brings the truth of that event even closer to us. Arguably, the visual replication on stage imbues the *The Aristocrats* with more power among all the Belomor texts; it buttresses word with deed, thereby enhancing the power of the play's message and, by extension, the power of the discourse. This contention does not imply that the dramatic treatment of Belomor is more effective that other narratives; it implies only that the dramatic discourse exerts enough of an influence so as to make its depiction of the event worthy of serious consideration.

While our contemporary reception of Pogodin's play is tempered by the clarity of hindsight, that reception should not ignore the fact that *The Aristocrats* also provides an unusual opportunity to understand how an actual event was simultaneously dramatized and historicized. It was left to Pogodin to recreate the reality of Belomor on the stage, a reality that sought to capture some of the spirit and energy of the project. As Markov correctly concludes, "When we now read Pogodin's plays, one after the other, before us opens the pages of the history of our country" (Markov, 8).

The Poetics of Reforging: Belomor in Verse

Just as Pogodin viewed Belomor as an appropriate topic for the comic mode, so, too, did a variety of poets use the poetic mode as the means through which they addressed the project. The response of poetry originated from three distinct sources: officially sanctioned, inmate, and officially unacceptable poets. The majority of Belomor verse flowed from the pens of inmate poets, a group comprised of both expert and fledgling writers. Their poetic responses turned on the theme of the greatness and success of the project; the writers infused the poems with laudatory rhetoric copied from contemporary newspapers and public speeches. While the heavily prosaic nature of the Canal project did not necessarily lend itself to the poetic mode, the very fact that it was poeticized imbued the event with greater significance and legitimacy. Poetic treatments of Belomor elevated it to a level that was considered fitting for such an important construction project. It was in this spirit that Konstantine Simonov produced his Belomor poems; he stands as the single non-inmate poet who praised the waterway project in verse.

A popular novelist, poet, playwright, journalist, and literary functionary, Konstantine Simonov (1915–1979) enjoyed a successful career in Soviet literature. Everything from his work as a war correspondent to his editorship of *Literaturnaya gazeta* (*The Literary Gazette*), as well as his membership in the Communist Party and position as secretary of the Union of Soviet Writers bespoke his total commitment to the Soviet Union and its ideology. Simonov is probably best known for his novels, most of which focused on the war. They include *Days and Nights* (1943–44), the first novel in a trilogy about the battle for Stalingrad that included *The Living and the Dead* (1959–71) and *Soldiers Are Not Born* (1963–64).

During World War II, Simonov emerged as one of the best-loved, most admired war correspondents who chronicled life and war on the front for the newspaper *Krasnaia zvezda* (*The Red Star*). His experiences inspired him to write novels, plays, and poems on the war theme. Perhaps more than any other literary creation, Simonov's wartime love poem "Wait for Me and I'll Return" etched itself on the psyche of Russian readers and became a classic of war literature and song. Within this context his authorship of Belomor poetry proves to be a natural outgrowth of his beliefs.

Although not a member of the Writers Brigade, Simonov traveled to the

Canal site to observe firsthand what had been accomplished; however, this trip did not necessarily translate into success in composing poems. In biographical accounts, references to this period of Simonov's career are rare, with greater attention paid to his lack of success with his early literary attempts. One recent biographer, A. V. Karaganov, notes, "The early verses did not end up in print—the editorial board did not accept them. For several years he struggled with the epic poem 'Pavel Black'—about the 'reforging' of a criminal on a construction site. The poem began to take shape, but never really came together; even a trip to the Belomor Canal in a group of worker-poets who were working for the State Literary Publisher didn't help" (Karaganov, 7). The lack of the success of the Belomor poems probably stemmed from a combination of the author's inexperience and a paucity of interesting themes in the project. As Karaganov also notes, "There was little success with other works, although a few of them made it into print: Simonov never included them in his later collections" (ibid.). Indeed, it is well-nigh impossible to find extant versions of these early verses in any of Simonov's collected works. They seem to appear only in multiauthored poetry collections from the early 1930s.

The apparent lack of success of these poems, coupled with the facts of Simonov's biography did not prevent him from considering what the Belomor project actually represented. As he later noted about his Belomor experience: "Both the construction of the Belomor Canal and the Moscow–Volga Canal, the construction of which was begun immediately after the completion of the first project, were, in my view, not only construction projects, but a humane school for reforging people from bad into good, from criminals into builders of the First Five-Year Plan. And through newspaper articles, and through the book that writers created after a large, collective trip in 1933 along the newly built Canal, that very theme resounded—the reforging of common criminals" (Simonov, 19). Significant in Simonov's comments is his focus on common criminals, not on political prisoners. It would have been impossible, especially writing some forty years later, for him not to know about the political prisoners on the Belomor Canal. His omission of a reference to them signals either that it was still taboo for him to mention them at the time or that politicals did not need to be reforged. Whatever the reason, the omission suggests a conscious effort not to mention this group.

In addition, in these comments Simonov notes the theme of reforging and that its optimism captured the public's imagination; former criminals were receiving commendations for their work on the Canal. According to him, this was the general mood of the country, a mood that also influenced his perception of the Belomor event, for he went to the Canal, "not to see how people lived in a prison camp, but how they were being reforged on the construction site. It sounds naive, but that's the way it was" (ibid.). As a result he dispels the myth that Belomor could not have been greeted with anything but scorn and condemnation. Instead, for many people, including Simonov, Belomor projected success, even if that success was tempered by the many abuses of man and nature on the Canal.

Simonov reached these conclusions only with the benefit of forty years of hindsight. That there could have been anything wrong with applauding the Canal project seems to have occurred to him only long after the event. Such a response is typical because the energy and rhetoric of that era tended to overshadow any doubts or concerns about the true nature of the project.

Simonov's youthful enthusiasm reverberates in his epic poem dedicated to the Canal's builders, *The Belomorists* (*Belomortsy*), which echoes the same sentiments found in newspaper articles about the construction project, as well as in the literary endeavors of Belomor camp inmates. In a fragment from this poem, Simonov writes:

> The country was spread like a white bird.
> Boulders guard the tranquility.
> Everything is silent.
>   Only the wind rushes
> And whirls above the river.
> In the cold darkness of a pine forest,
> Making shadows behind every tree trunk,
> The sun was shining . . .
>   The lakes froze over:
>   Vyg . . .
>   Vadl . . .
>   Vol . . .
>   *   *
>   *
>
> Silence . . .
>   And then at once
> An explosion rang out.
> And another
>   and another . . .
> And along the scattered diabase
> A rumble,
>   drawing near,
>   began
> (*Belomortsy*, 129).

In comparison with the poetry of inmates (cited below), Simonov's verses are more technically sound and not as overtly propagandistic. Yet the concluding stanza of a different poem reiterates if not the rhetoric then the sentiment attached to the achievement of Belomor:

> The polar sky hangs like mica.
> From Onega a steamship roars . . .
> And so our youthfulness with a feeling of pride,
> That this, the republic of joyous labor,
> Youth itself, waits for us there
> With gold ("Belomorskie stikhi," 62).

These brief excerpts exude the intensity of feeling that motivated Simonov to write about Belomor. Arguably, he could also have been taking advantage of an opportunity to cast his lot with an officially acceptable project, not a bad choice for a fledgling writer trying to get published. But there can be no doubt that he was, to a certain extent, captivated by the spirit of the time; he joined in praising the project, even if these early attempts at verse were not especially successful. That his later comments (cited above) convey his fuller understanding of the event does not lessen the fact that at the time of its construction the Canal project seemed to infuse him with the same enthusiasm as it did many of his peers.

The complexity of Simonov's response emerges in the way he romanticizes and poeticizes the Belomor project; while appropriate within the context in which he was working, his poetic depiction of the explosions on the Canal does not coincide with the reality of the situation: these explosions were responsible for hundreds of unnecessary deaths among the camp inmates.

In the same vein, inmate literary compositions conveyed one kind of reality about the Belomor project. Poems published in the camp newspaper and those extant in Russian archives describe a Belomor similar to the one we find in Pogodin's and Simonov's works.

In this regard, *Perekovka* served as the conduit through which inmates could submit poems, stories, puzzles, and cartoons that applauded the success of the Belomor project. By encouraging inmates to submit their work, the editorial staff supported the work of the cultural-education cells, whose instructors taught inmates how to read and write. As a result, the newspaper reinforced these new skills and encouraged inmates to practice by writing poems that were then submitted to the *Perekovka* staff, either on an ad hoc basis or through newspaper-sponsored competitions. Without fail, those inmates who were published dedicated their poems to the construction successes on the Canal, or they used their poems as propaganda to inspire Canal workers to greater feats. Of course, the editors of *Perekovka*, under the supervision of Sergei Alymov, controlled the thematic content of the poems so as to promote official ideology.

Examples of inmate writing, along with official mandates and a variety of articles designed to motivate inmates to greater productivity, fill the pages of *Perekovka*. The titles of the poems—"Remember Quality," "We Will Give the Canal," "We Are Canalarmyists," "Deliver It on Time!"—all reflect the thematic singularity of the verses. (This focus on productivity and reforging resounded in Alymov's poems as well, many of which were included on the pages of the newspaper.) Each poem exhorted Canal workers to labor more intensively. Yet the frequent mention of quality and efficiency in the titles suggests that these two areas were problematic. Otherwise why would so many poems be dedicated to those goals?

The selections that follow are from two of the most prolific poets in *Perekovka*—V. Lidin (by all accounts not the Soviet writer Vladimir Lidin) and Nikolai Shkred. The first example, the opening stanza of Lidin's poem "Deliver It on Time!" typifies the tone and rhetoric found in all of his poems.

"Deliver It on Time!"
(A Song of the Canalarmyists)
On the Belomor site this is our signal:
 —Assault [the project] higher than any lesson!
You will deliver to the republic a giant canal—
On time![3]

Shkred's poem echoes Lidin's sentiment. Entitled "To a New Life," it applauds the feats that the canalworkers achieved in building Belomor. He writes:

How
 the bright banner
  stands
   in the East.
The Karelian sun
 in the rough
  current.
The river Povenchanka
 froths like beer.
To Onega

>   the water crowds
>   hurriedly.
>   The water is foaming
>   The shorelines tremble.—
>   The river
>   feels
>   something
>   alarming.
>   Explosions
>   from the pine
>   forest
>   reach it—
>   A matter of heroism
>   of the brigades
>   of the B.M.S.

The B.M.S. to which Shkred refers is the BeloMorStroi, an acronym for the White Sea Construction project.

An interesting aside to Shkred's poem reveals how submissions were selected for publication in *Perekovka*. On the manuscript version of the poem we find, in red, the comment "Good" written twice by two different readers. After "Good" the reviewer added, "This is material for an issue of the newspaper."[4] These comments typify the manner in which submissions were reviewed for publication. If editors considered a poem, song, or puzzle unsuitable, they would mark it with a red *n* for *nyet* (no), thereby rejecting it for future use. In most instances more than one reader reviewed a poem for publication, as evidenced by comments in different handwriting.

The group of prisoner-poets on the Canal included the futurist poet Igor Terent'ev (1892–1937), a writer of great imagination and talent. In the late teens and early 1920s, he actively worked in futurist poetry and theater with Alexei Kruchenych and others in Georgia. In 1923 he moved to Petrograd (St. Petersburg) and worked intensively in the theater, first in the Agitstudio, then in the Red Theater, and finally in his own theater, the Theater of the House of Printing. Although the theater enjoyed a successful run in Moscow in 1928, Terent'ev was not able to sustain it. He moved to Ukraine, where he organized another successful theater company, the Dnepropetrovsk Workers' Theater. As his daughter Tatiana notes, "And so Terent'ev realized his dream—he organized a new youth theater in which he staged plays on current themes" (Terent'eva, 354).

Shortly thereafter Terent'ev applied for membership in the Communist Party and was accepted. Yet his Party membership ultimately did not save him, for in 1931 he was arrested and sentenced according to the infamous Article 58, receiving a term of five years. He spent one year in prison and then three years on the Belomor Canal, from which he was freed in 1933 thanks to his outstanding work as a shock-worker. (This information is validated by Terent'ev's file card, located in the Belomor prisoner card catalogue at the Ministry of Internal Affairs in Petrozavodsk, Russia.)

After his release from Belomor, Terent'ev moved on to the Moscow–Volga Canal construction project, where he worked until 1935. From 1935 to 1936 he lived in Kerch and attempted to shoot a film, *The Uprising of the Stones*, but the project was never realized. He voluntarily returned to the Moscow-Volga project, where he worked from 1936 to 1937. Terent'ev was rearrested on 28 May 1937 and was shot on 17 June 1937 in the Butyrka Prison in Moscow.[5]

In addition to the fact that Terent'ev had organized his own hugely successful and popular agitational-propaganda brigade, he also composed verse while at Belomor. Archival materials indicate he submitted a poem to *Perekovka* for a poetry competition.[6] The poem was originally titled "Canalsoldiers," but Terent'ev changed it to "The Army of Labor." Written in August 1932, the twelve-stanza poem is clearly superior to the other entries in terms of its technical and artistic features. Each four-line stanza is tightly composed. The lexicon is more complex, as is the presentation of ideas. Unlike other inmate submissions, Terent'ev's poem is comprised of full sentences with little jargon and publicistic rhetoric. Instead, each tightly constructed stanza presents the logical progression of ideas that culminates in the concluding lines:

> We are canalsoldiers.
> According to the plan
> A place will be found for us on the world's construction site!
> We trust ourselves: our heart beats evenly—
> To us the phrase "New Construction Project"—
> is our native land.[7]

The poem was rejected in favor of nonprofessional submissions. This decision is to have been expected, because the cultural-education cells emphasized the basic instruction and ideological indoctrination of common criminals, not the education of political prisoners. The work of the cells developed and refined the writing skills of those without any formal connection to the literary establishment. Precisely these "writers" provided fertile soil in which to plant the seeds of both Marxist-Leninist ideology and the program of perekovka.

Perhaps Terent'ev's fate and experience at Belomor captures best the arbitrary nature of the time. While he probably was arrested because he was a futurist, he still used his incarceration as an opportunity to continue to practice his art. His enthusiasm and success within Belomor did not save him, but at least these qualities provided him with an outlet for his creative energy. Looking back on Terent'ev's situation we comprehend the full nature of his tragedy. Yet if we examine his work within the context of the time, we find evidence of his irrepressible creative spirit, which enabled him to manipulate the situation to his advantage.

Terent'ev's unorthodox theatrical practices found success and expression in a most orthodox environment: the Belomor prison camp. In this regard, his experience provides a different side of the truth that was Belomor, for his ability to create was never squelched completely, in spite of his circumstances. And his adaptability suggests that some inmates were able to carve out their own paths, a perspective of Belomor about which we rarely hear. This contention does not suggest that Terent'ev enjoyed full artistic freedom; obviously that was impossible. His artistic success at Belomor probably owes more to his own abundant creativity, as well as to his ability to compromise in a difficult situation, rather than to the conditions that allowed him to show this attribute. In exchange for propagandizing the predominant ideology of Belomor, he was granted a modicum of independence in practicing his art, a result that certainly defies much of the accepted thinking about early camp life.

Like Terent'ev, the Russian poet Nikolai Kluyev (1887–1937) was a victim of the Stalinist terror. Active before and after the revolution, and a controversial figure in his own right, he is best known as a people's poet whose work is laden with Russian dialect and folk imagery that even many native Russians find difficult to understand. Rooted in religious mysticism and nature, Kluyev's poetry brings to life a kind of Russian language that is now all but extinct. As Vitaly Shentalinsky points out, "Kluyev's poetry is difficult to comprehend: Our loss is that today our native language has become just as poor as our natural resources, and we not only no longer possess our previous wealth, we've forgotten it. Kluyev's verses are difficult for us because of their rare multitonal, multicolored, multithematic qualities" (*Ogonyok*, 21–28 October 1989, 10).

The richness of his language and imagery marks his poetry as technically sophisticated. Thematically he often focuses on the demise of Russia, the beauty of Russian nature, and the importance of the Russian Orthodox faith. In Shentalinsky's view, "The poetry of Nikolai Kluyev is not only a lament for the passing of Russia, but a terrible prophesy" (ibid.). He continues, "Kluyev's poetry is more prophetic—it preserves the living roots of Old Russian mysticism and mystery. It is not a stylization of [the language of] the people (we've already heard our fill of that!), but an authentic epic literature, and Kluyev, perhaps, is the last Russian myth-maker" (ibid.).

Kluyev's career was cut short by his arrest in 1933. The poem cited below was found as an addendum to his KGB interrogation file of 15 February 1934. He was sentenced according to Article 58 "for the production and dissemination of counterrevolutionary literature" (ibid.) and was exiled to Kolpashev in Siberia. His friends succeeded in getting his sentence lightened, and in 1934 he was permitted to move to the city of Tomsk, where he remained until his second arrest and death before a firing squad in 1937. According to Shentalinsky it is unknown where Kluyev is buried; he was fully rehabilitated only in 1988.

The poem in which Kluyev mentions the Belomor Canal is entitled "Razrukha" (Ruin) and is addressed to Russia and all Russians. Throughout the work, which had never been published prior to the article about Kluyev in *Ogonyok*, the poet laments the demise and destruction of Russia at the hands of the Soviet regime. The land and the people suffer from the exploitation of natural and human resources, which ultimately ruins the entire country. But this suffering could, in fact, be the just punishment for Russia's refusal to avoid progress and embrace its own rich traditions and philosophies. Kluyev writes, in part:

> This is the new, invisible Kitezh . . .
> This is the Belomor death-canal,
> Dug by Prov from Vetlugi and aunt Fekla,
> and Akimushka.
> Great Russia got soaked to the skin
> By a red downpour
> And in the dense bogs, hid its tears from people,
> From the eyes of strangers.
> With a wheelbarrow, a spade, and a handful,
> With Belomor's molten metal
> They, as an immeasureable, woeful mass,
> Raise the waters in the locks and the dams.
> They [the waters] are cut by ships
> From Povenets to Rybia Sol'—

This is a monument to great pain,
A punishment from heaven for the sin
Of the person who, having drunk up the sweet wineskin
Filled with grandfather's vintage nectar,
Did not want to be in the virgin forest
In a simple, old house,
Did not want to lullaby the sun as was required
According to fate and according to the Christian faith.

[To Kitezh novyi i nezrimyi . . .
To Belomorskii smert'-kanal,
Ego Akimushka kopal,
S Vetlugi Prov i tetka Fekla.
Velikorossiia promokla
Pod krasnym livnem do kostei
I slezy skryla ot liudei,
Ot glaz chuzhikh v glukhie topi.
V nemerennom goriuchem skope
Ot tachki, zastupa i gorstki
Oni rasplavom belomorskim
V shliuzakh i dambakh vysiat vody.
Ix rassekaiut parokhody
Ot Poventsa do Ryb'ei Soli,—
To pamiatnik velikoi boli,
Metla nebesnaia za grekh,
Tomu, kto vypiv sladkii mekh
S napitkom dedovskim stoialym,
Ne voskhotel v boru opalom,
V napetoi, kondovoi izbe
Baiukat' solntse po sud'be,
Po dole i po krestnoi strazhe . . .]. (ibid., 11)

This rendition of the poem into English does not, cannot, do justice to the beauty of the verse in Russian. Kluyev fashions the poem after the Old Russian epics and lays, such as the *byliny* and *The Lay of Igor's Campaign*. As such, the meter and rhyme parallel the earlier forms; in fact, the poem reads like a lament, a choice consistent with Kluyev's themes.

In order to preserve the authenticity of the traditional genres that he employs, Kluyev includes old Russian phrases and images to evoke the spirit of Old Russia. For example, words such as *mekh* for wineskin, *skop* for throng or mass of people (derived from the more commonplace *skoplenie*), or the nicknames Fekla, Akimushka, and Prov all infuse the poem with the sound of the language of the countryside, of peasant villages, of times past. Words such as *napetyi*, which is translated here as *old* but is in fact derived from the verb *to sing, pet'*, and implies a house that has been long and well sung in, present a challenge to convey accurately in English.

Each word or phrase in the poem is laden with meaning and cultural associations for Russians. When Kluyev writes about the "new, invisible Kitezh," he evokes for Russian readers an image similar to that conjured up by "Atlantis" for English speakers. Carried within the phrase is the sense of a mythical, captivating place that no longer exists but nonetheless conveys some mystery. The phrase "A punishment from heaven for the sin" ["Metla nebesnaia za grekh"], translated literally as "a heavenly broom for the sin," pivots on the use of the common word *broom* (*metla*), which in this context gains a symbolic meaning as the broom used to sweep clean sin and evil. In these examples, as in others, Kluyev carefully crafts each word or turn of phrase so that it exudes the beauty and soul of old Russia.

As a result, his choice of form, style, and lexicon all contribute to the total thematic effect, for the author juxtaposes the modern construction, Belomor, with Old Russia. In so doing, he laments the construction of the Canal and questions the price that was paid for so-called progress. Kluyev's description of Belomor as a "death-canal" drenched in "a red downpour" (most probably an allusion, both to blood and to Soviet power) and "a monument to great pain" all create an image of destruction, evil, and suffering. Only when Kluyev describes what could have been—the old, worn house, the vintage nectar of past generations, the notions of fate and Christian faith—do the images of suffering and terror dissolve.

Precisely this poetic juxtaposition marks Kluyev's brilliance as a poet and thinker, for through it he reveals one of the truths of Belomor. He astutely notes how the Canal was constructed: a tightly packed throng of people built the Canal with wheelbarrows, shovels, and handfuls of dirt mixed in with molten metal, showered in blood, all in the name of progress. In identifying the chief tools of construction, he underscores the hypocrisy of the supposed progress, for it did not include modern technology. Moreover, he alludes to the chief promoter of the Canal—Stalin—as "the person who, having drunk up the sweet wineskin / Filled with grandfather's vintage nectar, / Did not want to be in the virgin forest / in a simple, old house, / Did not want to lullaby the sun as was required / According to fate and according to the Christian faith." Kluyev underscores Stalin's arrogant, blasphemous behavior; rather than embracing Russian traditions and

Christian beliefs, the dictator chooses to defy and reject them, only *after* he has partaken of their bounty. This turns out to be the ultimate insult to Russia and the sin for which they all must pay. Kluyev's words imply that the happiness of one (Stalin, who enjoyed the "vintage nectar") has been paid for by the suffering of many (the Russian people).

Consequently, as a Christian, Kluyev believes that any contemporary progress paid for by blood and suffering and the sacrifice of human life is not worth the cost. With this belief he continues the tradition of Russian writers and thinkers, most prominent among them Dostoevsky, who, arguing the *converse* of Kluyev's position, questions whether the suffering of one is justified to assure the happiness of the majority. In this regard, Kluyev echoes Dostoevsky's famous dialogue between the brothers Ivan and Alyosha Karamazov in *The Brothers Karamazov*. Ivan asks Alyosha: "Tell me yourself, I challenge you—answer. Imagine that you are creating a fabric of human destiny with the object of making men happy in the end, giving them peace and rest at last, but that it was essential and inevitable to torture to death only one tiny creature—that baby beating its breast with its fist, for instance—and to found that edifice on its unavenged tears, would you consent to be the architect on those conditions? Tell me, and tell me the truth."[8] To this Alyosha answers, "No, I wouldn't consent." At this Ivan responds, "And can you admit the idea that the men for whom you are building it would agree to accept their happiness on the foundation of the unexpiated blood of a little victim? And accepting it would remain happy forever?" And to this Alyosha replies, "No, I can't admit it, Brother"(ibid.). If even one person suffers for the happiness of everyone else, then the happiness earned on the suffering of another is unacceptable, even impossible.

For Kluyev this philosophy underpins the Canal project and casts in doubt any positive gains from it. His position emerges as the opposite of those writers who strove to couch Belomor in affirming, glorifying terms. For him there can be no glory based on suffering, and any success thus earned is doomed to failure and punishment. Arguably, Kluyev viewed Bolshevism as the punishment levied on Russia for surrendering to progress and Western influence. He would have preferred that Russia remain undeveloped and outside world culture. Perhaps the fittest testament to Kluyev's prophecy in "Ruin" is the fact that presently the Belomor Canal is hardly used and considered by many to be utterly worthless. In Kluyev's world-view, this is the natural result of a philosophically ill-conceived project that neglected the true roots of Russianness: Russian Orthodoxy and Old Russian peasant life. Without these bases, such a project was doomed to failure.

The emphasis on Old Russian traditions and Russian Orthodoxy casts

Kluyev's response to Belomor as the antithesis of any literary piece sympathetic to the project. Less obvious is the fact that his view is ultimately an extreme one, as extreme as those positions held by writers who maintained that Belomor was a totally positive, affirming experience, devoid of suffering and injustice. Remember that Kluyev, here and elsewhere, advocates *no* progress. In his view, Russia must remain the way it was hundreds of years before in order to assure for its citizens peace and happiness. That his philosophy is rooted in a *religious* rather than a totalitarian *political* system makes his views more palatable to contemporary sensibilities.

Philosophically Kluyev makes a potentially sound argument; practically, such an approach would be unable to sustain itself. It is questionable whether a lack of progress would ensure happiness for all, in the same measure that it is questionable whether a total reforging of criminal and political prisoners would assure a new, better Soviet society and happier citizens. That Kluyev's stance is so persuasive attests both to the philosophical system underpinning his beliefs and his exquisite artistry, which conveys the philosphy so powerfully.

Precisely this power enables the poetic discourse about Belomor to exert itself in the interpretive scheme. As such, it provides a narrative voice as forceful as documentary, dramatic, and prosaic discourse, while bringing to our reading of the event yet another perspective. The confluence on the Belomor event of poetic with other kinds of discourse encourages a fuller understanding of the project, while mirroring the variety of response, each infused with its own philosophical agenda, that the Canal engendered.

Mikhail Prishvin's response to Belomor posits itself on an equally persuasive philosophical system. It should come as no surprise that the other less sympathetic portrayal of Belomor would be produced by a writer, like Kluyev, whose sensibilities were formed before the revolution.

Prosaic Truth

It is fitting that Mikhail Prishvin should address the topic of the Belomor Canal and its construction. With the exception of the prose writer Ivan Sokolov-Mikitov and the poet Nikolai Kluyev, few writers knew the Russian north as well as Prishvin. Nor did any other Russian writer revere the uncommon natural beauty of the Russian north in his prose work as did Prishvin. In his oeuvre, nature and man's interdependency and relationship to each other occupied a central position. The mystical beauty of nature imbued Prishvin's work with an almost fairy-talelike quality. Indeed, he subtitled *The Tsar's Road* a "novel–fairy tale," a generic classification that stitched two distinct discourses into a seamless whole.

Mikhail Prishvin (1873–1954) was born into a merchant's family in the Russian north. He studied in Riga and Leipzig; in later life he lived in Moscow. Throughout his career he was an inveterate traveler who journeyed throughout Russia, central Asia, and the Far East. Always a nature lover, Prishvin was an avid fisherman and hunter who frequently wandered alone through some of the most remote areas in the Russian north. His interest in folklore, ethnography, and nature penetrates all his work, and *The Tsar's Road* is no exception. This appreciation for and understanding of the natural world provided him with a unique perspective from which to observe the construction of the Canal through territory he knew extremely well.

Prishvin produced sketches, short stories, and novels. His first collection of short stories, *In the Land of Brave Birds* (1907), remains one of his most

18. Front side of a file card of the Karelian Ministry of Internal Affairs for Fyodor Dostoevsky's grandson, Andrei Andreevich Dostoevsky, who was imprisoned at the Belomor Canal. This card is one of thousands housed in the Belomor card catalogue at the Karelian MVD in Petrozavodsk. The front of the card lists (numbers 1–14) the inmate's last name, first name, patronymic, year and place of birth, address, profession, place of employment, nationality, citizenship, date of arrest and nature of the crime, the criminal code statute according to which the arrest was made, who filled out the card, and, on the right side, the number of the archival form from which the information was taken with the note "destroyed." Used by permission of Ivan Chukhin.

popular and beloved works. Other collections followed, each locating the narrative in the world of nature and man's relation to it. One of his most famous works, *Ginseng: The Root of Life,* appeared in 1936. Perhaps the most remarkable aspect of his career was his ability to preserve his literary approach, a path from which he rarely deviated, even in the midst of the extreme conformism of the 1930s. This steadfastness might have had something to do with the official refusal to allow him to participate in the Belomor Brigade, although there is no direct evidence to support this contention. In terms of the literary responses to Belomor, Mikhail Prishvin had the elegant last word.

His final and longest novel, *The Tsar's Road* [*Osudareva doroga*] (1957), serves as a counterpoint to *The History of Construction,* as well as to other pro-Soviet literary renderings of Belomor, for it argues neither for perekovka nor for socialist ideology. Instead, the novel traces the effects of the construction of the Belomor Canal on the north country. While Prishvin

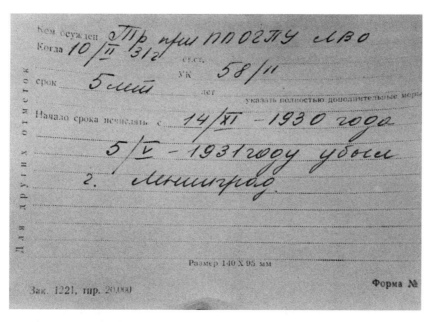

19. The reverse side of Andrei Dostoevsky's Karelian MVD card, which notes who sentenced him (in this case an OGPU tribunal or troika), when he was sentenced, according to which statute of the criminal code, and for what term (five years). Also noted is the date his sentence commenced and the date of his release (May 1931), a date that suggests that inmates were being arrested and sent to Belomor six months before the documented start of construction.

does not neglect discussing the OGPU and construction personnel who invade the area to build the waterway, his narrative focuses on the destruction of both nature and of Old Believer communities that lay in the path of the new Canal.

In so doing, Prishvin brings to the discussion a perspective that other literary works fail to consider. As a result, his contribution to the discourses on Belomor broadens the presentation of the project to include issues less consonant with the accepted approach to the Canal at that time. It is no accident that he was unable to publish the novel during his lifetime; it appeared in 1957 only after both Stalin's death and his own. As Prishvin claimed, "Truth and fairy tales—that is the theme of my whole life, and it will be primary in *Canal* [*The Tsar's Road*], and this is my life" (Kiselev, 84).

The genesis of *The Tsar's Road* dates back to the time of the Belomor construction project. Although he was already quite familiar with Karelia and the Russian far north, he reportedly still wanted to participate in the Writers Brigade to Belomor; but his request was refused. Subsequently he traveled to the construction site independently and collected materials for his proposed writing on the subject. In an entry to his diary for 16 July 1935, he wrote, "Packing for a trip to the Onego–White Sea Canal and Solovki" (*Diaries*, 252). An entry for 12 July 1937 notes that "I have started work on a book *Canal* and must squeeze out of it all the juices there are. My canal. The end: So where are the people? I don't look far, they are here. And they gave their best, and so much that you won't remember their names. Here the names flow together into the population, like drops into a waterfall" (ibid., 324). In the 6 September 1939 entry, he recorded, "I am returning to my theme, to write about the total person, as he appears in *Padun*" (ibid., 360).

Prishvin originally planned to write a novel about Belomor entitled *Canal*, but later he changed the title to *Padun*, the name of a waterfall that was dammed on the path of the Belomor project. Although that title never materialized, he did publish introductory chapters for it in the first issue, in 1939, of the journal *Molodaia gvardiia*. The selections were subtitled "Belomor Fairy Tales," with a note from the editor that stated: "Here we are printing the beginning of a large work of M. M. Prishvin on the construction of the White Sea–Baltic Canal" (*Molodaia gvardiia*, 96). *Padun* contained the beginnings of the novel *The Tsar's Road*.

The 1939 publication of the novel's first chapters was preceded by the release of Prishvin's remarkable little book, *Fathers and Children*. Written in 1933 but not published until 1937, this work presents an abbreviated version of the basic story line on which he would expand in *The Tsar's Road*. In addition to these fictional sections, *Fathers and Children* also contains a discussion of the history of the Belomor project prior to its implementation under the Soviets, as well as a detailed calendar of the construction of Belomor, with comparative statistics on the Belomor Canal and the Moscow–Volga Canal. His concluding chapter, entitled "The Padun of Mikhail Prishvin," presents a personal discussion of the significance of the waterfall for him.

The novel's title, *The Tsar's Road*, refers to the path originally carved out by Peter the Great in his effort to transport ships over land from the Baltic to the White Sea. Certainly comparisons may be made between the cruelty and single-mindedness that both Peter and Stalin employed in making their plans for a northern sea route a reality. When the construction of the Belomor Canal commenced, remnants of Peter's path remained (and do to the present day).

This comparison is further implied in *The Tsar's Road*, where Prishvin deftly contrasts the life of the Old Believers with the new life under the Soviet regime. While not portraying the OGPU personnel in an entirely negative light, he conveys to the reader that his sympathies lie not with the new Soviet system but with nature and the Old Believers. He achieves this effect not so much through what his characters say but through what they do not say. Prishvin chooses to highlight the problems associated with Belomor, a presentation that deviates from the more acceptable approach, which portrayed the dominant ideology in a positive light. In this regard, Prishvin defied the spirit of an age that promoted large construction projects in spite of the damage they could inflict.

Unlike *The History of Construction* and *The Aristocrats*, Prishvin's Belomor focuses on nature and the people who coexist with it; nature becomes a character in the narrative. He imbues his descriptions of the environment with majesty and vividness. The author consciously manipulates this approach; in raising nature to an almost sacred level, he underscores the strong ties between the Old Believers and their natural surroundings. Conversely, he emphasizes the lack of these ties among the young Soviet Chekists, most sharply personified in the character Sutulov, who supervises the construction of the Canal. By linking nature with the Old Believers, Prishvin emphatically describes their demise and subtly condemns the waterway's construction. By building the Canal, the OGPU not only destroyed nature but a way of life as well. In *The Tsar's Road* Prishvin champions the cause of conservation and, perhaps unwittingly, challenges the contention that underpinned every large-scale Soviet construction project, that development, no matter the cost, was worth pursuing to uphold the ideology and to make the Soviet Union competitive with the West.

In essence, he presents a clash of philosophies that appears most forcefully in his main protagonist, Zuek, who, according to Prishvin, represents the artist himself (Prishvin, *Osudareva doroga,* 10). Zuek feels drawn simultaneously to his roots in Old Believer society and to the determined, cool-headed, leather-jacketed Sutulov, who leads the contingent in charge of building a particular section of the Canal. The contrast between Zuek and Sutulov reveals for the reader the true conflict that the Belomor construction project raised for Prishvin. He admitted that *"The Tsar's Road* was written based on materials gathered through the personal experiences of the author. I won't hide from the reader that the experience of intertwining history, autobiography, and the contemporary construction project was difficult for me. In the story I want to show the birth of a new consciousness of a Russian person through the depiction of the soul of a peasant boy" (ibid., 12). Precisely the confrontation of these two worlds provides the dramatic tension in the novel.

The sharpest images of the results of progress affect the Old Believers in two significant ways. First, the waterfall, a huge, fantastically beautiful waterfall that the locals refer to as "our happiness," falls silent as a result of the Canal project. The workers succeed in damming the river to form a reservoir, thereby stopping the flow of water over the waterfall. The ensuing silence is deafening and deadening to the locals. When Zuek's grandfather realizes that the waterfall is no longer making noise, he is stupefied. How can that happen? As he tells his grandson, "I don't hear it . . . I don't hear it, do you?" (ibid., 141). When Zuek looks out the window he sees that the waterfall has been blocked: "In one night these gates were finished and immediately everything changed" (ibid.). To his remark that they "closed" the waterfall, his grandfather replies, "Well, well, everything is finished. The waterfall doesn't make noise and there's no end of the world" (ibid.).

The world does end, however, when the islands and lowlands on which the Old Believers live are flooded. Prishvin describes in painful detail how the water slowly overtakes everything in its path: "The water ran over the banks of the pond and began to spill over the entire island. . . . Everything around became as if in a dream and the sorceress—the foaming water— began to endow all of nature with dreams and fairy tales" (ibid., 195). A peasant woman, Marya Mironovna, watches as the last vestiges of her home disappear. "Only one chimney stack remained above the water. Mironovna stopped holding herself back and, sobbing, fell into her boat, and the boat floated aimlessly in one place for a long time" (ibid., 199).

With the loss of her home, Mironovna loses her reason to be; she, like her boat, becomes aimless.

In these scenes Prishvin captures what happened in reality. The ultimate travesty of the flooding—coffins floating away from cemeteries—calls forth only sympathy for the Old Believers and disdain for progress. By flooding the islands, the Belomor project actually profanes holy ground. This image begs the question—how can such a project be justified and succeed in the face of such desecration?

Note that Prishvin never takes up the ideas of perekovka, socialist construction, or Bolshevik ideology directly. Instead, and therein lies the power of the novel, he chooses to convey his overall perception of Belomor through the interaction among nature, the Old Believers, and the new Soviet men and women. When a river that had been dammed begins to flow again, the project boss exclaims, "There are no more questions, no more arguments, look out the window yourselves. Out there is one and the same answer: the river has begun to flow" (ibid., 185). The narration continues, "Thus began this strange battle of eternally uniting the power of the water with the power of human will and reason. 'I order it!' said the person having power over nature" (ibid.). Prishvin presents this conflict not as an issue of Soviet will versus the environment but as *human* will versus the environment. In so doing, he raises the discussion to a higher level beyond the juxtaposition of texts supportive or unsupportive of the ideology.

He offers a view of Belomor that differs markedly from its official interpretation and questions the very tenets that were used to justify the project. It is as if two metaphorical worlds collide—the industrial versus the natural—and battle to a draw. Progress does proceed, but nature continues to assert itself. That the Old Believers fall victim to the very nature they so respect makes the ending of the novel even more tragic and nullifies any positive effect that industrial progress might have realized. In this regard, his understated conclusion to the novel captures a certain reality of the situation more truthfully than any other Belomor account.

The tension between the two ways of life that Prishvin illustrates moves beyond the conflict between industrialization and nature. In pursuing industrialization, the Soviet Union sought to achieve parity with, even superiority, over the West. But the model that propelled this industrial push was a *Western* model of progress, against which *The Tsar's Road* appears to protest. The poignancy and persuasiveness of his narrative underscores his dislike of that progress, and his affinity for Russian thought and Russian traditions. In this regard he reiterates Kluyev's active opposition to Western inroads and to the forsaking of inherently Russian traditions. While Kluyev concentrates his disapproval in a dense, poetic framework, Prishvin sustains the intensity of his message through a longer, more complicated narrative. As a result, Prishvin produces a work that no less aggressively illustrates his philosophy.

He achieves this result because he relies on actual, documented occurrences during the construction of the Belomor Canal. The damming of waterfalls, the flooding of Old Believer settlements, the destruction of houses, livestock, and cemeteries all occurred. The officially accepted ideology does not motivate the progression of the narrative; Prishvin's own philosophical musings do.

If each discourse on Belomor engages in a power struggle with the others, then Prishvin's narrative emerges as one of the most powerful, precisely because it contrasts so sharply with other literary responses. *The Tsar's Road*, the most formally fictional of the accounts, provides a kind of truth that the most documentary, and therefore supposedly most factual account, *The History of Construction*, could not.

Taken as a whole, each of these literary responses to the Belomor project brings to the discussion an added perspective and dimension of truth. In addition, each reaction manipulates its mode of discourse in order to accommodate and convey its author's point of view. Interestingly, a last example of literary response tries to achieve this goal in a unique way. The English translation of *The History of Construction* seems to parallel the original text, but ends up adjusting the resulting narrative in such a way that it almost outpropagandizes the original. In so doing, it asserts itself in the power struggle among the texts that sought to capture the essence of Belomor.

Reforging in Translation

At one time or another we all have struggled with a translation that does not succeed. Try as we might, we simply cannot get the words right, or we think we are not doing justice to the spirit of the original, or we convince ourselves that there is no adequate equivalent for a word or phrase. In common parlance, something often gets "lost in the translation." Such difficulties with interpreting a text are commonplace, and a variety of critical studies on translation discusses these problems in great detail.[9] But what is less commonly discussed, though no less important, are the issues that obtain when a problematic text faces translation.

The term *problematic* presupposes that certain writings, in their original language, carry with them particular moral, ethical, or ideological concerns that cannot be separated from the text. To ignore these concerns produces a translation that, while falling under the general rubric of "equivalence," fails to capture adequately the content, form, and context of the original. Some contend that such omissions are "immoral" (Bassnett-McGuire, 22); the translator must understand that the text is part of a system from which it cannot be divorced, even in another language (ibid., 77). In effect, to quote Susan Bassnett-McGuire, "the translator is first a reader then a writer, and in the process of reading he or she must take a position" (ibid., 78). As Bassnett-McGuire further argues, "Quite clearly, the idea of the reader as translator and the enormous freedom this vision bestows must be handled responsibly. The reader/translator who does not acknowledge the dialectical materialist basis of Brecht's plays or who misses the irony in Shakespeare's sonnets . . . is upsetting the balance of power by treating the original as his own property. And all these elements can be missed if the reading does not take into full account the overall structuring of the work and its relation to the time and place of its production" (ibid., 79–80). A successful translation can never stress content at the expense of its total structure; we need to understand the totality of a work before we translate even the first word. As she concludes, "If the translator . . . handles sentences for their specific content alone, the outcome will involve a loss of dimension" (ibid., 115).

Based on this reasoning, it is clear that the English version of *The History of Construction,* rendered as *Belomor: An Account of the Construction of the Great Canal between the White Sea and the Baltic Sea,*[10] while not a successful translation, presents one more literary response to Belomor. Unlike the Russian original, the English translation of the Belomor volume stresses content at the expense of the total structure and the context in which it was written. On contextual, structural, lexical, and ideological levels the anonymous translators have taken certain liberties with the text, thereby prompting the loss of dimension of which Bassnett-McGuire writes. While the translation preserves many of the Belomor volume's original themes, especially the theme of reforging, it dilutes the impact of the text to the point of creating a "new" text that sabotages the integrity of the original.

The inadequacy of the English version is compounded by the fact that there is a paucity of background information concerning how the Belomor volume came to be translated at all. Never are the translators, always referred to in the plural, identified by name. The only clue to their identities appears in the publisher's note, which prefaces the text and stipulates, "The English translation used in ths edition was prepared in Moscow from the Russian edition" (*Belomor,* ii). Since the text was prepared in Moscow, it is likely that the translators were Russians who were operating under strict ideological guidelines at the behest of the Soviet regime. Hence, the English version of the book was intended as a propaganda ploy to present the Belomor episode to English readers in a palatable version. This conclusion is not unjustified, given the Soviet propaganda campaign directed at the West and the apparent need to legisimize events like the construction of the Canal.

While we continue to learn more about the Soviet context in which the Belomor volume was published, the context that produced the English version is less clear. Data that document the non-Russian participants in the project are scant. To date, there is no evidence to suggest that the American Communist Party in some way funded the publication of *The History of Construction* in English. Aside from the publishers, Harrison Smith and Robert Haas, only two other contributors are cited as having helped prepare the manuscript. The publisher's note thanks a certain May O'Callaghan who helped "in the work of collating the translation with the Russian edition, and checking and reading the proofs" (ibid.). Both the identity of May O'Callaghan and the reasons behind her participation in the project remain a mystery. In addition, we must take O'Callaghan to task for improper collation, given the English version's complete disregard for the narrative progression of the Russian original.

Less is known about Amabel Williams-Ellis, the editor of the English version and author of its introduction. In it Williams-Ellis affirms that "the authors' own notes on the writing of the book (including an amazing time schedule) seem to the present writer so novel and so interesting that she has persuaded the translators to include them in the English edition" (ibid., vi), which suggests that she had contact with the Russian translators as well as input into the translation project. Where these meetings took place or how the interactions occurred are unclear. But her familiarity with the translators suggests a certain closeness to the ideology and the purveyors of it.

More important, Williams-Ellis's introduction reveals her position vis-à-vis the text and casts the narrative in a positive light, a further indication of her ideological bent. To her credit, she focused on two valid aspects of *The History of Construction:* its description of the program of reforging and its status as a work of collective authorship. As she asserts, "This book answers two questions: the first, and most often asked is, 'What happens to political prisoners in the USSR?' . . . Of the second less is heard, but it is one that I, as a writer, have often asked, and to which I had not until now managed to get a comprehensible answer. What—I wanted to know—is this method that Russian writers have of writing a book as a group? What is 'group composition'?" (ibid., v). She poses valid questions; however, her answers to these questions are less satisfying.

In response to her first question, Williams-Ellis notes, "This tale of the accomplishment of a ticklish engineering job, in the middle of primeval forests, by tens of thousands of enemies of the State helped—or should it be guarded—by only thirty-seven GPU officers, is one of the most exciting stories that has ever appeared in print" (ibid., vi). Such an assessment buttresses the translators' positive disposition toward the Belomor project in spite of countless inaccuracies. In fact, the contingent of OGPU officers standing guard on the Canal numbered far above thirty-seven. In addition, the choice of "ticklish" to describe the engineering feat accomplished at Belomor and the hardships that accompanied it does not even begin to characterize the enormous physical challenge that the construction of the Canal posed. In fact, Williams-Ellis concludes, "For the first time we are here told the story of what goes on in a Russian labour camp, and gain some insight into the motives and trains of thought which led skilled and intelligent engineers to take up the dangerous work of sabotage" (ibid., vii). The opposite is, in fact, true, for the Belomor volume, regardless of what language it is in, presents only one carefully scripted variant of life in a Soviet labor camp.

While the vantage point of the late twentieth century makes it difficult to believe that Williams-Ellis could have been so naive as to sympathetically embrace the Belomor volume, it is not beyond the realm of possibility. Any number of factors, ranging from genuine belief in the cause to limited access to information could have shaped her interpretation. More important, she shares the dilemma faced by any reader of the English version—she is at the mercy of translators who, for all intents and purposes, wrote a new book. The lack of lexical consistency in translation, coupled with the total rearrangement of every segment of the text, produces a work that only marginally mirrors the original *The History of Construction*.

Williams-Ellis's enthusiastic assessment of the Belomor volume extends to the idea of collective authorship. She claims that "if group composition can produce this sort of thing it is worth enquiring into" (ibid., vi). According to her, collective authorship "enshrine[s] some of the best pieces of comic writing that even Russian literature can afford" (ibid.). Her judgment that parts of *The History of Construction* are comic both shocks and perplexes. And no single narrative in the Belomor volume, perhaps except for Zoshchenko's contribution, contains any linkage with the rich tradition of the comic in Russian literature. Nevertheless, she concludes that "for the first time a book composed by the new and peculiar method of group composition is available to the English reader. Finally, this tale of Belomorstroy gives us the thing of which no reader ever tires, a series of exquisitely observed, sometimes comic, sometimes tragic stories of vivid individual experience" (ibid., vii). Such a conclusion is not far-fetched if examined in light of the argument that the writers indeed succeeded in creating an innovative literary work that defied conventional classification.

While there is little background information to definitively establish Williams-Ellis's political and ideological positions, data regarding the publishing house that produced the English version of the Belomor volume lend some insight into how and why the book was produced.[11] The Harrison Smith of Harrison Smith and Robert Haas Publishers originally worked for Harcourt Press but quit over their refusal to publish William Faulkner's *The Sound and the Fury*. After a brief partnership with the British publisher Jonathan Cape, Smith founded his own publishing house in 1931, bringing several authors, including Faulkner, with him. Robert Haas joined the firm in 1932, and they remained an independent company until they were acquired by Random House in 1936. In addition to Faulkner, Smith and Haas published works by Isak Dineson, Antoine de Saint Exu-péry, and André Malraux, as well as the Babar the Elephant books. Imagine—from Belomor to Babar!

Two key elements in Harrison Smith's career stand out and suggest that, in addition to his liberal views, he had a more than passing interest in Russia. Prior to his hiring at Harcourt in the late twenties, he spent six months writing freelance magazine articles in Russia and the Far East; immediately prior to his employment at Harcourt he was editor of the *Foreign Press Service*. In addition, while he was Jonathan Cape's partner, Smith published Maurice Hindus and Maxim Gorky, among others. It is highly probable that Smith pursued the Belomor project because of his familiarity with the young Soviet state and a genuine interest in things Russian.

This background information surrounding the publication of the English version does little to ameliorate the dissatisfaction we feel when comparing it with the Russian original. Numerous structural and lexical deviations, as well as ideological exclusions, mar the translation. While it is impossible to elaborate on each one, the following discussion introduces those elements that immediately strike the reader and recast the entire structure of the text. In these examples, lexical items cannot be divorced from their places in the structure of the narrative.

Consider, for example, the title of the volume in Russian, *Istoriia stroitel'stva Belomorsko-Baltiiskogo Kanala imeni Stalina*, which appears in the English variant as *Belomor: An Account of the Construction of the*

Great Canal between the White Sea and the Baltic Sea. No mention of Stalin is made, in spite of the fact that the English translation appeared in 1935 and that Stalin was credited with initiating the Belomor project. In addition, the English list of contributors omits two authors, Mikhail Kozakov and A. Tikhonov; Tikhonov's name appears in all three Russian printings of the book, while Kozakov's appears in two, not unexpected in light of Koza-kov's impending arrest. Yet the translators never note which Russian edition was used. Are we to assume that the translators based their work on the third Russian printing of the Belomor volume, the one that omits Koza-kov's name? Or were they privy to another edition, perhaps unpublished, that omitted Tikhonov's name as well as Kozakov's? The translators neglect to explain any of their choices.

To the translators' credit, they include elements of the original text that are important to the overall apprehension of the work. For example, they accurately present a "Calendar of the Work" (ibid., ix), which highlights the dates in the history of the writing of the book and the rapidity with which it was written. In addition, the translators provide a bibliography that cites source materials that the Belomor authors consulted in producing the text. While the Russian version lists the sources in telegraphic, numerical order, the translators create a three-paragraph narrative that lists both specific documents and general sources of information; however they omit any direct references to the GULag or to specific OGPU officers, while including a discussion of the illustrators and printers. From an ideological standpoint, it is as if the translators were striving to de-politicize and de-ideologize the translation in an effort to make it more approachable and less didactic. Perhaps they believed that this didactic function, while appropriate for a Soviet audience, held no purpose for English readers because they did not live in the Soviet Union or did not share the ideology. An overtly didactic tone might alienate readers, a risk not worth taking in such a stridently propagandistic piece.

The translators include a paragraph of profound importance to readers. Their "Note on the Method of Writing 'Belomor'" parallels a brief note that accompanies the list of authors in the Russian version. The English version states: "All the thirty-four authors take full responsibility for the text. They helped one another, corrected one another. On this account it is difficult to indicate just who wrote the various sections. But the fact must be stressed that the real authors of the entire book are the workers who collaborated in the construction of the historic White Sea–Baltic Canal, dedicated to Stalin" (ibid.).

The translation of this passage deviates from the original in two significant ways. Whereas in the Russian no mention is made of the number of writers in the collective, the translator adds the figure thirty-four (it should have been thirty-six). In addition, while the paragraph concludes with the sentence, "But the fact must be stressed that the real authors of the entire book are the workers who collaborated in the construction of the historic White Sea–Baltic Canal, dedicated to Stalin," the Russian version reads, "Here we point out the authors of the basic sections that went into this or that chapter, while reminding [the reader] once again, that the real authors of the entire book are members of the whole team that worked on *The History of the Stalin White Sea–Baltic Canal* ["My ukazyvaem zdes' avtorov osnovnykh chastei, voshedshikh v tu ili inuiu glavu, eshche raz napominaia, chto deistvitel'nym avtorom vsei knigi iavliaetsia polnyi sostav rabotavshikh nad *Istoriei Belomorsko-baltiiskogo kanala imeni Stalina*"] (*HC*, vii). The translators incorrectly ascribe the authorship of the Belomor volume not to the writers' collective but to the actual workers on the Canal, thereby modifying how English readers perceive the nature of collective authorship. These minor translation inconsistencies recur in the English version and produce subtle shifts in meaning.

Moreover, the Russian edition lists every author who participated in the writing of a particular chapter, from single-author chapters such as those penned by Gorky and Zoshchenko to chapters with multiple authors. The English translation omits the list of authors ascribed to each chapter, thereby weakening the impression of collective authorship. The English-language reader fails to realize the precise nature of collective authorship because, aside from the brief paragraph cited and the editor's comments elsewhere, no structural element of the text calls attention to it.

Other, seemingly harmless structural changes litter the English translation, all of which contribute to the overall inaccurate rendering of the text from Russian into English. For instance, the translators increase the number of chapters from fifteen to thirty-five, frequently calling several textual segments chapters, when in the Russian original they are discrete sections within a larger chapter. The English version's final chapter, chapter 35, is rendered as "Maxim Gorky Sums Up." It serves as the English counterpart to chapter 15 in the Belomor volume, "First Experience" [Pervyj opyt]. While correctly attributing this segment to Gorky, the translators include only part of the Russian original, thus disrupting the entire structure of the text; Gorky authored the first and last chapters of the Belomor volume, thereby framing the entire narrative both structurally and ideologically. It is no small matter that Gorky, the inspiration behind not only the Belomor volume but the whole History of Factories and Plants series as well, should command the first and last word of *The History of Construction*.

Gorky's framing texts are crucially important when we consider that his chapter 1, "The Truth of Socialism" [*Pravda socializma*], sets the ideological tone of the Belomor volume; it includes the directives of the Central Committee of the CPSU (Communist Party of the Soviet Union) that mandated the production of *The History of Construction* under the direction of the OGPU. The translators omit this chapter entirely, opting to begin their version with a chapter entitled "The Problem," a segment that corresponds not to the actual opening chapter of the Belomor volume but to selected paragraphs from the Russian version's chapter 3, "The GPU, the Engineers, the Project." Segments of this same chapter reappear as chapter 2 of the English translation. Even then, the translator neglects to "begin at the beginning" and instead opens the English version with narrative that in the Russian original is found in section 3 of chapter 3, "The OKB" [The Special Construction Bureau]. Because the English version operates under a different agenda, the ideological underpinnings of the Belomor volume are sacrificed in order to avoid an overtly didactic, overideologized tone.

As the preceding description attests, the organization of the material is so confused and disordered in relation to the Russian original that at times it is difficult to believe the translators based their work on the Russian text. As a result, these structural deficiencies sufficiently indict the entire translation. Yet a look at *how* the translators decoded and recoded the language from Russian into English suggests that, while they generally adhered to the content, the text still bears witness to certain liberties taken at the expense of lexical and narrative accuracy. While space limits us from examining the whole narrative, any given excerpt illustrates this point quite well.

Consider the brief part of the concluding section of the Russian version's chapter 6, "People Change Professions" [*Liudi meniaiut professii*], which appears as section 4 of chapter 15, "The Stable." (See Appendix VI.) A quick perusal reveals that the translators have generally adhered to the spirit and content of the original. Certain structural differences emerge, though, when we note that the translators did not preserve the telegraphic sentence structure that prevails in the second half of the section. Instead they opt to combine a number of sentences into longer paragraphs. While we could argue that the telegraphic sentences in Russian create a more direct, emphatic tone, the basic sense of the passage still translates into the English.

More problematic, however, are the insertions of sentences or phrases that seem to provide additional explanation, but in fact add a value judgment or personal opinion to the narrative. Note the opening lines of the section that in Russian read: "Tak dereviannyi vek Belomorstroia rodil vek zheleznyi. Liudi, kotorye rabotali na mekhbaze, v bolshinstve sluchaev byli liudi ili iz vorovskoi ili iz dereviannoi proselochnoi staroi Rossii" [And so the wooden age of Belomorstroi gave birth to the iron age. In the majority of cases people who were working in the fur factory were from either (circles of) thieves or from the wooden settlements of Old Russia" (*HC*, 278). In the English version this becomes: "The wooden age of Belomorstroy brought forth an age of iron, but sometimes the transition was very difficult, as witnessed by the story of Balabuk and his ox" (*Belomor*, 199). Arguably, there is nothing in the Russian original that suggests the conclusion that the translators draw; while the reader might assume that the transition from the wooden age to the iron age is difficult, the simple statement in Russian that the bulk of workers at the fur factory were thieves and peasants does not necessarily prompt the inference that their transformation into Soviet workers was difficult. In this instance the translators add a value judgment by excluding the direct references to thieves and old Russian rural life, as if to pretend that there are no thieves in the Soviet Union and that old Russian rural life, an allusion to prerevolutionary Russia, need not be included in this "Soviet" text.

Similarly, the second sentence in the third paragraph in the Russian original differs markedly in tone and lexicon from its English equivalent. Russian words such as *naemnyi*, which means *hired*, and *drat' shkuru*, which means *to flay*, are softened in the English to *laborers* and *overwork* or *sweated* respectively. This stylistic softening is applied consistently throughout the entire translation, e.g. the narrator's rendering of the two most prominent Chekists' names at Belomor, Kogan (misspelled in the English as *Kagan*) and Firin, both of whom become "our old friend Kagan" (ibid., 327) and "another old friend comrade Firin" (ibid., 328) in the English. It is highly unlikely that any inmate on the Belomor site considered Firin or Kogan his "old friend," and the Russian version does not refer to them as such.

A final example of mistranslation occurs in the paragraph beginning "Okolo Medvezhei gory . . . " [Near Bear Mountain]. The last sentence reads: "Vspakhannoe pole navelo na nego tosklivye vospominaniia" [The ploughed fields brought him anguished memories] (*HC*, 278), which is translated into English as: "The ploughed fields to his left brought him sad memories" (*Belomor*, 200). While it is debatable whether or not *tosklivye* is best translated as *sad, melancholy,* or *depressed* (although in this instance *melancholy, depressed,* or *anguished* seem less-diluted variants and more appropriate to the context than *sad*), we can only conclude that the translators accidentally transposed *navelo* to *nalevo* and rendered it incorrectly.

Many elements of the text imply that the translators not only applauded the Belomor project but strove in the English text to make the whole episode more palatable to their readers. This inference suggests that the translators could have feared that without this modification of language and tone, English-language readers might surmise that the Belomor episode really was a life-threatening, highly questionable, terror-inducing project. Softening certain elements and altering the presentation of the material would serve to mitigate reader perception of the event, thereby making it less damnable.

That *The History of Construction* was translated at all attests to the perceived importance of Belomor both in Russia and, to a certain extent, abroad. In fact, only a few contemporary American and British newspapers reported on the Belomor Canal.[12] Yet familiarity with the Russian text makes its English version unsatisfying. While we benefit from knowing how the Belomor Canal was constructed and how the program of reforging was implemented, we lose the artistic and ideological concerns that were vital to the overall presentation of material.

Yet an analysis of the English translation is not without value. We can consider the English variant yet another literary response to the Belomor project, perhaps no less important than the other literary responses discussed previously. Its translators seemed to have a good understanding of the ideology and expectations of an English-speaking audience. By presenting Belomor as a success in reforging prison inmates, *The History of Construction* provides a tempting alternative to the American prison system. Using forced labor on large construction projects with the goal of turning those inmates into new citizens had merit. Perhaps the translation's unstated intent also was to depict the USSR as a "normal" country that was not a dictatorship but a forward-thinking state that worked to improve the lot of its citizens.

At least the English translation made *The History of Construction* accessible to English readers so that they could glean these suppositions from the Belomor volume. Publicizing these achievements of Soviet industrialization to an English-speaking audience would serve to promote the USSR among some of the world's greatest powers—England and the United States. The Belomor volume in English potentially had vast propaganda value, a possibility clearly not lost on those who organized its publication in the United

States. The English translation did advertise a remarkable construction feat; the twist was that the Belomor Canal was a stunning feat of manual labor, not of technological progress.

The Documenting of History as a Power Relationship

As Foucault argues, an event, presumably any historical event, can be more broadly and fully interpreted if we examine the sum total of its constituent discursive parts. This kind of analysis means that the richest interpretation of an historical event occurs when the discourses surrounding it are analyzed and perceived as a totality. Initially no single narrative dominates, for each narrative brings to the interpretation of the event an insight into the true nature of the whole. As Foucault demonstrates in *I, Pierre Riviere,* discourses "battle" each other to become the dominant narrative about a particular event.[13] According to Foucault, this process results in a discursive power struggle in which the strongest discourse wins out and presents itself as the narrative closest to the truth.

This supposition begs the issue of context. In the Soviet context the dominant narrative was *The History of Construction,* because during the time in which it was written the Soviet readership had access to neither Kluyev's nor Prishvin's account of the Canal. In the context in which the Belomor event unfolded there was a very real power struggle for control of Soviet literature. Therefore, if we use the Foucault model within the narrow confines of the actual time in which the Belomor project was first presented and analyzed, then *The History of Construction* without question emerges as the dominant discourse on the subject, with journalistic accounts a distant second. Inmate poems were not read by the general public, and, given the limited circulation of Simonov's poems, many readers probably did not know of them either. An analysis of the convergence of discourses would have been impossible at the time.

The more interesting and knotty interpretive problem obtains in our contemporary context because we enjoy the luxury of both hindsight and of access to previously inaccessible materials. The diversity of response to which we have access expands the interpretive possibilities far beyond that which was permissible and feasible in 1934.

When we, as late twentieth-century readers, closely examine the companion works to *The History of Construction,* we find texts that equal, even surpass it in terms of the power of the message and its presentation. Certainly Prishvin's and Kluyev's contributions to the discourse about Belomor convincingly and elegantly convey their vision of the reality of the Canal project.

Does this mean, then, that they emerge victorious in the present struggle among the texts for discursive supremacy? Arguably, they are the most technically and thematically sophisticated and well crafted; but they are also the texts most consistent with the traditional Western view of the Belomor Canal project and its attendant issues, and therefore to many readers the most appealing or comprehensible presentations of that event. As such they describe one kind of reality in the waterway project but not the complete reality.

We gain a wider view of the reality of Belomor if we accept that each Belomor narrative brings to the event a particular truth, that, when added to the other truths provided by other narratives, forms a more complete picture of this historical moment. Conversely, the relationship of language and discursive method forces us to view this particular historical moment from distinct standpoints that are shaped by the form through which the author chooses to present his reading of the event. Each discrete part not only contributes to our comprehension of the event but also problematizes the Belomor project even more and challenges any traditional view. In effect, even though the early 1930s was a very complex era, the process through which we can make sense of that era is now more complicated.

In addition, each kind of discourse illuminates one segment of reality. For example, while *The History of Construction,* as a prime example of socialist realism, illustrates the spirit of the times—the energy behind and enthusiasm for industrialization and reforging—Prishvin's novelistic discourse brings to the fore the conflict between progress and nature, between Russian and Western traditions. Kluyev's poetic treatment injects an even stronger view of the Russian versus Western dichotomy. To borrow Bakhtin's term, the polyphony of voices produces not the monopoly of one discursive voice, but truth. The most startling by-product of the polyphonic reading of the event is that even socialist realism, a discursive approach that has often been thought of as monologic, contributes to our understanding of the truth of what happened at Belomor: Thousands of people were enthusiastic about remaking people and nature, and this element of the Belomor (hi)story cannot be forgotten.[14] In spite of the discursive tactics and the thematic intent of the authors, no one text monopolizes (or monologizes) the truth.

5
The Legacy of Belomor

> In our attempt to re-create the historical landscape of the "Great Terror" through its "intimate" chronicles, we certainly share a certain helplessness in regard to the "mystery" of those times that cannot be thoroughly explained, but we also have the responsibility of listening to those voices that have come to us and should remain, as much as possible, the subjects of their stories.
>
> "Editors' Introduction," *Intimacy and Terror*

While the diaries the editors of *Intimacy and Terror* collected were written during the years 1934–1939, the editors' comments are no less appropriate to the earlier period discussed in this book. For many readers and commentators the Belomor volume and the Belomor episode were and remain a mystery, in the sense that we probably will never know what motivated the writers to participate—was it fear, cowardice, real belief in the new system?—nor will we ever know exactly what went on during the twenty months of the construction of the Canal. I, too, have felt a certain "helplessness" in trying to reconstruct the construction of the Belomor Canal and the production of the Belomor volume and other literary works dedicated to the Canal. By the same token, it is hoped that the voices of those who built the Canal, wrote the Belomor *History*, and responded in other ways to the waterway project have been heard.

But to hear these voices is not enough if we are to probe more deeply into the Belomor project in the hope of achieving a better understanding of it. While it might be impossible to reach a complete understanding of the event and its texts, this exploration of Belomor has demonstrated that it is possible to uncover a certain kind of truth that has been all but neglected in previous scholarship and critical literature on Belomor. The issue here is not whether it is a truth that we find compatible with our sensibilities. Rather, the issue is that the Belomor project is a much more complicated and significant moment in Soviet literary history and history in general than has been previously realized.

In addition to the moments of truth revealed in this discussion, other conclusions can be drawn that bring some closure to this particular chapter in the Belomor history. Is there something we can learn from the Canal beyond the traditional lessons of moral outrage and ethical indignation? Does Belomor still have some significance and relevance in our contemporary milieu, be it Russian or Western? These questions can be answered in the affirmative; in considering the answers, we contemporize Belomor with our own age.

Writers, Workers, and OGPU Men

The interaction among these three groups formed the basis for the discourse on Belomor. Yet the results of that interaction played out differently for each group in spite of their common bond in the project.

For writers, and for literature in general, Belomor proved to be a fundamental event in shaping the response of writers to large construction projects, the strategies of collective authorship, and the role of literature in the "new" Soviet society. As we have seen, *The History of Construction* remains the epitome of collective authorship based not only on the fact that the Writers Brigade wrote it, but also on the fact that it truly was a collaborative work. The goal of this collaboration was to encourage writers to work not as individuals but as a unified whole to produce a literature worthy of the accomplishments of the young Soviet state and reflective of the prevailing political program. That the collaboration worked at all is quite remarkable; that it was unsustainable is no surprise.

Beyond the success or failure of collaborative authorship is the notion that collaboration can be a positive way to channel the enthusiasm of a particular moment so as to capture both the moment and the enthusiasm in all of its shades of intensity. Ostensibly collective authorship had the power to do that but fell victim to the shift in politics and literary policy in the mid-thirties. Instead of a collective mass of indistinguishable faces, individual heroes who accomplished great deeds were to be the models for new Soviet citizens.

Nevertheless, *The History of Construction*—as the most successful work of collective authorship in Soviet literature and the first text devoted to Belomor—remains the pivot around which all other narratives on the subject coalesce. In documenting the actual event, *The History* informs all narratives produced subsequent to it. As a result, we are left with a potentially rich intergeneric and intertextual dialogue that, while suggested by this study, has yet to be fully explored and remains a rich source for further inquiry.

In addition, privileging *The History of Construction* as the primary text on the Belomor Canal allows us to draw some conclusions as to the nature of literary life and the repercussions for literary history that such a troubling work produces. Most obviously, how the book came to be written demonstrates the complex, often contradictory nature of literary life in the early 1930s. The history of *The History of Construction* further buttresses the widely accepted notion that this period in Soviet literature marked a time of upheaval in the attempt to subjugate literature to ideology. The background of the Belomor volume further supports recent scholarship on Soviet literary history in that it shows the attempt, most prominently by Gorky, to join disparate parts into a unified whole for the purpose of creating a new literature. This theme of newness, discussed extensively by Katerina Clark, resonates in the writing process of the Belomor volume. It marked the culmination of the drive to have "new" Soviet writers compose the "new" history of the "new" Soviet Union through "new" construction projects that produced "new" Soviet men and women. Belomor, both the event and the history of it, epitomized this push toward the new.

This push contributed to the production of an original literary prototype that would continue to operate throughout the course of Soviet literature. The reforged worker, the quintessential new Soviet man, was a product of Belomor, both in a literal and figurative sense. The Canal project literally produced new men and women, who had arrived at Belomor unskilled and illiterate and who left the project with modest literacy and job skills; this reforging applied uniformly to common criminals but was not the case for all Belomor inmates. Nevertheless, according to inmate testimonials, there were people who left Belomor feeling as if they had accomplished a great task and were the better for it. One inmate, Aleksandra Ivanovna Ivanova, wrote in a letter of thanks to the head of the GULag, Matvei Berman: "Comrade Director, I hurry to thank you for helping me to move to the correct path of life. . . . Now I'm working. . . . I have lots of free time. I signed up for the club ROKK [No indication as to what this was, CR] and for the athletic club Dynamo where I'll be learning how to ice-skate. They've also given me books and newspapers from the library. I read and I like it much better that I am a working member of society, and I study and see what use I will be to the state. . . . I give you my word that I will work honestly."[1] Although some might question the authenticity of Ivanova's letter, the archival document is written in longhand and in a few spots contains misspellings in Russian. Was she coached to write this letter? Quite possibly. Does this circumstance at all lessen the level of her enthusiasm for the project or the genuiness of her sentiment? No, because this document, like many others cited in this book, speaks to the natural enthusiasm that was evident in the Belomor project, in spite of our expectations to the contrary. Ivanova's letter captures some of the spirit of the time, and as such presents a valuable insight into one person's experience.

On the figurative level, writers were able to create a literary type who epitomized the program of reforging. *The History of Construction* is full of the accounts of those who were reforged and those who became models of reforging. The focus on the Belomor volume is not to suggest that it was the only literary source for this kind of role model. That its type recurred in other works, most prominently in Pogodin's *The Aristocrats,* testifies to the adaptability of the model and its appropriateness for the time. Other novels, such as Ostrovsky's *How the Steel Was Tempered* and Kataev's *Time, Forward!*, not only developed the type but added new dimensions to the portrayal of it. Nonetheless, the Belomor volume, thanks to its documentarian style and devotion to the idea of reforging, stands as the central work in locating this literary "positive hero" in real circumstances.

Similarly, the Belomor volume also contributed the "mentor" type, which would be a recurring feature in socialist realist narratives. OGPU men such as Kogan and Rapoport were presented as living paragons to emulate. In their leather jackets and with their keen intellect (according to the Belomor volume), they represented all that was positive and worthy in a mentor. What the authors of *The History of Construction*, like the OGPU men themselves, could not know was that almost the entire Belomor administration was obliterated in the purges. As a result, this particular model that was engendered by Belomor needed to be expunged from collective consciousness, the very same collective consciousness that the Canal project and its OGPU leaders had sought to foster. The disappearance of *The History of Construction* from availability to the reading public was a way to prevent these purportedly troublesome mentor types from reaching a wider audience.

Yet, just as we know that, as Bulgakov wrote, "manuscripts don't burn," we also know that the legacy of a project the magnitude of Belomor could not and would not disappear from public consciousness. The lingering psychological and ideological effects, like the physical manifestations of the project—the Canal itself and the cigarettes named after it—have not disappeared; they are simply more difficult to detect.

The Broader Perspective

Part of the picture that emerges from the Belomor episode is the totality of the project: It was all-encompassing and included work, a modest amount of job training, a newspaper, music, theater, poetry, ideologically based projects, supervision by the highest levels of government (Yagoda and Berman), education for some, and struggles with nonbelievers.[2] The Canal project marked the first organized attempt to reforge people, to transplant one psychology, one set of attitudes and values, with another.

As a result of this massive effort, Belomor was, perhaps, the first and last great attempt to reforge; it was abandoned because the human cost was too high and because it was impossible to sustain such a high level of energy and enthusiasm for a prolonged period of time. Dissent could be quelled only by drowning it out with a huge push to build or produce, but the enormous effort needed to keep up this intense degree of construction and production was too much. However, the grandiosity of the project, the desire to make it bigger and better, is consistent with the Russian character. We recall other efforts reminiscent of Belomor, not least of which was the construction of St. Petersburg.

What is missing in the Canal project that was very much present in the construction of St. Petersburg was a dominant leader who remained visible throughout the endeavor. In the written accounts about the waterway, Stalin is strangely absent. We hear about him only as the great generator of global ideas. Stalin never visits the construction in progress, and when he finally sees the completed Canal, he complains about its size. While his name is referred to in *The History of Construction,* he is very much missing from any other narrative on Belomor. He is not the focus; the people who carry out his ideas are. The texts examined here that are sympathetic to Soviet power ultimately support the argument that the implementation of policy during Stalinism did not necessarily operate from the top down. Contrary to the totalitarian model, lesser figures played important roles in the implementation of programs, plans, and ideas that could have been, but were not necessarily, spawned at the top.

Instead, in every text about Belomor we find the emphasis on the person whom Clark calls the "little hero," the canalworker, engineer, or criminal who is reforged and contributes to the completion of the project. Even those narratives not sympathetic to the cause—Kluyev's "Ruin" and Prishvin's *The Tsar's Road*—while condemning the larger picture, do not condemn the man. Rather they focus on the people who do the work, face the inevitability of the project, or suffer from its excesses. Precisely the portrayals of these little heroes who accomplish big deeds bring to the reader the kind of truth about Belomor that has gone unnoticed. Even *The History of Construction,* for all its emphasis on the grandeur of the project and its reflection of the ideology, distills away to a series of stories about the "little people" who make the project work.

As a result of all these factors, Belomor presents itself to us as a new paradigm that requires a new framework for analysis. The preceding chapters have attempted to apply different kinds of analytical models, from White's vision of emplotment to Foucault's model of converging discourses, in order to tap into the different kinds of insights that Belomor can provide. But what are some of those insights?

First, the Belomor project legitimized, even if only for those who participated in it, the practice of using forced labor for large-scale construction projects. As such, it bred an entire cultural phenomenon—Soviet camp literature and culture—that survives today, predominantly in its literary manifestations and survivors' memories. On a more subtle level, the Canal project engendered the promotion of collective literary production. Even if no other work of literature was produced in a collective fashion like the Belomor volume, the whole motivation for collective authorship—the attempt to subjugate many voices to one—persisted throughout the Stalinist epoch and beyond. Arguably, the practice of literary censorship sustained the practice of collective authorship in its own peculiar way.

The legacy of such a practice continues in two diametrically opposed ways. On the one hand, the subjugation of many voices to one in fact promoted the opposite effect, for individuality and creativity could not be suppressed forever. Eventually, as more recent Soviet literary history suggests, individual creativity won out. On the other hand, the whole notion of a collective mentality that unquestionably has prerevolutionary roots was institutionalized in part as the result of Belomor. The most shocking recent manifestation of this psychology was apparent in the comments of the first lock operator on the Canal. When reminded of the immense suffering and atrocities that marked its construction, he retorted, "Nothing happens without some victims."[3] According to this thinking, as long as the collective good does not suffer, then any means can be used to achieve the stated goals, a rationale quite contrary to Kluyev's, Prishvin's, and that of many of their predecessors and successors.

In addition, the emphasis on the OGPU so readily apparent in the Canal project cannot be understated, especially given subsequent events in the Soviet Union. The OGPU assumption of responsibility for building the Belomor Canal and for producing the Belomor volume justified the use of terror to achieve any other goal in Soviet society. While the use of terror reached its apex in the late 1930s, it did not disappear until the demise of the Soviet Union. Even today, the spectre of an all-powerful KGB still haunts many Russians and non-Russians alike.

The true legacy of Belomor persists, even to this day, in the last shreds of the program of perekovka. On the most obvious level, perekovka helped redefine literary production, physically changed the Russian landscape, and reforged thousands of criminals by turning them into workers. The most dynamic and essential element of perekovka, however, emanated from its impulse to change a person's attitudes toward his work, his society, his country, and, most important, himself. While perekovka did not and probably could not reshape everyone whom it encountered, it nonetheless set in motion the idea that people could be changed and remolded to fit an ideology. The process of perekovka, although officially downplayed after the First Five-Year Plan, remained in force in society and continued to propel not only positive heroes in socialist realist literature but average citizens in daily life as well.

Lest we think that perekovka represents a relic of faulty ideology and broken social systems, we need to simply look around at our own circumstances. Perekovka obtains every time one group tries to remake another in its image or attempts to bend someone's thinking in order to bring them in line with a predominant ideology. The difference, however, between perekovka as it was implemented in the early 1930s and its implementation now is one of circumstance and perspective. While we might not admit to it, miniature reforgings occur each time a political or religious group tries to remake prospective followers into the prototypical member of the organization. This objective is achieved not so much through deed as through thought; the significant difference between it and the perekovka of Belomor is a difference in how we perceive the reforging. That some writers in the Writers Brigade endorsed perekovka and believed in its potential reinforces this contention.

Arguably, current events in Russia demonstrate even more forcefully the lingering influence of perekovka. Witness the recent celebration of the 850th anniversary of Moscow's founding. The city's mayor, Yuri Luzhkov, spared nothing in trying to (re)create, for all intents and purposes, a new Moscow. In fact, it has been suggested that the massive rebuilding and refurbishing of Moscow, from the reconstruction of churches and cathedrals razed by Stalin to modern shopping malls and underground parking lots, signifies an attempt to create a new Russian past.[4] The impulse to remake Russia and reconstitute Russian history in service to the government hints at a continuity, if not of practical application, then of psychological disposition. (No one would ever accuse Luzhkov of resorting to Stalinist tactics to finesse sizeable funding for Moscow's restoration, and rightly so.) These most recent efforts to make Russia new—massive building projects and ongoing efforts to encourage a fresh attitude toward work, country, and self—resonate with the not-so-distant strains of perekovka, sans the terror and forced labor that accompanied the program in its original form. The resilience of the idea has not weakened with time.

Does this argument excuse the excesses of Belomor? Absolutely not. But it does suggest that the Canal project can function as a prototype, not only in the Soviet Russian context, for much of what followed it. As such, it invites further consideration of Stalinism, the 1930s, and the legacy of both, within and beyond the confines of Soviet Russian society.

Appendix I

The following list, in Russian alphabetical order, represents the most complete compilation to date of the writers who participated in the Belomor Brigade. While no specific record exists that delineates precisely who participated, this list has been culled from every public pronouncement and personal document that testified to a writer's participation in the brigade. Of the 120 participants, sixty-six are listed here. (It was not possible to find first initials for all the writers.)

A. Avdeenko	M. Kozakov
L. Averbakh	Ia. Kolas
B. Agapov	G. Korabel'nikov
A. Aleksandrovich	Krylov
A. Bezymensky	Kulik
A. Berzin'	Ia. Kupala
S. Budantsev	Kuprianov
S. Bulatov	B. Lapin
P. Vasiliev	A. Lebedenko
E. Gabrilovich	L. Leonov
N. Garnich	V. Lidin
S. Gekht	Liubenko
G. Gauzner	G. Madarev
K. Gorbunov	A. Malyshkin
S. Dikovsky	Maraf
N. Dmitriev	D. Mirsky
K. Zelinsky	N. Nikitin
M. Zoshchenko	L. Nikulin
Vs. Ivanov	V. Pertsov
I. Il'f	E. Petrov
V. Inber	B. Pil'niak
L. Kassil'	N. Pogodin
V. Kataev	Ia. Rykachev
V. Kirshon	M. Ryl'sky
Kovalev	M. Svetlov

L. Seifullina
(?) Selivanovsky
L. Slavin
K. Sobolev
Sokolov
M. Shaginian
Shishkov
A. Tolstoy

K. Trenev
I. Utkin
K. Finn
Z. Khatzrevin
A. Erlikh
N. Iurgin
Iu. Yanovsky
B. Jasensky

Appendix II

The members of the writers' collective that coauthored *The History of Construction*, listed in Russian alphabetical order as they appear in the Belomor volume:

L. Averbakh	V. Kataev
B. Agapov	M. Kozakov
S. Alymov	G. Korabel'nikov
A. Berzin'	B. Lapin
S. Budantsev	A. Lebedenko
S. Bulatov	D. Mirsky
E. Gabrilovich	L. Nikulin
N. Garnich	V. Pertsov
G. Gauzner	Ia. Rykachev
S. Gekht	L. Slavin
K. Gorbunov	A. Tikhonov
M. Gorky	A. Tolstoy
S. Dikovsky	K. Finn
N. Dmitriev	Z. Khatsrevin
K. Zelinsky	V. Shklovsky
M. Zoshchenko	A. Erlikh
Vs. Ivanov	N. Iurgin
Vera Inber	Bruno Jasensky

Appendix III

The Table of Contents of *The History of Construction*, including the authors of each chapter, taken from the first edition prepared for the Seventeenth Party Congress in January 1934.

Chapter 1. The Truth of Socialism
  M. Gor'ky
Chapter 2. The Country and Its Enemies
  G. Gauzner, B. Lapin, L. Slavin
Chapter 3. The GPU, the Engineers, the Project
  S. Budantsev, N. Dmitriev, G. Korabel'nikov, D. Mirsky, V. Pertsov, Ia. Rykachev, V. Shklovsky
Chapter 4. The Prisoners
  K. Gorbunov, Vs. Ivanov, Vera Inber, Z. Khatsrevin, V. Shklovsky
Chapter 5. The Chekists
  S. Alymov, A. Berzin', Vs. Ivanov, V. Kataev, G. Korabel'nikov, L. Nikulin, Ia. Rykachev, V. Shklovsky
Chapter 6. People Change Their Professions
  S. Alymov, A. Berzin', E. Gabrilovich, N. Dmitriev, A. Lebedenko, Z. Khatsrevin, V. Shklovsky
Chapter 7. Canalarmyists
  S. Alymov, A. Berzin', S. Budantsev, S. Dikovsky, N. Dmitriev, Ia. Rykachev, V. Shklovsky
Chapter 8. Tempo and Quality
  B. Agapov, S. Budantsev, N. Garnich, N. Dmitriev, Vera Inber, Ia. Rykachev, V. Shklovsky, N. Iurgin
Chapter 9. Finish Off the Class Enemy
  B. Agapov, K. Zelinsky, Vs. Ivanov, Vera Inber, Z. Khatsrevin, Bruno Jasensky
Chapter 10. The Storming of the Watershed
  K. Gorbunov, N. Dmitriev, Vs. Ivanov, Ia. Rykachev, V. Shklovsky
Chapter 11. Spring Tests the Canal
  B. Agapov, S. Alymov, A. Berzin', S. Dikovsky, N. Dmitriev, Vs. Ivanov, Vera Inber, L. Nikulin, V. Shklovsky, A. Erlikh

Chapter 12. The Story of One Reforging
  M. Zoshchenko
Chapter 13. In Stalin's Name
  S. Bulatov, S. Gekht, Vs. Ivanov, Ia. Rykachev, A. Tolstoy,
  V. Shklovsky
Chapter 14. Comrades
  L. Averbakh, S. Budantsev, G. Gauzner, Vera Inber, B. Lapin, K. Finn,
  N. Iurgin
Chapter 15. The First Experience
  M. Gor'ky

List of Technical Terms and Other Words

Short Bibliography

Appendix IV

Listed below are the names of the administrators and directors of the Belomor Canal construction project and concentration camp.

Genrikh Yagoda, head of the OGPU of the USSR

Belomor Camp

Matvei Berman, director of the GULag system for the USSR
Semyon Firin, assistant director of the GULag, director of the Belomor GULag
Iakov Rapoport, assistant director of the Belomor GULag

Belomor Construction Project

Lazar Kogan, director of the Belomor construction project
Iakov Rapoport, assistant director of the Belomor construction project
Nefteli Frenkel, assistant to the director of the Belomor construction project/director of labor
Nikolai Khrustalev, chief engineer of the Belomor construction project

Appendix V

Shown below are the final and draft versions of a brief excerpt of chapter 4 from *The History of Construction*, "The Prisoners" (145).

Medgora rabotala, ne otkhodia ot stolov, s bessonnitsei, s nepreryvnymi zasedaniiami, s neustannymi telefonnymi zvonkami. Neustanno ona sozdavala kadry, neustanno ikh iskala. Kadrov bylo malo. Vo vse kontsy Soiuza mchatsia upolno mochennye vybirat' nyzhnye kadry iz drugikh lagerei.
    Naprimer nuzhno otpravit' v Voronezh na verbovku. Kogo? Chto ego s konvoem otpravliat'?
    -Doverit'.
    I doveriaiut. I edut.
    V Belbaltlage nachali soveshchat'sia. Unichtozhiv otseplennyi lager', doveriv eti gigantskie prostrantsva byvshim prestupnikam, im skazali dobavok:
    -Davaite soveshchat'sia, kak zhe nam rabotat' vmeste?
    Vspominaiut ob etom kratko: "Kogan vnes shirokuiu struiu khoziaistvennosti". Trudno naiti v mnogochislennykh zapisiakh, prochitannykh nami, opisanie pervykh zasedanii chekistov s zakliuchennymi. Eto molchanie mozhno poniat', no ochen' trudno opisat'. Barak, krasnyi ugolok ili palatka, ili novyi, tol'ko chto otstroennyi klub, ili proektirovochnoe biuro—vse ravno, komnaty napolnilis' i priobreli tsveta neobychaino legkoi novi-zny.
    Chekisty ne uspokaivalis'. Oni trebovali initsiativy. Skazat', chto voz'mem shturmom prirodu, legko, no nuzhno ponimat', kak ee brat'. Ona, eta priroda, khitraia shtuka, ona podvedet takie neozhidannosti, ona zagnet takoe, chto i ruki opustish' i rot raskroesh'. A ona tebe kamen' v rot i ruki tvoi i v topi na veki vechnye.
    Eshche veter ne raskidal zolu ot pervykh kostrov, no na polianakh uzhe poiavilis' vozle barakov bani, prachechnye, iz okon pekaren zapakhlo svezhim khlebom, dveri kukhni shiroko raskryty, povar v belom kitele gromadnoi lozhkoi meshaet v kotle, i kotel pakhnet tak, chto na velikoe mnozhestvo verst krugom ne tol'ko u cheloveka—u murav'ia veselitsia zhivot.
    No chekisty opiat' povtoriaiut:

-Proiavliaite initsiativu! Dvigaites' dal'she!..

Chekisty ne ochen' khvaliat. Oni znaiut kakuiu-to osobuiu meru pokhvaly. Pokhvaly otpuskaetsia stol'ko, chtoby ona pereshla v deistvie, chtoby chelovek rabotal, a ne pyzhilsia i ne pokrikival na drugikh samodovol'no.

No ne nuzhno osobenno obol'shchat'sia. Eshche mnogie iz tridtsatipiatnikov vysmatrivaiut tropy i sostavliaiut marshruty begstva. Pravda, ne tak-to daleko granitsa, burzhuaznye strany, no tridtsatipiatniku khochetsia v svoi goroda. Znakomye ulitsy, znakomye vyveski, znakomye den'gi, no chuzhoi iazyk znaiut . . .

Draft manuscript of the excerpt cited above which contains editorial cuts and comments, as well as Vs. Ivanov's name in the left margins. (GARF, f. 7952, op. 7, d. 59, ll. 23-25).

– 10 –

и ржаньем лошадей, но пришел совсем другим.

Медгора работала, не отходя от столов, с бессонницей, с непрерывными заседаниями, с неустанными телефонными звонками. Неустанно она создавала кадры, неустанно их искала. Кадров было мало. Во все концы Союза мчатся уполномоченные выбирать нужные кадры из лагерей. Например, нужно отправить в Воронеж на вербовку. Что его с конвоем отправлять?

— Доверить?

И доверяют. И едут.

Нужно быстро срудить бараки. А сил нехватает. Что же тратить силы на конвой? Но конвой конвоем, а вот если без конвоя, полной доверенностью так ребята вдвое лучше и вдвое быстрее работают.

В Белбалтлаге уже не напутывали вокруг бараков услаговской проволоки.

В Белбалтлаге начали осмеяться. Разрезав проволоку, уничтожив оцепленный лагерь, доверив эти гигантские пространства бывшим преступникам, им сказали вдобавок

— Давайте осмеяться, как же нам работать вместе, как же брать штурмом природу.

Вспоминатели говорят об этом кратко: "Коган внес широкую струю хозяйственности." Трудно найти в многочисленных записях, прочитанных нами, описание первых заседаний чекистов с заключенными. Это молчание можно понять. Это, наверное, очень трудно описать. Барак, красный уголок или палатка или новый, только что отстроенный клуб или проектировочное бюро, все равно,

20. First page of three-page excerpt, which contains editorial cuts and comments from the draft manuscript for chapter 4, "The Prisoners," in *The History of Construction*.

- II - 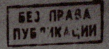 27

эти комнаты наполнились и приобрели цвета необычайно
легкой новизны. Люди сидели бодрые, прямые. Они весело
пальцами закручивали толстые папироски и пускали толстые клубы дыма. Чрезвычайно приятные ощущения от этого
курева. В окно они видят новый пейзаж. Неожиданно
легкие сосны держат охапки снега, легкомысленно стряхивая легкие пушинки. Ребята - думает он: - небось
возле дома исполосовали весь снег салазками, а то
вдруг - по дороге папанька шагает...

Он поднимает руку:

- Мое следующее предложение, - говорит он. Чеспрекословно, первая боевая задача, чтобы думать в смысле
соревнования и ударничества...

Опять таки вспоминатели говорят об этом чрезвычайно
кратко и, по моему, выразительно. " Отношение соловчан
к чекистам, как к охраняющей власти, было сломлено".

Но чекисты не успокаивались. Они требовали инициативы
от соловчан. Сказать, что возьмем штурмом природу, легко
но нужно понимать, как ее брать. Она, эта природа хитрая штука, она подведет такие неожиданности, она загнет
такое, что и руки опустишь и рот раскроешь. А она тебе камень в рот и руки твои в топи на веки вечные. Тут
надо зрок переправлять на другие соображения.

Еще ветер не раскидал золу от первых костров, но
на полянах уже появились возле бараков бани, прачешные
из окон пекарен запахло свежим хлебом, двери кухни
широко раскрыты, повар в белом кителе громадной лужёной ложкой мешает в котле и котел пахнет так, что на

21. Second page of three-page excerpt, which contains editorial cuts and comments as well as Vs. Ivanov's name in the left margins for the draft manuscript for chapter 4, "The Prisoners," in *The History of Construction*.

- 12 -

великое множество верст кругом, не только у человека, у муравья веселится живот.

Но чекисты опять повторяют:

- Проявляйте инициативу. Двигайтесь дальше...

Чекисты не очень хвалят. Они знают какую то особую меру похвалы. Похвалы отпускается столько, чтобы она перешла в действие, чтобы человек работал, а не пыжился и не покрикивал на других самодовольно.

- Вы, каналоармейцы, — говорят чекисты.

И это не только перемена слова "заключенный" на "каналоармеец", это как бы замок на прошлое, это как бы выкинутые в болота ножницы, которыми перерезаны колючие проволоки вокруг лагерей. Вместо охраны, вместо злоискателей, перед ними встали друзья, старшие начальники и, самое главное, перед ними встала иная жизнь, в которую они там, на воле, войти не могли.

Но не нужно особенно обольщаться. Еще многие из тридцатипятников высматривают тропы и составляют маршруты бегства. Правда, не так то далеко граница, буржуазные страны, но тридцатипятнику хочется в свои города. Знакомые улицы, знакомые вывески, знакомые деньги, опять же не всякий язык знает. Чужой язык знают редкие, почтенные люди, вроде "медвежатников": взламывателей несгораемых шкафов, а домушник, скокарь, куда ему за границу.

Каэры, вредители, офицерики думают по другому. Пристально рассматривают они санки или телегу, на которой
    лагерники

22. Third page of three-page excerpt, which contains editorial cuts and comments, from the draft manuscript for chapter 4, "The Prisoners," in *The History of Construction*.

Appendix VI

Comparison sample of the Russian and English versions of a passage from *The History of Construction*. The Russian version is from chapter 6 (278), while the English version was extracted from Stage IV, chapter 15 (199–200).

Muzhik i vol

Tak dereviannyi vek Belomorstroia rodil vek zheleznyi.

Liudi, kotorye rabotali na mekhbaze, v bol'shinstve sluchaev byli liudi ili iz vorovskoi ili iz dereviannoi proselochnoi staroi Rossii.

Byl na Ukraine kulak Balabukha. Byli u nego sivye voly so spokoinoi postup'iu, s raskidistymi rogami. Bylo u nego khoziaistvo s naemnymi rabochimi, s volov trekh shkur ne dral, a s batrakov dral.

Kogda raskulachivali Balabukhu, on sil'no agitiroval, soprotivlialsia s oruzhiem v rukakh i okazalsia na Belomorstroe. Na Belomorstroe sperva delal on tachki okolo mekhbazy, a potom razduval v mekhbaze gorn, a potom stal slesarem. Rabotal u stanka ne khuzhe drugikh.

Okolo Medvezh'ei gory est' sovkhoz. Balabukha byl udarnikom, imel pravo vykhoda iz lageria. Poshel guliat' v vykhodnoi den'. Idet. Vspakhannoe pole navelo na nego tosklivye vospominaniia.

A tut stado, a v stade sivyi vol.

I idet etot vol k nemu, mychit, lizhet emu laskogo ruki.

I uznal Balabukha svoego vola. Vzial Balabukha vola za roga, polozhil goluvu mezhdu rogami i na-chal plakat'.

Poplakav, prishel na mekhbazu k Rudenko i stal prosit'sia: otpustite menia rabotat' v sovkhoz. Tam u menia vol—zemliak.

Govorit emu Rudenko:

-Rabotal vsiu zhizn' vol na muzhika, muzhik—na vola. Krutilis' oni nemazanym kolesom,-zachem tebe eto delo, kogda ty slesar' vtoroi ruki?

Podumal Balabukha i skazal:

-Ladno. Budu ia khodit' k volu v gosti po vykhodnym dniam.

Tak konchalsia na Belomorstroe dereviannyi vek, i nastupal vek metallicheskii.

4

The wooden age of Belomorstroy brought forth an age of iron, but sometimes the transition was very difficult, as witness the story of Balabuk and his ox.

In the Ukraine, there was a Kulak, Balabuk. He had grey long-horned, quiet-stepping oxen. He tired out the labourers who worked on his farm. He didn't overwork his oxen, but he sweated his workers.

When Balabuk was "de-kulakised," he put up a fierce resistance, and was sent to Belomorstroy. At Belomorstroy he first made wheelbarrows near the mechanical base, and then worked the bellows for the forge at the base, and finally became a fitter. He worked at his machine as well as anyone.

There is a State farm near Bear Hill. Balabuk was an Udarnik, a specially privileged shock-brigader, and had the right to go beyond the limits of the camp. He went for a walk on his free day. He walked. The ploughed fields to his left brought him sad memories. And there was a herd of oxen, and in the herd a grey ox. This ox came up to him, lowed and licked his hands. And Balabuk recognized his ox. He took the ox by the horns, laid his head betwen the horns and began to cry.

Then he came to Rudenko, a G.P.U. man in command at the base, and asked him: "Let me go to the State farm to work! There's an ox of mine there—a fellow-countryman."

Rudenko said: "The ox has worked all his life for the peasant, and the peasant for the ox. They went along like an unoiled wheel. What do you want with all that, when you're a fitter already, a skilled man?"

Balabuk thought it over, and said:

"All right. I'll go and visit the ox on my free days."

And thus the wooden age ended in Belomorstroy and an age of metal began.

Notes

Introduction. Constructing the Problem Historically and Theoretically

1. I am indebted to Edward Lee for this perceptive interpretation of Jester's comments.
2. Edward Lee, letter to the author, 8 August 1996.
3. See note 1.
4. For the full discussion of both these projects see Stephen Kotkin, *Magnetic Mountain: Stalinism as a Civilization*; Anne D. Rassweiler, *The Generation of Power: The History of Dneprostroi*; Michael Jakobson, *Origins of the GULag: The Soviet Prison Camp System 1917–1934*. GULag refers to the penal camp system that existed in the USSR for most of its seventy years. The acronym GULag [*Gosudarstvennoe upravlenie lagerei*] stands for the State Directorate of Camps.
5. For the complete text of Solzhenitsyn's comments on Belomor, see Aleksandr I. Solzhenitsyn, *Arkhipelag GULag, 1918–1956*, I–II, 78–102. In the English translation see III–IV, 86–105.

Chapter 1. Reconstructing the (F)Actual History of the Belomor Canal

1. The *American Heritage Dictionary* defines *diabase* as "dark-gray to black, fine textured igneous rock, composed mainly of feldspar and pyroxene, and used for monuments and as crushed stone."
2. Russian State Archive of Literature and Art (RGALI), f. 1885, op. 3, d. 36, l. 262.
3. For all these accounts see S. Ia. Alymov, RGALI, f. 1885, op. 3, d. 47, l. 16; A. C. Insarov: 12; I. Isakov, 144.
4. For brief accounts of this journey see Insarov, 12; Isakov, 144; B. Lepin, 8; Alymov, RGALI, f. 1885, op. 3, d. 33, l. 1 and d. 47, l. 16.
5. For additional details see Insarov, 12; Isakov, 144; Lepin, 6: Alymov, ibid.
6. For further details see S. Ia. Alymov, RGALI, f. 1885, op. 3, d. 47, l. 18. Alymov provides a detailed chronology that lists each step of the Canal's tortuous history prior to Soviet rule. Alymov's source for all this information is unclear. Presumably his position as editor of the camp newspaper, *Perekovka*, afforded him access to documents.
7. Ibid.
8. Personal interview, 17 July 1993.
9. Dmitrii Likhachev, *Ia vspominaiu* [I remember], 94.

10. A growing body of memoir literature on the life of political prisoners on the Canal continues to appear. In addition to Losev's and Antsiferov's memoirs cited in the Introduction, other sources provide equally riveting testimony to life on Belomor. Some of these accounts include D. Vitkovsky's "Polzhizni" [Half a life], as well as a variety of interesting articles and notes about Igor Terent'ev's time on Belomor in his *Sobranie sochinenii* [Collected Works], 18–21, 72–73, 331–32, 463–69. The notes that accompany these selections are replete with additional information about Terent'ev's art and life on Belomor. Two classic narratives devoted to camp life in Solovki and Belomor are M. Z. Nikonov-Smorodin's *Krasnaia katorga* [Red hard labor] and I. L. Solonevich's *Rossiia v kontslagere* [Russia in a prison camp].

11. Personal interview, 18 July 1993. As a measure of how relaxed the atmosphere around the Canal had become, I was permitted into the first lock's control tower and actually witnessed a ship traversing the first lock. As late as 1992 the Canal was still considered a security installation and was guarded by Soviet soldiers. The only remnant of this practice was the sign on the gate leading up to the lock that warned: Entrance Strictly Forbidden. As a further testament to the laxity of the security procedures, I entered the control tower to the strains of the Rolling Stones' song "Ruby Tuesday" blaring from a radio. The irony of the situation was not lost on either me or my Russian colleagues.

Chapter 2. Mythmaking and Mythbreaking: The (Hi)Story behind *The History of the Construction of the Stalin White Sea–Baltic Canal*

1. This discussion of art and life shaping each other owes much to comments made by one of the anonymous reviewers of the manuscript for this book.

2. RGALI, f. 1604, op. 1, d. 21, ll. 51–146. Kornelly Zelinsky, "Beseda I. V. Stalina s pisateliami, 26 oktiabria 1932 g." Repression meant that the writer (or painter, journalist, composer, military officer, for repression touched many professions) disappeared from both the literary scene and Soviet literary history. While not all repressed writers perished in the purges, those who survived faced ruined careers and condemnation by their more zealous colleagues throughout the Stalinist period. The advent of "The Thaw" (1953–63) began to lessen the stigma attached to many of these people, and they were rehabilitated, a professional and personal resurrection of sorts.

3. RGALI, f. 1604, op. 1, d. 21, l. 146.

4. RGALI, f. 1604, op. 1, d. 21, l. 21.

5. RGALI, f. 1604, op. 1, d. 21, ll. 32–33.

6. Evgeny Gabrilovich, interview by the author, Moscow, Russia, 9 June 1992. When I asked Gabrilovich about his participation in the Belomor Writers Brigade and volume, he initially said that he could not remember anything about that time or the event. After gentle prodding he began to describe the writers' voyage along the Canal and spoke in particular about Zoshchenko's behavior. At no time, however, did Gabrilovich offer an opinion as to the validity of the project or the volume.

7. Andrew Wachtel, *An Obsession with History: Russian Writers Confront the Past*.

8. My thanks to one of the anonymous reviewers of the manuscript for this book, who suggested the industrial metaphor and its conceptual possibilities. In addition, this discussion relies heavily on and echoes Katerina Clark's arguments in "Little Heroes and Big Deeds: Literature Responds to the First Five-Year Plan."

9. For an additional discussion of the move to document collective endeavors, see Lazar Fleishman, *Boris Pasternak v tridtsatye gody*, 135–40, as well as the collectively written work *Liudi stalingradskogo traktornogo zavoda* [The People of the Stalingrad Tractor Factory], compiled by Iakov Il'in (Moscow: OGIZ Istoriia fabrik i zavodov, 1934). Another excellent literary source that addresses the theme of collective labor is Valentine Kataev's novel *Time, Forward!* translated by Charles Malamuth (Bloomington: Indiana University Press, 1976); the novel was originally published in Russian in the USSR in 1931.

10. See note 6.

11. RGALI, f. 2268, op. 2, d. 153, l. 1.

12. The term *Potemkin Villages* originated during the reign of Catherine the Great (1762–96). In 1787, Catherine's then-current favorite, Grigory Potemkin, constructed fake villages in sparsely populated areas in southern Russia so as to deceive Catherine, Emperor Joseph II of Austria, and the Polish king Stanislaw Poniatowski into believing that the area was developing. Catherine and her guests were touring the region. In fact, Potemkin ordered that facades be contructed, behind which there was nothing. Since that time the term Potemkin Villages has come to mean any false facade erected for the sake of deceiving the viewer.

13. See note 6.

14. RGALI, f. 2268, op. 2, d. 40, ll. 1–33, and d. 159, ll. 1–34.

15. Vitaly Bronislavovich Mileiko, interview by the author, St. Petersburg, Russia, 3 July 1993.

16. V. V. Shklovskaya-Kordi, interview by the author, Peredel'kino, Russia, 10 July 1993.

17. The discussion of the true author of the song "Over the Hills and Dales" is found in A. Isaev's article "Zabytyi avtor liubimoi pesni" [The forgotten author of a beloved song].

18. RGALI, f. 1885, op. 3, d. 41, l. 1.

19. Alla Iurievna Gorcheva, interview by the author, Moscow, Russia, June 1993.

20. See note 16.

21. See note 16.

22. See note 16.

23. The full text of Shklovsky's speech to Leningrad writers about the work of the Belomor brigade is found in his personal file in RGALI, f. 562, op. 1, d. 205, ll. 1–40.

24. For complete discussions of this phenomenon, see Clark, "Little Heroes," and Sheila Fitzpatrick, "Culture and Politics under Stalin: A Reappraisal."

25. See Clark, "Little Heroes," and Karen Petrone, "Life Has Become More Joyous, Comrades!"

26. RGALI, f. 2268, op. 2, d. 153, l. 7.
27. RGALI, f. 2268, op. 2, d. 90, l. 10.
28. Ibid.
29. Ibid.
30. RGALI, f. 2268, op. 2, d. 39, l. 29.
31. RGALI, f. 2268, op. 2, d. 40, l. 33.
32. RGALI, f. 2268, op. 2, d. 39, l. 52.
33. Irina Erenburg, interviews by the author, Moscow, Russia, 1988–93.
34. Evgeny Gabrilovich, interview by the author, Moscow, Russia, 9 June 1992.
35. For more complete information on Zoshchenko's life and work, see Linda Scatton's recent biography, *Mikhail Zoshchenko: Evolution of a Writer* (Cambridge: Cambridge University Press, 1993).

Chapter 3. Literary Text as Historical Narrative: *The History of the Construction of the Stalin White Sea–Baltic Canal*

1. For a more detailed discussion of the English translation of the Belomor volume, see chapter 4 of this study.

2. Kozakov's Belomor writings are found in RGALI, f. 1517, op. 1, d. 91 and 105.

3. For a more detailed discussion of this distinction, see Linda Hutcheon, "The Pastime of Past Time: Fiction, History, Historiographic Metafiction." Of particular interest to any discussion of Stalinism and the GULag system are Matt F. Oja's insightful comments in "Fictional History and Historical Fiction: Solzhenitsyn and Kish as Exemplars."

4. Perhaps the most extensive discussion of the interplay of history and literature is found in Hayden White, beginning with the work in which he launched his theories on history and literature, *Metahistory: The Historical Imagination in Nineteenth-Century Europe*. He pursues the idea of metahistory and modifies some of his arguments in two subsequent works, *Tropics of Discourse: Essays in Cultural Criticism* and *The Content of the Form: Narrative Discourse and Historical Representation*. White's work has been the source of a great deal of debate and criticism, especially from historians who dispute his basic contention that the writing of history is essentially a literary act.

5. Everyone familiar with Russia knows about or has witnessed the great Russian passion for reading and the respect bestowed upon writers. This point was made especially clear to me as I was discussing the Belomor volume with Ivan Chukhin. When I expressed incredulity at the fact that readers truly believed what Soviet writers were reporting about Belomor, Chukhin replied that readers believed it because it was written down. This is more than a "passion for reading." The committing of words to paper somehow confirmed the truthfulness and accuracy of their content, even if what was written turned out to be false.

Such a comment was especially appropriate coming from Chukhin given his knowledge of the Belomor episode and his own approach to the material. In fact,

Chukhin's book exemplifies precisely what White intends by the concept of emplotment.

6. I am indebted to one of the anonymous reviewers of my manuscript who contributed this insight.

7. The first scholar to call attention to this change was Katerina Clark in her article "Little Heroes and Big Deeds: Literature Responds to the First Five-Year Plan." While she has approached this phenomenon from a literary scholar's point of view, Karen Petrone is pursuing the topic from an historian's vantage point. Her work, including her dissertation "Life Has Become More Joyous, Comrades," explores just this issue—the shift from collective to indiviual heroism.

8. The State Archive of the Russian Federation (GARF) houses the files that document the writing of the Belomor *History*. Located in the archive of the History of Factories and Plants series, the documents include draft manuscripts for the Belomor volume, as well as newspaper articles about the Canal that were culled from a variety of sources. In addition, archival materials include a variety of discrete texts that illustrate how the Belomor volume was written. This repository serves as the basis for much of the information that will be discussed in this section. For the actual documents see GARF, *Gosudarstvennoe izdatel'stvo "Istoriia fabrik i zavodov" Ogiz'a*, f. 7952, op. 7, d. 25–96.

9. The bulk of these articles appeared in *Literaturnaia gazeta*, 24 August 1933–26 January 1934, *Leningradskaia Pravda*, 1 June–15 October 1933, and *Pravda*, 29 June 1933–12 January 1934. Of course, such articles were most prevalent immediately following the Writers Brigade to Belomor in mid-August 1933, and prior to and during the Seventeenth Party Congress in January 1934.

10. GARF, f. 7952, op. 7, d. 75, l. 8.

11. GARF, f. 7952, op. 7, d. 79, l. 9.

12. Ibid.

13. GARF, f. 7952, op. 7, d. 75, ll. 10–11a.

14. GARF, f. 7952, op. 7, d. 75, l. 15.

15. GARF, f. 7952, op. 7, d. 75, ll. 11b-12.

16. For the full discussion of photomontage in the Soviet context see Matthew Teitelbaum, preface to *Montage and Modern Life, 1919–1942,* and Margarita Tupitsyn, "From the Politics of Montage to the Montage of Politics: Soviet Practice 1919 Through 1937."

17. For the full treatment of this argument, see Boris Groys, *The Total Art of Stalinism: Avant-Garde, Aesthetic Dictatorship, and Beyond*.

18. RGALI, f. 562, op. 1, d. 205, l. 9.

19. RGALI, f. 562, op. 1, d. 96, ll. 4–5.

20. RGALI, f. 562, op. 1, d. 1, l. 27.

21. RGALI, f. 562, op. 1, d. 205, ll. 5–6.

22. RGALI, f. 562, op. 1, d. 205, l. 19.

23. RGALI, f. 562, op. 1, d. 96, l. 3.

24. For a fuller discussion of the origins and development of socialist realism, see

C. Vaughan James, *Soviet Socialist Realism: Origins and Theory*, and Herman Ermolaev, *Soviet Literary Theories 1917–1934: The Genesis of Socialist Realism*. In addition to Groys's book cited in note 17, other treatments of this issue include Clark's *The Soviet Novel: History as Ritual* and Regine Robin, *Socialist Realism: An Impossible Aesthetic*.

Some of the texts posited as precursors to the official adoption of socialist realism include Gorky's novel *Mother* (1906), Gladkov's novel *Cement* (1925), and Chernyshevsky's *What Is to Be Done?* (1863).

25. Pyrite is also known as fool's gold, a yellow to brown mineral sulfide that is used to produce sulfur dioxide for sulfuric acid.

26. GARF, f. 7952, op. 7, d. 83, l. 12.

27. GARF, f. 7952, op. 7, d. 83, ll. 31–32.

28. GARF, f. 7952, op. 7, d. 84, ll. 49–52.

29. The word *kulak* in Russian means *fist*. As used in the Soviet Union, it denoted wealthy, productive peasants whose land, livestock, and agricultural products were confiscated during the period of "de-kulakization" in the drive to collectivize agriculture in the First Five-Year Plan, 1928–32. Kulaks were removed from their farms, exiled, imprisoned in concentration camps, or killed outright.

30. The Internal Guard or VOKHR (*Vnutrennaia OKHRana*) was comprised of prison inmates who were chosen to guard their fellow inmates in the camps.

31. GARF, f. 7952, op. 7, d. 84, l. 19.

32. RGALI, f. 2302, op. 1, d. 35, ll. 6–8.

33. GARF, f. 7952, op. 7, d. 61, l. 25.

34. My thanks to one of the anonymous reviewers of the manuscript for contributing this insight.

35. For a fuller treatment of Prishvin and Belomor see chapter 4.

36. GARF, f. 7952, op. 7, d. 62, l. 1.

37. My thanks to an anonymous reviewer for sharing this insight.

38. RGALI, f. 562, op. 1, d. 391, l. 94.

39. RGALI, f. 562, op. 1, d. 183, l. 1.

40. For a fuller discussion of Terent'ev's activities and poetry while at Belomor, see chapter 4.

41. GARF, f. 7952, op. 7, d. 76, ll. 152–156.

42. GARF, f. 7952, op. 7, d. 71, l. 26.

43. GARF, f. 7952, op. 7, d. 71, l. 45a.

44. See note 17.

45. Ivan Nikolaevich Rusinov, interview by the author, Moscow, Russia, July 1993.

46. Natalya Kuziakina has provided the most complete account of the theater and theatrical productions on Belomor in her book *Theatre in the Solovki Prison Camp*, esp. 103–29. In a related vein, Erika Wolf, at the University of Michigan, is working on a dissertation in art history that will focus on the visual arts at Belomor in general and on Rodchenko's photographic work on the Canal in particular, as depicted in the journal *The USSR on Building Sites* [SSSR na stroike].

47. Solzhenitsyn discusses the plight of camp musicians in *The GULag Archipelago*, 105.

Chapter 4. Converging Narratives and the Emerging Truth

1. All citations from *The Aristocrats* are taken from volume 3 of Nikolai Pogodin's *Sobranie dramaticheskikh proizvedenii v piati tomakh* [The collected dramatic works in five volumes]. Translations are mine unless noted otherwise.

2. My thanks to Edward Lee for helping me develop these insights.

3. Both of the cited poems were found among Sergei Alymov's papers in the Russian State Archive of Literature and Art. In fact, Alymov's file contained a few of the extant copies of the newspaper *Perekovka*, as well as numerous inmate submissions, including suggestions for puzzles and games. It is unclear from the manuscripts whether or not any of the puzzles were printed in the newspaper. For further examples, see Sergei Alymov, RGALI, f. 1885, op. 3, d. 34, l. 201, Shkred's poem; l. 262, Lidin's poem.

4. RGALI, f. 1885, op. 3, d. 34, l. 201.

5. This biographical summary is based on an introduction to the only published collection of Terent'ev's work. For a more complete account, as well as examples of Terent'ev's publications and theoretical works, see Igor Terent'ev, *Sobranie sochineii* [Collected works], and *Moi pokhorony* [My funeral] (Moscow: GILEIA, 1993).

6. The complete text of the poem is found in Sergei Alymov's archival file in RGALI, f. 1885, op. 3, d. 34, ll. 192–93.

7. RGALI, f. 1885, op. 3, d. 34, ll. 192–93.

8. This and all the following citations are taken from Fyodor Dostoevsky, *The Brothers Karamazov*, trans. Constance Garnett (New York: Modern Library, 1950), 291–92.

9. There is a sizeable body of literature devoted to detailed discussions of the field of translation studies. This discussion has relied on Susan Bassnett-McGuire's *Translation Studies* as its critical base in part because she outlines and integrates the various approaches to translation in common practice. For additional insights see Rachel May, *The Translator in the Text* (Evanston, Ill.: Northwestern University Press, 1994); Peter Newmark, *Approaches to Translation* (Oxford: Pergamon Press, 1981); and Newmark, *A Textbook of Translation* (New York: Prentice Hall, 1988).

10. All subsequent references to the English text are from *Belomor: An Account of the Construction of the Great Canal between the White Sea and the Baltic Sea*.

11. This discussion is a synopsis of material taken from John Tebbel, *The Golden Age between Two Wars, 1920–1940*, 569–71, and *American Literary Publishing Houses, 1900–1980*.

12. Although noted in source materials, newspaper articles that discuss the Belomor volume in the foreign press have been difficult to document, thus suggesting that the event and book were not perceived as important. One article—Ralph W. Barnes, "Soviet Pardons 12,484 Convict Canal Builders"—discusses the Canal project rather than the volume itself. So, too, does Walter Duranty in his article

"Soviet Releases 12,484 in Record Amnesty; 59,616 Sentences Also Cut for Canal Work." Throughout August 1934 the *Moscow Daily News* printed various articles about the first anniversary of the canal.

13. For a fuller discussion of Foucault's approach, see *I, Pierre Riviere, having slaughtered my mother, my sister, and my brother* . . . , edited by Michel Foucault.

14. I am again indebted to Edward Lee for his cogent comments on this issue, many of which were incorporated into my thinking about the converging discourses.

Chapter 5. The Legacy of Belomor

1. GARF, f. 7952, op. 7, d. 28, l. 20.

2. My thanks to Edward Lee for helping me shape this insight.

3. First lock operator, Belomor Canal, conversation with the author, Povenets, Russia, 18 July 1993.

4. I am indebted to Dan Davidson for this insight.

Bibliography

Al'tman, Iogann. "Kniga o bol'shom pobede" [A Book about the great victory]. *Literaturnyi kritik* 6 (1934): 253–62.

American Literary Publishing Houses, 1900–1980. Vol. 46 of *Dictionary of Literary Biography*, edited by Peter Dzwonkoski, 349–51. Detroit: Gale Research Company and Book Tower, 1986. Trade and paperback.

Antsiferov, N. P. *Iz dum o bylom. Vospominaniia*. [From thoughts about the past. Recollections]. Moscow: Feniks, Kul'turnaia initsiativa, 1992.

Avdeenko, Aleksander (a). *I Love*. Translated by Anthony Wixley. Moscow: Cooperative Publishing Society of Foreign Workers in the USSR, 1935.

———. (b). "Otluchenie" [Excommunication], parts 1 and 2. *Znamia* 3 (1989): 5–73; 4 (1989): 80–133.

Bakhtin, Mikhail. *Rabelais and His World*. Translated by Helene Iswolsky. Cambridge, Mass.: MIT Press, 1968.

"Baltic–White Sea Canal Celebrates First Year." *Moscow Daily News*, 3 August 1934, 4.

Barnes, Ralph W. "Soviet Pardons 12,484 Convict Canal Builders." *New York Herald Tribune*, 5 August 1933, late edition, 1.

Bassnett-McGuire, Susan. *Translation Studies*. London: Methuen, 1980.

Belomor: An Account of the Construction of the Great Canal between the White Sea and the Baltic Sea. Edited by Maxim Gorky, L. Averbach, and S. G. Firin. Introduction by Amabel Williams-Ellis. New York: Harrison Smith and Robert Haas, Inc., 1935.

"Belomorsko–Baltiiskii Kanal gotov" [The White Sea–Baltic Canal is ready]. *Ogonyek*, 5 July 1933, 5.

Belomorkso–Baltiiskii Kanal imeni Stalina: Istoriia stroitel'stva [The history of the construction of the Stalin White Sea–Baltic Canal]. Edited by M. Gorky, L. Averbakh, and S. Firin. Moscow: Istoriia Fabrik i Zavodov, 1934.

Belomorsko–Baltiiskii Kanal imeni tov. Stalina: Karta-putevoditel' [The Stalin White Sea–Baltic Canal: map-travel guide]. Moscow: TSS OSVOD, 1934.

Boiarskii, Ia. O. "Zritel' zhdet" [The viewer is waiting]. Review of *Aristokraty*, by Nikolai Pogodin. Realisticheskii teatr, Moscow. *Vechernaia Moskva*, 9 March 1935, n.p.

Bolotnikov, A. "Kniga dostoinaia svoei temy" [The book is worthy of its theme]. *Literaturnaia gazeta*, 26 January 1934, 2.

Boshko, V. I. "Otkrytie Belomorskogo Kanala i ego znachenie v sviazi s problemoi bol'shogo Dnepra" [The opening of the Belomor Canal and its significance in connection with the problem of the Big Dnepr]. *Sovetskii Sever* 4 (1933): 114–15.

Bragin, Vladimir. "Ne ochen'-to podkhodiashchee vremia dlia iskusstva" [Not a very appropriate time for literature]. *Tallin* 65, no. 2 (1989): 85–9.

Brooks, Jeffrey. "Socialist Realism in *Pravda*: Read All About It." *Slavic Review* 53, no. 4 (1994): 973–91.

Bulgakova, Elena. *Dnevnik Eleny Bulgakovoi* [The diary of Elena Bulgakova]. Moscow: Izdatel'stvo Knizhnaia palata, 1990.

Carleton, Greg. "Genre in Socialist Realism." *Slavic Review* 53, no. 4 (1994): 992–1009.

Chukhin, Ivan. *Kanaloarmeitsy* [Canalarmyists]. Petrozavodsk: Kareliia, 1990.

Clark, Katerina. (a) "Little Heroes and Big Deeds: Literature Responds to the First Five-Year Plan." In *Cultural Revolution in Russia, 1928–1931*, edited by Sheila Fitzpatrick, 189–206. Bloomington: Indiana University Press, 1978.

———. (b) *The Soviet Novel: History as Ritual*. Chicago: University of Chicago Press, 1985.

Dallin, David J., and Boris I. Nicolaevsky. *Forced Labor in Soviet Russia*. New Haven: Yale University Press, 1947.

Danin, Daniil. "Zaitsy ne dolzhny begat' s fonariami" [Rabbits should not run with lamps]. *Literaturnaia gazeta*, 27 January 1993, 6.

Dashkov, B. B. "Baltic–White Sea Canal." *The Great Soviet Encyclopedia*, 1973 edition.

Duranty, Walter. "Soviet Releases 12,484 in Record Amnesty; 59,616 Sentences Also Cut for Canal Work." *New York Times*, 5 August 1933, late edition, 1.

Eco, Umberto. "The Frames of Comic 'Freedom'." In *Carnival!* edited by Thomas A. Sebeok, 1–9. Berlin: Mouton Publishers, 1984.

Erenburg, Ilya. *Eve of War 1933–1941*. Vol. 4, *Men, Years, Life*. Translated by Tatiana Shebunina with Yvonne Kapp. London: Macgibban and Kee, 1963.

Erlikh, A. "Chudo v Karelii" [The miracle in Karelia]. *Khudozhestvennaia literatura* 4 (1934): 8–10.

Ermilov, V. "Teatral'nye pis'ma" [Theatrical letters]. *Krasnaia nov'* 4 (1935): 234–40.

Ermolaev, Herman. *Soviet Literary Theories, 1917–1934: The Genesis of Socialist Realism*. University of California Publications in Modern Philology, no. 69. Berkeley: University of California Press, 1963.

Eventov, I. "Komandiru o sovetskoi khudozhestvennoi literature. (Obzor)" [To the commander about Soviet literature. A review]. *Krasnaia nov'* 6 (1934): 150–58.

Fin, S. "Kniga o 'chude' na Karel'skikh ozerakh" [A book about the "miracle" on the Karelian lakes]. *Komsomol'skaia pravda*, 24 January 1934, 4.

Firin, S. *Itogi Belomorstroia* [The results of Belomorstroi]. Moscow: Partiinoe Izdatel'stvo, 1934.

Fitzpatrick, Sheila. "Culture and Politics under Stalin: A Reappraisal." *Slavic Review* 35, no. 2 (June 1976): 211–31.

Fleishman, Lazar. *Boris Pasternak v tridtsatye gody* [Boris Pasternak in the thirties]. Jerusalem: The Magnes Press, 1984.

Foucault, Michel, ed. *I, Pierre Riviere, having slaughtered my mother, my sister and my brother* . . . . Pantheon Books: New York, 1975.

Golomshtock, Igor. (a) "Problems in the Study of Stalinist Culture." In *The Culture of the Stalin Period*, edited by Hans Günther. New York: St. Martin's Press, 1990.

———. (b) *Totalitarian Art in the Soviet Union, the Third Reich, Fascist Italy and the People's Republic of China*. Translated by Robert Chandler. London: Collins Harvill, 1990.

Gorcheva, Alla Iurievna. "Ne podlezhit rasprostraneniiu" [Not subject to dissemination], parts 1–3. *Sovetskaia bibliografiia* 5 (1991): 56–78; 6 (1991): 63–84; 1 (1992): 99–112.

Gorky, Maksim. "Istoriia fabrik i zavodov'" [The history of factories and plants]. *Sobranie sochinenii*, v. 26, 141–46. Moscow: Gosizdat khudozhestvennoi literatury, 1953.

———. "Kak sobaka: vse ponimaiu, a molchu" [(I'm) like a dog: I understand everything, but am silent]. *Literaturnaia gazeta*, 3 August 1994, 6.

———. "O kochke i o tochke" [About hillocks and hummocks]. In *O literature*, 169–77. Moscow: Khudozhestvennaia literatura, 1935.

———. "O rabote po 'Istorii fabrik i zavodov'" [About the work on the History of Factories and Plants]. *Sobranie sochinenii*, v. 26, 270–79. Moscow: Gosizdat khudo-zhestvennoi literatury, 1953.

———. "Za rabotu!" [To work!]. *Sobranie sochinenii*, v. 26, 172–75. Moscow: Gosizdat khudozhestvennoi literatury, 1953.

Gromov, V. "Put' prolozhennyi Bol'shevikami (Belomorsko–Baltiiskii Vodnyi Put')" [The path laid out by the Bolsheviks (the Belomor–Baltic Waterway)]. *Partrabotnik* 11 (June 1933): 49–52.

Groys, Boris. *The Total Art of Stalinism: Avant-Garde, Aesthetic Dictatorship, and Beyond*. Translated by Charles Rougle. Princeton: Princeton University Press, 1992.

GULag v Karelii. Sbornik dokumentov i materialov, 1930–1941. [The GULag in Karelia. A collection of documents and materials, 1930–1941.] Petrozavodsk: Karel'skii nauchnyi tsentr RAN, 1992.

Günther, Hans. "Education and Conversion: The Road to the New Man in the Totalitarian Regime." In *The Culture of the Stalin Period*, edited by Hans Günther. New York: St. Martin's Press, 1990.

Gurvich, O. "Vtoroe rozhdenie" [Second birth]. *Krasnaia nov'* 4 (1935): 172–93.

Hutcheon, Linda. "The Pastime of Past Time: Fiction, History, Historiographic Metafiction." In *Postmodern Genres*, edited by Marjorie Perloff, 54–75. Norman: University of Oklahoma Press, 1989.

Iakovlev, S. "Belomorsko–Baltiiskii Vodnyi Put' i ego rol' v ekonomike Soiuza" [The White Sea–Baltic Waterway and its role in the economy of the Union]. *Sovetskaia Kareliia* 8–9 (1933): 49–63.

Insarov, A. S. *Baltiisko–Belomorskii Vodnyii Put'* [The Baltic–White Sea Waterway]. Moscow: OGIZ GOSTRANSIZDAT, 1934.
Intimacy and Terror: Soviet Diaries of the 1930s. Edited by Veronique Garros, Natalia Korenevskaya, and Thomas Lahusen. Translated by Carol A. Flath. New York: The New Press, 1995.
Intourist. *The White Sea–Baltic Canal.* Leningrad: Vneshtorgizdat, 1935.
Isaev, A. "Zabytyi avtor liubimoi pesni" [The forgotten author of a beloved song]. *Dal'nyi Vostok* 5 (1960): 158–59.
Isakov, I. (a) "Belomorsko–Baltiiskaia vodnaia magistral'" [The White Sea–Baltic water magistrate]. *Morskoi sbornik* 11 (1932): 138–42.
———. (b) *Belomorsko–Baltiiskaia vodnaia magistral'* [The White Sea–Baltic water magistrate]. Leningrad: Izdanie Upravleniia Voenno-Morskikh Sil RKKA, 1932.
Ivanova, Tamara. "Eshcho o 'Nasledstve,' o 'Dolge,' i 'Prave': Byl li Vsevolod Ivanov 'Zhdanovtsem'?" [More about "heritage," "debts," and "rights." Was Vsevolod Ivanov a "Zhdanovist"?]. *Knizhnoe obozrenie* 34 (1989): 6.
Izvestiia, 21 June–24 September 1933.
Jakobson, Michael. *Origins of the GULag: The Soviet Prison Camp System, 1917–1934.* Lexington: University Press of Kentucky, 1993.
James, C. Vaughan. *Soviet Socialist Realism: Origins and Theory.* New York: St. Martin's Press, 1973.
Jester, Art. "Truman Was Right; Nuclear War Is Wrong. Read On." *Lexington (Ky.) Herald-Leader*, 6 August 1995, E4.
Karaganov, A. V. *Konstantin Simonov: vblizi i na passtoianii* [Konstantine Simonov: Up close and from a distance]. Moscow: Sovetskii pisatel', 1987.
"Karelian Autonomous Soviet Socialist Republic." *Collier's Encyclopedia*, 1991 edition.
"Karelian Autonomous Soviet Socialist Republic." *Great Soviet Encyclopedia*, 1976 edition.
Kenig, E. L. "Ne Skazka-a Byl' (Belomorsko–Onezhskii Vodnyi Put')" [Not a fairy tale, but reality (the White Sea–Onega Waterway)]. *Izvestiia*, 28 December 1932, 2.
"Khronika: Belomorsko–Baltiiskii Kanal imeni Stalina" [Chronicle: the Stalin White Sea–Baltic Canal]. *Zemlevedenie* 36, no. 1 (1934): 99–100.
Kiselev, A. *Prishvin—khudozhnik* [Prishvin—The Artist]. Khabarovsk: Khabarovskoe knizhnoe izdatel'stvo, 1978.
Kluyev, Nikolai. "Razrukha" [Ruin]. *Ogonyek* 43, no. 3248 (21–28 October 1989): 11–12.
Koganer, Z. "'Belomorstroi' sozdal novykh liudei" [Belomorstroi created new people]." *Leningradskaia Pravda* 10 June 1933, 2.
———. "Vorota v Beloe More" [The gates to the White Sea]. *Leningradskaia Pravda*, 12 June 1933, 4.
Kolchevska, Natasha. "Toward a 'Hybrid' Literature: Theory and Praxis of the Faktoviki." *Slavic and East European Journal* 27, no. 4 (1983): 452–64.

Kommunisticheskaia molodezh' [Communist youth] 34, 4 (1934): 60.

Kotkin, Stephen. *Magnetic Mountain: Stalinism as a Civilization.* Berkeley: University of California Press, 1995.

Kren, N. "Chudo na Vyge" [The miracle on the Vyg]. *Nashi dostizheniia* 1 (1933): 23–35.

———. "Soedinenie Morei" [The joining of the seas]. *Leningradskaia Pravda,* 5 November 1932, 3.

Kuziakina, Natalia. *Theatre in the Solovki Prison Camp.* Translated by Boris M. Meerovich. Russian Theatre Archive, vol. 3. Luxembourg: Harwood Academic Publishers, 1995.

Lage (no first name given). "Chelovek i priroda" [Man and nature]. *Kommunisticheskaia molodezh'* 7 (1934): 60–2.

Lapin, Boris, and Evgeny Gabrilovich. "Krokus Prim" [Crocus Prim]. In *Moskovskii parnas. Vto-roi sbornik* [Moscow Parnassus. Second collection], 64–83. Moscow: Moskovskii parnas, 1922.

Leningradskaia Pravda, 1 June–15 October 1933.

Lepin, B. "K Voprosu ob istorii i ekonomike Baltiisko–Belomorskogo vodnogo puti" [Concerning the question of the history and economy of the Baltic–White Sea waterway]. *Sovetskaia Kareliia* 5–6 (1932): 8–14.

Lepin, K. "Baltiisko–Belomorskii Vodnyi Put' i rekonstruktsiia Mariinskoi Sistemy" [The Baltic–White Sea waterway and the reconstruction of the Marinsky System]. *Vodnyi Transport* 7 (1932): 12–15.

Likhachev, Dmitrii. *Ia vspominaiu* [I remember]. Moscow: Progress, 1991.

Literaturnaia gazeta, 24 August 1933–26 January 1934.

Losev, A. F. *Zhizn'. Povesti, Rasskazy, Pis'ma.* [Life. Novellas, Short Stories, Letters]. St. Petersburg: AO "Komplekt," 1993.

Mandelshtam, Nadezhda. *Hope Abandoned.* Translated by Max Hayward. New York: Atheneum, 1974.

———. *Hope Against Hope.* Translated by Max Hayward. New York: Atheneum, 1976.

Markov, P. "O dramaturgii Nikolaia Pogodina" [About the drama of Nikolai Pogodin]. Introduction to *Sobranie dramaticheskikh proizvedenii v piati tomakh,* 1: 7–14. Moscow: Iskusstvo, 1960.

"Metro, Baltic Canal, Tolstoi Novel in New Films." *Moscow Daily News,* 16 August 1934, 2.

"Nachal'nik GULag NKVD Tov. M. D. Berman v Belbaltkombinate" [The head of the GULag NKVD Com. M.D. Berman in the Belbaltcombinat]. *Belomorsko–Baltiiskii Kombinat: Ezhemesiachnyi tekhniko-ekonomicheskii zhurnal* 9 (1935): 3.

"New Kombinat to Utilize the Resources of Karelia." *Moscow Daily News,* 5 August 1934, 2.

Nikonov-Smorodin, M. Z. *Krasnaia katorga* [Red hard labor]. Sofia: Izdatel'stvo NTSNP, 1938.

Oja, Matt F. "Fictional History and Historical Fiction: Solzhenitsyn and Kish as Exemplars." *History and Theory* 27, 2 (1988): 111–24.

Pervyi vsesoiuznyi s"ezd sovetskikh pisatelei. Stenograficheskii otchet [The first all-union congress of Soviet writers. Stenographic record]. Moscow: Sovetskii pisatel', 1990.

Petrone, Karen. "Life Has Become More Joyous, Comrades." Ph.D. diss., University of Michigan, 1994.

Pogodin, Nikolai. *Aristokraty* [The aristocrats]. In *Sobranie dramaticheskikh proizvedenii v piati tomakh* [The collected dramatic works in five volumes], 3:85–171, notes 481–86. Moscow: Iskusstvo, 1960.

———. "Avtobiograficheskie zametiki" [Autobiographical notes]. In *Sobranie dramaticheskikh proizvedenii v piati tomakh* [The collected dramatic works in five volumes], 1: 15–25. Moscow: Iskusstvo, 1960.

———. "Sodoklad N. F. Pogodina o dramaturgii" [The speech of N. F. Pogodin about drama]. In *Pervyi vsesoiuznyi s"ezd sovetskikh pisatelei. Stenograficheskii otchet* [The first all-union congress of Soviet writers. Stenographic record], 385–94. Moscow: Sovetskii pisatel', 1990.

Polovtsova, K. A. "Arkhitektura i stroitel'stvo: Dereviannaia arkhitektura Belomorsko–Baltiiskogo Kanala" [Architecture and construction: Wooden architecture of the White Sea–Baltic Canal]. *Belomorsko–Baltiiskii Kombinat: Ezhemesiachnyi tekhniko-ekonomicheskii zhurnal* (April 1935): 47–9.

Pravda, 29 June 1933–12 January 1934.

Prishvin, Mikhail. "Dnevniki, 1905–1954" [Diaries, 1905–1954]. *Sobranie sochinenii v vos'mi tomakh,* vol. 8, Moscow: Khudozhestvennaia literatura, 1986.

———. *Osudareva doroga* [The tsar's road]. Moscow: Izdatel'stvo Sovetskaia Rossiia, 1958.

———. *Otsy i deti* [Fathers and children]. Moscow: Khudozhestvennaia literatura, 1937.

———. "Padun" [The waterfall]. *Molodaia gvardiia* 1 (1939): 96–109.

Protasova, Metallina Petrovna, and Irina Iakovlevna Temkina. *Puteshestvie dlinoju v zhizn'* [The journey of life is long]. Moscow: Sovetskii pisatel', 1972.

Rassweiler, Anne D. *The Generation of Power: The History of Dneprostroi.* New York: Oxford University Press, 1988.

Raymond, Ellsworth. "White Sea–Baltic Canal." *Encyclopedia Americana,* 1992 edition.

Robin, Régine. *Socialist Realism: An Impossible Aesthetic.* Translated by Catherine Porter. Stanford: Stanford University Press, 1992.

Rozental', S. "*Aristokraty*" [The aristocrats]. *Pravda,* 3 October 1934, 6.

———. "Aristokraty N. Pogodina" [The aristocrats of N. Pogodin]. *Pravda,* 11 March 1935, 4.

Ruder, Cynthia. "Master Traveller and Forgotten Survivor: The Life and Works of Boris Matveevich Lapin." Ph.D. diss., Cornell University, 1987.

Rykachev, Ia. *Inzhenery Belomorstroia* [The engineers of the Belomor construction project]. Moscow: Zhurnal'no-Gazetnoe Ob"edinenie, 1934.

"S&S Festival Tours '97 Presents Waterways of Russia." Brochure. S & S Folk Festival Tours, 1997.

Shaginian, Elena. "Mikhail Zoshchenko–Marietta Shaginian: Iz perepiski" [Mikhail Zoshchenko–Marietta Shaginian: from correspondence]. *Tallin* 65, no. 2 (1989): 89–109.

Shentalinsky, Vitaly. *Arrested Voices: Resurrecting the Disappeared Writers of the Soviet Regime*. Translated by John Crowfoot. Introduction by Robert Conquest. New York: Martin Kessler Books, Free Books, 1996.

———. "Gamaiun-ptitsa veshchaia" [The prophetic gamyun-bird]. *Ogonyek* 43 (21–28 October 1989): 9–10.

Sheskin, Ira. "Suez Canal." *Grolier's Multimedia Encyclopedia*, 1992 edition.

Shidlovskii, A. "Opisanie Onego–Belomorskogo Vodnogo Puti po zapadnomy variantu" [A description of the Onega–White Sea Waterway according to the Western variant]. *Izvestiia Obshestva izucheniia Olonetskoi Gubernii* [Proceedings of the Society for the study of the Olonets Province] 7, 3–4 (1916): 73–102.

Shklovsky, Victor Borisovich. *O teorii prozy* [On the theory of prose]. Moscow: Federatsiia, 1929.

———. *Sentimental Journey: Memoirs, 1917–1922*. Ithaca: Cornell University Press, 1984.

———. *Zoo' or, Letters not about Love*. Ithaca: Cornell University Press, 1971.

Simonov, Konstantine. "Belomorskie stikhi" [Belomor verses]. In *Sbornik molodykh poetov*, 57–62. Moscow, 1935.

———. "Belomortsy" [Belomorists]. In *Smotr sil. Sbornik 2* [A public showing of power], 129–36. Moscow, 1934.

———. "Glazami cheloveka moego pokoleniia" [Through the eyes of a person of my generation], part 2. *Znamia* 4 (1988): 49–121.

Smirnov, G. "Kak snizit' stoimost' stroitel'stva" [How to lower the cost of the construction project]. *Pravda* 11 September 1934, 2.

"Soedinenie Morei" [The joining of the seas]. *Karelo-Murmanskii Krai* 7–8 (1932): 7–12.

Solonevich, I. L. *Rossiia v kontslagere* [Russia in a prison camp], vols. 1–2. Sofia: Izdatel'stvo NTSNP, 1936.

Solzhenitsyn, Aleksandr I. *Arkhipelag GULag, 1918–1956*, I–II [The Gulag Archipelago, 1918–1956]. Paris: YMCA Press, 1973.

———. *The Gulag Archipelago, 1918–1956*, III–IV. Translated by Thomas P. Whitney. New York: Harper & Row, 1975.

Stalin, Joseph. Letter to Viacheslav Molotov, 7 September 1930. In *Stalin's Letters to Molotov*, edited by Lars T. Lih, Oleg V. Naumov, and Oleg V. Khlevniuk, 212–13. New Haven: Yale University Press, 1995.

———. *Works*, 13:414–15. Moscow: Foreign Language Publishing House, 1955.

"Stalinskaia trassa (K 15-letiiu Sovetskoi Karelii)" [The Stalin worksite (for the 15th anniversary of Soviet Karelia)]. *Belomorsko–Baltiiskii Kombinat: Ezhemesiachnyi tekhniko-ekonomicheskii zhurnal* 6–7 (1935): 17–19.

Starchkov, A. "Vtoroe rozhdenie" [Second birth]. *Izvestiia*, 14 February 1933, 3.

Starkov, A. *Mikhail Zoshchenko: Sud'ba khudozhnika* [Mikhail Zoshchenko: the fate of the artist]. Moscow: Sovetskii pisatel', 1990.

Stepanov, V. "Zritel' zhdet" [The viewer is waiting]. Review of *Aristokraty*, by Nikolai Pogodin. Realisticheskii teatr, Moscow. *Vechernaia Moskva*, 9 March 1935, n.p.

Stroud, Matthew D. "The Comedia as Playscript." In *Approaches to Teaching Spanish Golden Age Drama*, edited by Everett W. Hesse, with the assistance of Catherine Larson, 27–42. York, S.C.: Spanish Literature Publications Company, 1989.

Tebbel, John. *The Golden Age Between Two Wars, 1920–1940*. Vol. III of *A History of Book Publishing in the United States*, 569–71. New York and London: R. R. Bowker Company, 1970.

Teitelbaum, Matthew, ed. Preface to *Montage and Modern Life, 1919–1942*, 6–18. Cambridge, Mass.: MIT Press, 1992.

Terent'ev, Igor. (a) *Moi pokhorony* [My funeral]. Moscow: GILEIA, 1993.

———. (b) *Sobranie sochinenii* [Collected works], 18–21, 72–73, 331–32, 463–69. Bologna: S. Francesco, 1988.

Terent'eva, Tatiana. "Moi otets Igor' Terent'ev" [My father Igor Terent'ev]. *Zaumnyi futurism i dadaism v russkoi kul'ture* [Zaumist Futurism and Dadaism in Russian culture], 353–60. Edited by Luigi Magarotto, Marco Marciaduri, and Daniela Rizzi. Bern: Peter Lang, 1991.

Tsimbal, S. "Pogodin-Okhlopkov i Pogodin-Vakhtangovtsy" [Pogodin and Okhlopkov and Pogodin and the Vakhtangovists]. *Rabochii i teatr* 9, no. 5 (1935): 6–9.

Tupitsyn, Margarita. "From the Politics of Montage to the Montage of Politics: Soviet Practices, 1919–1937." In *Montage and Modern Life, 1919–1942*, ed. Matthew Teitelbaum, 82–127. Cambridge, Mass.: MIT Press, 1992.

Troshchenko, E. "Zametki o 'Belomorstroe'" [Notes about the Belomor project]. *Znamia* 4 (1935): 244–55.

Usievich, E. "Razgovor o geroe" [A conversation about the hero]. *Literaturnyi kritik* 9–10 (1938): 154–88.

Vikhman, A. "Belomorsko–Onezhskie Rabotiagi i Belomorsko-Baltiiskii Morskoi vodnyi put'" [The White Sea–Onega hard workers and the White Sea–Baltic Sea Waterway]. *Izvestiia*, 15 January 1934, 1–8.

Vitkovsky, Dmitry. "Polzhizni" [Half a life]. *Znamia* 6 (1991): 107–16.

Vozdvizhensky, Viacheslav. "Put' v kazarmu, ili eshche raz o nasledstve" [The road to Caserma, or one more time about (our) heritage]. *Oktiabr'* 5 (1989): 176–84.

Wachtel, Andrew. *An Obsession with History: Russian Writers Confront the Past*. Stanford: Stanford University Press, 1994.

Weisstein, Ulrich. "Collage, Montage, and Related Terms: Their Literal and Figurative Use in and Application to Techniques and Forms in Various Arts." *Comparative Literature Studies* 15, 3 (1978): 124–39.

White, Hayden. *The Content of the Form: Narrative Discourse and Historical Representation.* Baltimore: Johns Hopkins University Press, 1987.

———. *Metahistory: The Historical Imagination in Nineteenth-Century Europe.* Baltimore: Johns Hopkins University Press, 1973.

———. *Tropics of Discourse: Essays in Cultural Criticism.* Baltimore: Johns Hopkins University Press, 1978.

"White Sea–Baltic Canal." *Encyclopedia Britannica: Macropaedia,* 1991 edition.

Williamsen, Amy R. *Co(s)mic Chaos: Exploring "Los trabajos de Persiles y Sigismunda."* Newark, Del.: Juan de la Cuesta, 1994.

Wortman, Richard. "Epilogue: History and Literature." In *Literature and History,* edited by Gary Saul Morson, 277. Palo Alto: Stanford University Press, 1986.

Zarkhi, N. A. "Zritel' zhdet" [The viewer is waiting]. Review of *Aristokraty,* by Nikolai Pogodin. Realisticheskii teatr, Moscow. *Vechernaia Moskva,* 9 March 1935, n.p.

Zelinsky, Kornelly. "Beseda I. V. Stalina s pisateliami, 26 oktiabria 1932 g" [The conversation of I. V. Stalin with writers, 26 October 1932]. RGALI, f. 1604, op. 1, d. 21, ll. 1–146.

Zoshchenko, Mikhail. "The Bathhouse." In *Russian Literature of the Twenties* introduction by Robert Maguire, edited by Carl Proffer, Ellendea Proffer, Ronald Meyer, and Mary Ann Szporluk, 289–91. Ann Arbor: Ardis, 1987.

Zubkov, Iu. "Uslovnost' i pravda" [Conventionality and truth]. *Sovetskaia kul'tura,* 3 January 1957, n.p.

Zven'ia. *Istoricheskii al'manakh. Vypusk 1.* [Links. A historical almanac. Part 1]. Moscow: Progress Feniks Atheneum, 1991.

Index

agitbrigady [agitational brigades], 149
Alymov, Sergei, 14, 69, 144, 215–17;
    biography of, 54–56; contributions to
    The History of Construction, 115,
    119–22, 123–24, 132, 138
Antsiferov, N. P., 7, 25, 147
The Aristocrats: carnival, 156, 169–70;
    comic mode in, 168, 170; discussion
    of, 159–66, 172–73; linguistic
    peculiarities in, 166–67; literary
    misquotes in, 167–68; OGPU men in,
    159, 160, 161, 171; Okhlopkov
    staging of, 169–70; reviews of, 169–
    70, 171; theme of perekovka in, 155,
    158, 159, 163–66; Vakhtangov
    staging of, 170–71. *See also*
    perekovka; Pogodin, Nikolai
Avdeenko, Aleksandr, 46, 69, 108, 213;
    analysis of Gorky's position on the
    Belomor volume, 45; analysis of
    participation, 67–68; biography of,
    64–66; recollections of writers
    brigade, 48, 55, 59–64
Averbakh, Leopold, 87, 121, 132, 213,
    215

Bakhtin, Mikhail, 150, 156, 203
*Belomor: An Account of the Construction of the Great Canal between the
    White Sea and the Baltic Sea*, 87,
    114, 225; analysis of, 193–202
Belomor Prison Camp (BelBaltLag), xv;
    artifacts from, 33; formation of, 20–
    28; museum at, 33
Belomorsko-Baltiiskii Kanal imeni
    Stalina [Stalin White Sea–Baltic
    Canal] (Belomor Canal/BBK), xv;
    camp theater at, 147–48; comedic
    response to, 155–73; comparison of,
    to the Suez and Panama Canals, 34–
    35; construction statistics of, 30; cost
    of construction of, 35–36; decree to
    build, 20; dimensions of, 12;
    engineers of, 73; history of, 12–38;
    legitimization of forced labor at, 209;
    map of, 15; memoirs about, 7;
    musical ensembles at, 149; official
    opening of, 30–31, 33–34; poetic
    response to, 173–85; portrayal of, in
    popular press and literature, 12–13;
    pre-Soviet history of, 14–9; prose
    response to, 185–92; reasons for
    construction of, 36–38; and reduction
    in travel time, 34; Soviet history of,
    19–34; taboo about, 1; variety of
    written response to, 40; writers
    brigade to, 213–14. *See also Istoriia
    stroitel'stva Belomorsko-Baltiiskogo
    Kanala imeni Stalina*; perekovka;
    Teplitsky, Leopold
Berman, Matvei, 21, 206, 218
Budantsev, Sergei, 69–70, 86, 213, 215–
    17; and archival materials on writers
    brigade, 50; Belomor as history and

literature, 72; biography of, 70; *The Great Waterways of the USSR*, 70–71; letter to Stalin, 71–73; literary profile of, 71; panegyric to Stalin, 75; work on the Belomor volume, 71–75, 103–4
Bulgakov, Mikhail, 52–3

Chernyshevsky, Nikolai: proto-realist models in relation to Belomor, 42
Chukhin, Ivan: analysis of Canal construction by, 37–38; book *Kanaloarmeitsy* [Canalarmyists], 6; and KGB archives on writers brigade, 48; research on GULag, 38
Clark, Katerina: and "little heroes," 208; mythmaking, 152–3; reasons for writer participation, 46–47; scholarship on Belomor, 46; shift in literary heroes, 67; on socialist realism, 4, 66, 141–42, 206
collective authorship, 3, 99–100, 205, 209; in *The History of Construction*, 89, 101–5, 111–12, 114–40, 140–41. *See also* montage

Dallin, David J., 8, 37–38
Dostoevsky, Andrei, 147

Eco, Umberto: carnival, 169–70. *See also The Aristocrats*
emplotment, 10–11, 94, 209; in relation to Gorky's theories, 96–97
engineers of human souls: in relation to industrial metaphor, 46; Stalin's formulation of, 44–45, 92
Ermolaev, Herman, 5

Firin, Semyon, 21, 50, 87, 218; editor of *The History of Construction*, 121, 132; as model of reforged Soviet, 146–47; repartee with Prince Mirsky and Valentin Kataev, 61–62
First Five-Year Plan, 9; Belomor in the context of, 13, 45–47

Fitzpatrick, Sheila, 3–4, 66
Foucault, Michel: and power relations among texts, 154, 172, 202–3, 209

Gabrilovich, Evgeny, 213, 215–17; contribution of, to *The History of Construction*, 132, 133–34; in writers brigade, 48, 50, 69; meeting at Gorky's, 44
Gauzner, Gleb, 213, 215–17; contribution to *The History of Construction*, 78, 105, 109, 130
Golomshtock, Igor, 5, 141
Gorbunov, Kuz'ma, 213, 215–17; contribution of, to *The History of Construction*, 130; speech to the First Congress of Writers by, 110, 150
Gorky, Maksim, 39, 48, 215–17; as brigade organizer, 53–54; contributions to *The History of Construction*, 87, 121, 132; meeting with Stalin and Soviet writers, 42, 44; opinion of Belomor, 98; and Soviet writers as historians, 94–98
Groys, Boris, 5; analysis of Stalinist art and culture by, 107, 140–41

The History of the Construction of the Stalin White Sea–Baltic Canal [*Istoriia stroitel'stva Belomorsko-Baltiiskogo Kanala imeni Stalina*], xv–xvi, 2, 192; analysis of, 86–153; collective authorship of, 89, 111–12, 114, 140–41, 142–43; conclusions about 205–6, 207; contents of, 216–17; critical response to, 142–43; description of, 86–90; English translation of, 192–202; excerpts from, 219–24; history vs. literature, 89, 90–100; list of contributors to, 215; as literary hybrid, 3, 8, 9, 113–14, 143; method of compilation of, 73–74, 100–105; montage in, 105–13; perekovka, 144–53; practical

History—continued
  application of montage in, 114–140;
  publication figures for, 86–87;
  relationship of, to other texts, 154–55, 202–3; as socialist realism, 142;taboo surrounding, 88–89;
  theoretical underpinnings of, 140–42;
  writer motivation for, 8, 46. *See also* OGPU; perekovka

Ilf: and Petrov, 47, 108, 213
Inber, Vera, 69, 105, 109, 213, 215–17;
  contributions to *The History of Construction*, 115, 130, 138; poem to Belomor, 12–13
Istoriia fabrik i zavodov [The History of Factories and Plants], 86, 88;
  development of the series, 94–98
Istoriia stroitel'stva Belomorsko-Baltiiskogo Kanala imeni Stalina. See The History of the Construction of the Stalin White Sea–Baltic Canal
Ivanov, Vsevolod, 39, 46, 73, 213, 215–17; contributions to *The History of Construction*, 115, 131, 138, 221–23; on writers as historians, 98
Ivanova, Tamara, 39–40, 41; recollections of writers brigade by, 50; on Zoshchenko's and Ivanov's participation, 81–82, 83

Jakobson, Michael, 4, 6, 25; discussion of penal policy, 10
Jasensky, Bruno, 69, 214, 215–17

kanaloarmeitsy [canalarmyists]:
  construction feats of, 30–31;
  derivation of name of, 34
Karelia: geography of, 14; GULag in, 7
Kataev, Valentin, 47, 69, 213, 215–17;
  contributions to *The History of Construction*, 115; conversation with Semyon Firin, 62; *Time, Forward!*, 91, 113, 117

Khatsrevin, Zakhar, 214, 215–17;
  collaboration of, with Lapin, 75;
  contribution to *The History of Construction*, 129–30, 132
Khrustalev, N. I., 50, 73–74, 218
Kliuyev, Nikolai, 9, 155, 185, 202–3;
  analysis of response, 184–85; literary biography, 180–81; "Ruin," 181–84, 208
Kogan, Lazar, 34, 115, 117, 129, 218;
  as literary type, 118–19; with Mikoyan at Belomor, 127
Kotkin, Stephen, 4
KVO [Kul'turnye vospitatel'nye otdeli] (Cultural educational cells): in *The History of Construction*, 119–20, 121–22, 144

Lapin, Boris, 69–70, 213, 215–17;
  biography of, 75–78; husband of Irina Ehrenburg, 69, 76; participation in *The History of Construction*, 78–79, 102–3, 105, 107, 109, 130;
  recollections of Ilya Ehrenburg about, 76; recollections of Nadezhda Mandelshtam about, 76–77
Lebedenko, A., 213, 215–17; contribution to *The History of Construction*, 132–33
Likhachev, Dmitry, 25
Losev, A. F., 7, 25
Luzhkov, Yuri, 210

meeting of Soviet writers with Stalin et al. (26 October 1932), 43–44
mentor as literary type, 112, 207
Mikoyan, Anastas: visit by, to Belomor Canal, 127
Mileiko, V. B.: film on Belomor, 52–53
Mirsky, Prince Dmitry, 69, 213, 215–17; participation in writers brigade, 59–64, 67–68
Molotov, Viacheslav: correspondence with Stalin about Belomor, 19–20;

meeting at Maksim Gorky's with Soviet writers, 42
montage: practical application of, in *The History of Construction*, 114–40; theory of, in *The History of Construction*, 105–14, 140

Nicolaevsky, Boris I., 8, 37–38

OGPU, xv, 144, 207, 209; as arbiters of reforging, 146, 151–52; as literary type 112–13, 115–16, 207; charged with constructing Belomor Canal, 20–21; guarding Belomor camp, 26; in *The History of Construction*, 115–29, 143; in Pogodin's *The Aristocrats*, 159; in Prishvin's *The Tsar's Road*, 189–90; supervision of writers brigade, 50–51; supervision of writers collective, 88, 91–92
Old Believers, 14–16, 21–22; in Prishvin's *The Tsar's Road*, 189–92
Osudareva doroga. See *The Tsar's Road*

People of the Stalingrad Tractor Factory, 155
perekovka [reforging], 45, 208, 209–10; in *The Aristocrats*, 155, 159, 163–66; in context of literature, 3; definition of, 2–3; in *The History of Construction*, 89, 112, 126, 128, 132–34, 142, 143–44, 144–53; link to Marxism, 152; of Mirsky and Avdeenko, 63–64; program in the 1930s, 10. See also *The Aristocrats*; *The History of Construction*
Perekovka (camp newspaper), 55, 139–40, 144, 160, 161; inmate poetry in, 176–78; source for *The History of Construction*, 87; Terent'ev's submission to, 179–80
Peter the Great: and early path of the Belomor Canal, 18, 125, 189
Petrone, Karen: shift in literary heroes, 67

Pogodin, Nikolai, 9; literary biography of, 155, 156–58; plays of, 157, 168–69. See also *The Aristocrats*
positive hero: in *The Aristocrats*, 165; prototype in *The History of Construction*, 112, 146, 207
Povenets Steps, 31, 125; assessment of, 32. See also Belomor Canal
Prishvin, Mikhail, 101, 202–3; cited in *The History of Construction*, 135–38; *Fathers and Children*, 188–89; literary biography, 185–88; nonparticipation in the writers brigade, 52–53; *The Tsar's Road*, 188–92. See also *The Tsar's Road*

Rapoport, Yakov, 218; as literary type, 115–16
Rassweiler, Anne D., 4
Robin, Regine, 5
Rusinov, Ivan, 147–9

Seifullina, Lidia, 213; speech to the First Congress of Writers, 110
Shentalinsky, Vitaly: and KGB archives on Belomor writers brigade, 48
Shklovsky, Victor, 46, 53, 69, 73, 215–17; on the Belomor Canal, 57–58; biography of, 56–59; contributions to *The History of Construction*, 104, 105, 108–10, 115, 121, 130, 132, 138–39
Simonov, Konstantine, 9, 155, 202; Belomor poems, 174, 175–76; literary biography, 173–74; theme of reforging, 174–75
Smith, Harrison, 196
socialist realism: analysis of, by Boris Groys, 107, 140–41; analysis of, by Katerina Clark, 4, 141–42; as reflected in *The History of Construction*, 112–13, 129, 166; scholarship on, 5. See also positive hero
Sokolov-Mikitov, Ivan, 70, 185

Solzhenitsyn, Aleksander, 6, 25, 38, 41; atrocities on the Canal, 62; identification of authors of the Belomor volume, 78

Stalin, Joseph: absence from Belomor, 208; correspondence with Molotov about Belomor, 19–20; de-Stalinization, 6; engineers of human souls speech, 44–45, 92; mandate to writers, 47; reaction to Canal, 12, 13; voyage through the Canal, 32–33

Stroud, Matthew, 158

Teplitsky, Leopold: incarceration on Belomor, 22–23

Terent'ev, Igor, 25, 155, 180; Belomor poetry, 179; cited in *The History of Construction*, 138–40; literary biography of, 178–79

Tolstoy, Aleksei, 47, 69, 108, 213, 215–17

The Tsar's Road [Osudareva doroga], 101, 155, 185, 208; initial drafts of, 8–9. *See also* Prishvin, Mikhail

tufta: definition of, 28; incentives for curtailing, 29–30; problem on the Canal, 28–29; punishment for, 29

Vozdvizhensky, Vyacheslav, 39–40, 41

Wachtel, Andrew, 5; Russian writers as historians, 45, 91, 99

White, Hayden, 10–11, 93–94; in relation to Gorky's theories, 96–97

Williams-Ellis, Amabel, 194–96

Williamsen, Amy, 156

writer motivation, 85. *See also* Alymov, Sergei; Avdeenko, Aleksander; Budantsev, Sergei; Lapin, Boris; Shklovsky, Victor; Zoshchenko, Mikhail

writers brigade, 34, 46, 74; history of, 47–52; leading writers in, 53; in relation to authors of *The History of Construction*, 53

Zelinsky, Kornelly: literary biography of, 44, 213; record of writers' meeting with Gorky and Stalin, 42–44

Zoshchenko, Mikhail, 69–70, 213, 215–17; biography of, 79–80; narrative method of, 79–80, 81; participation in *The History of Construction*, 81–84, 87, 145; "Youth Restored," 82

Cynthia A. Ruder received her Ph.D. in Russian literature from Cornell University. She has taught at Occidental College and Bryn Mawr College. Currently she is an associate professor of Russian language and literature at the University of Kentucky. Her work includes publications on Soviet literature in the 1930s and on Russian language pedagogy.